# London in His Own Time

WRITERS IN THEIR OWN TIME

Joel Myerson, *series editor*

# LONDON

## *in His Own Time*

A Biographical

Chronicle of His Life,

Drawn from Recollections,

Interviews, and

Memoirs by Family,

Friends, and

Associates

EDITED BY

Jeanne Campbell Reesman

University of Iowa Press

Iowa City

*March 18, 2021*

*For Amy, with immense respect and great affection,*

*Hugs,*

*Jeanne*

University of Iowa Press, Iowa City 52242
Copyright © 2020 by the University of Iowa Press
www.uipress.uiowa.edu
Printed in the United States of America

Printed on acid-free paper

Library of Congress Cataloging-in-Publication Data
Names: Reesman, Jeanne Campbell, editor.
Title: London in His Own Time: A Biographical Chronicle of His Life,
Drawn From Recollections, Interviews, and Memoirs by Family, Friends,
and Associates / edited by Jeanne Campbell Reesman.
Description: Iowa City: University of Iowa Press, [2020] |
Series: Writers in Their Own Time |
Includes bibliographical references and index. |
Identifiers: LCCN 2020017800 (print) | LCCN 2020017801 (ebook) |
ISBN 9781609387129 (ebook) | ISBN 9781609387112 (paperback; acid-free paper) |
ISBN 9781609387112 (paperback; acid-free paper) | ISBN 9781609387129 (ebook)
Subjects: LCSH: London, Jack, 1876–1916. | London, Jack, 1876–1916—
Friend and associates. | Authors, American—20th century—Biography.
Classification: LCC PS3523.O46 (ebook) | LCC PS3523.O46 Z736 2020 (print) |
DDC 813/.52 [B]—dc23
LC record available at
https://lccn.loc.gov/2020017800

This book is dedicated to the memory
of Christian Pagnard (1951–2017)
*notre meilleur ami*

HE LOVED THE LIFE, the deep arctic winter, the silent wilderness, the unending snowsurface unpressed by the foot of any man. About him towered icy peaks unnamed and uncharted. No hunter's camp-smoke, rising in the still air of the valleys, ever caught his eye. He, alone, moved through the brooding quiet of the untraveled wastes; nor was he oppressed by the solitude. He loved it all, the day's toil, the bickering wolf-dogs, the making of the camp in the long twilight, the leaping stars overhead and the flaming pageant of the aurora borealis.

Especially he loved his camp at the end of day, and in it he saw a picture which he ever yearned to paint and which he knew he would never forget—a beaten place in the snow, where burned his fire; his bed a couple of rabbit-skin robes spread on fresh-chopped spruce-boughs; his shelter a stretched strip of canvas that caught and threw back the heat of the fire; the blackened coffee-pot and pail resting on a length of log, the moccasins propped on sticks to dry, the snow-shoes up-ended in the snow; and across the fire the wolf-dogs snuggling to it for warmth, wistful and eager, furry and frost-rimmed, with bush tails curled protectingly over their feet; and all about, pressed backward but a space, the wall of encircling darkness.

—JACK LONDON, "The Man on the Other Bank," *Smoke Bellew* (1911)

# Contents

# Acknowledgments

AS ONE CIRCULATES clockwise in the Huntington Library's Munger Center Ahmanson Room, where literary manuscripts from medieval times to the present may be examined by scholars, one notices the bronze busts of intellectual luminaries on top of the tall bookcases, evenly arranged around the large, luxurious wood-paneled room. Sir Richard Francis Burton rests comfortably next to George Gordon, Lord Byron, followed by Joseph Conrad, Dante Alighieri, George Dock, Albert Einstein, Benjamin Franklin, John Paul Jones, Abraham Lincoln, William James Potter, William Makepeace Thackeray, George Washington, Evelyn Waugh, and then Jack London, in a bust by his friend, sculptor Finn Froelich.

How fondly I recall my first time in the Ahmanson Room in the older library building, conducted by none other than Earle Labor and Milo Shepard, in 1990. I was so abashed and so proud to be there, and I was astonished that I was allowed to sit with them in one of the two glass-walled private rooms and talk as we pleased over Charmian's diaries (then somewhat restricted) or other items, in full view of the rest of the readers but in total silence from them. Sara S. "Sue" Hodson, curator of literary manuscripts at the time, became a close friend. I remember the old tradition while on fellowships at the Huntington in subsequent summers, how we were all kicked out of the manuscript room at 11:45 a.m., not to be readmitted until 1 p.m. I remember the first time going to lunch by myself and following the custom in those days of just sitting with a stranger at a table in the leafy garden where the tables rested under large trees and were visited by green jays and squirrels. With a walk in just a part of the entire Huntington Gardens to while away time planned for after lunch, I would ask my new friend what she might be working on. Something exotic and mysterious, requiring numerous languages, medieval incunabula. When politely asked in return, saying "Jack London," I remember that look: first bafflement, then a vague pity. The guy who wrote the dog books. Well, I could always go hide out in the basement of the old building, in secondary material, with its dark and scary stacks. However, until the recent accession of the papers of Octavia Butler, the Jack London Collection was the single largest author collection at the Huntington.

Beginning in the 1960s, post–Cold War, the socialism, the popularity, the naturalism that had kept him out of literary anthologies suddenly began to shift as Stanford University Press issued a three-volume collection of selected letters and then three volumes of the complete short stories. London had arrived. Over the ensuing decades, dedicated scholars made London into a staple of academia and he never left the public bookshelf. The Huntington is paradise for any scholar and a place to make and keep many friends. I remember the tales of the oddities of readers, especially eccentric locals, and legends of librarians of the past and present, curators current and retired, especially and of course Henry E. Huntington's surprising vision. For a so-called robber baron of the California Electric Railways, an example of Twain's "Gilded Age" attacked in Frank Norris's *The Octopus* (1900), Huntington strove to address social needs with projects especially for children, using the estate. But Huntington, as well as some of his family, also had a vision for a location far above Los Angeles that would preserve British and American art and literature based on the Huntington family's astounding if generally traditional collections. The locale was eventually made public, and its gardens were vastly expanded. Today it is a must-visit site in Pasadena, California, for its gardens, art galleries, library, and other amazing spaces. It has the best museum bookstore I have ever seen.

The very first people I wish to thank for this book are current and retired staff at the Huntington Library and at the Merrill-Cazier Library's Jack and Charmian London Collection at Utah State University. The items I have been able to include, which were not available electronically, reflect much research on Jack London and related collections at the Huntington and at Logan, combing through most — never all! — of it, finding hints on how he was spoken of by those who knew him from cross-referencing microfilm, ledgers, photo albums, photo negatives, digitized photos, and digitized and nondigitized primary resources going back many years. I received four Huntington fellowships to work in residence over the years, and these made a big difference. My heartfelt gratitude and eternal professional appreciation most of all go to now-retired Sue Hodson for her unwavering and stimulating support, coauthorship, and true friendship. I thank the members of Reader Services and all the other fine people who have made and continue to make the

Huntington so special. The Huntington has seen new developments, but one thing has not changed: the unmistakable sense of welcome and support the scholar receives is still there. I thank Roy Ritchie, who retired in 2010 after nineteen years as the Huntington Library's W. M. Keck Foundation Director of Research; David A. Zeidberg, Avery Director of the Huntington Library, who served from 1996 until 2017, when he retired; Natalie Russell, assistant curator of literary collections; Gayle Richardson, archivist; and Mona Shulman, assistant to the director of the library and library registrar. I also wish to thank the Andrew W. Mellon Foundation for one of the fellowships.

I got to know the superb Jack and Charmian London collection in Special Collections at the Merrill-Cazier Library at Utah State University a bit later in my research, but what a trove of wonders they hold, especially letters, London's Tramp Diary, and the logbook of the *Snark*. Warm thanks to Brad Cole and Clint Pumphrey of the Jack and Charmian London Collection, especially with letters from George Brett and Charmian London. They cohosted a Jack London Society Symposium, which allowed many of us to continue researching there and explore the mountains and canyons.

At the John Peace Library, University of Texas at San Antonio, I thank Tara Schmidt. I am also grateful to the Academy of Distinguished Scholars and our former UTSA provost, John Frederick; retired dean Dan Gelo of the College of Liberal and Fine Arts; and former chair of the Department of English, Mark Bayer, for their concerted support of my research and writing. I am deeply grateful to Jack and Laura Richmond of San Antonio for their support through their endowed faculty fellowship in American literature.

There was another librarian in Jack London's life who deserves special mention here, namely, Ina Coolbrith (1841–1928), a struggling poet in the last quarter of the nineteenth century but primarily librarian of the Oakland Public Library, where she began in 1874. This library became one of the first two city libraries in California to become free to the public instead of remaining private clubs. She was named Poet Laureate of California in 1915. London encountered her at the age of 10, and she allowed him to check out books, even though technically a patron had to be 14 years of age. She gave him his first request—a book about Pizarro and Peru—and many more. Having also known early poverty as a child, she, like London, was mostly self-educated. She began publishing in her twenties when she moved to San Francisco, first in the *Californian*, edited by a new friend, Bret Harte, and then in the *Overland Monthly*, where she regularly published poems and served as an editor.

She eventually published two book collections. Upon her sister's death she returned to Oakland to support the family with the library job. She offered London Tobias Smollett and his Scottish picaresques, then Horatio Alger and Washington Irving. A favorite of London's remained Irving's *The Alhambra*. Coolbrith was friends with Mark Twain and encouraged a young Isadora Duncan. When her time at the library ended in 1892, she completed a history of California literature whose only finished manuscript copy was destroyed in the 1906 San Francisco earthquake and fire. Asked to donate an item to a festschrift for Coolbrith, London sent her several signed first editions. When in 1919 she moved to New York, her Bay Area friends started the Ina Coolbrith Circle, which Joan London began to attend at the age of 14; it still exists today as a poetry society.[1] Along with Ina Coolbrith, I wish to thank most especially Tarnel Abbott, great-granddaughter of Jack and Bess London, retired as librarian at the Richmond Public Library in California. She kindly granted permission for the reprinting of Joan's letters to her father.

I thank the many Jack London scholars who have talked over parts of this book or guided me to find sources, especially Earle Labor, Noël Mauberret, Michel Viotte, Rudy Ciuca, Joe Lawrence, Richard Russo, Donna Campbell, Kenneth K. Brandt, Keith Newlin, Eric Carl Link, Steve Frye, and the late Milo Shepard, Russ Kingman, and Christian Pagnard.

I am grateful to the staff at the University of Iowa Press, especially my copy editor; Susan Hill Newton, managing editor; and James McCoy, acquisitions editor, for their patient and faithful support. I also thank two talented graduate research assistants on this project, now MA graduates of the University of Texas at San Antonio, Connor McBrearty and Brooke Haley. And to all of the students with whom I have shared Jack London—you are always on my mind.

Joel Myerson, Distinguished Professor Emeritus of English Language and Literature, University of South Carolina, and general editor of the University of Iowa Press series Writers in Their Own Times, has my endless gratitude. He has been extraordinarily patient and inspiring in shaping the course of this volume.

**NOTE**

1. George, "Ina Coolbrith."

# Introduction

The adventurous and sensational life of author Jack London (1876–1916) has often overshadowed his dramatic naturalistic tales: born illegitimate to a spiritualist and an astrologist in bohemian San Francisco, "Johnny" was wet-nursed by an African American former slave, Oakland neighbor Mrs. Virginia Prentiss, who in part raised him as a young child. He was adopted by his birth mother's Civil War–veteran husband and grew up in the lower class, moving from rental to rental, from boardinghouse to farm. He worked selling papers, setting pins in a bowling alley, doing whatever he could, from the age of 7. At 15, London ran away to the waterfront and joined a gang of oyster pirates, stealing, drinking, and carousing with them until nearly drowning in the icy bay one night. Joining the shore patrol, London nevertheless was tempted again by adventure and hit the road to hobo in 1892 and 1894, and then in 1897 joined the financially desperate in the frenzied Yukon Gold Rush, having meanwhile sailed the Pacific on a sealing ship as an able seaman. And all of this took place before he really began to write, returning to California and "hit[ting] the books," as he put it: he entered Oakland High School at age 21. London wrote out of his own hard experience. One should not forget, however, that another kind of experience provided a wellspring for his works, namely, his omnivorous reading, especially, from early on, any sort of adventure, Greek and Roman literature and history, and the epic in general. His attentive reading of British literature is clear. He found major philosophical influences in Darwin, Spencer, Marx, Freud, and Jung. London also read a good deal of science and later, in particular, psychology, as well as deeply and constantly in agrarian publications, and of course he followed numerous serials and newspapers. The Hawaiian and South Seas tales have two main sources: the Bible and early missionary accounts. He sought to tell the truth about life as he saw it, not only naturalistically and scientifically but also in its mystery and myth, in a shared humanity. Ironically, though there is no complete edition of his works in English, separate full editions in Japanese and French, for example, are common. London is probably America's most widely read and translated author. He wrote fifty books, encompassing novels, short fiction, poetry, drama, essays, newspaper correspondence, prizefighting and other sports stories, biography, and feminist works. London uses characters such as Buck in *The Call of the Wild* to express deep and widely shared human myths of identity and survival. He is the one American author people you meet abroad will know.

Professors and literary critics have disliked London for various reasons, but he has never needed them, though there has been a groundswell of critical interest in his works in the last fifty years, bringing him into the literary canon and university classroom. London made no secret of writing for money, but he also wrote for his own sense of art and truth. With him there is always duality: he relished the sense of the solitary with the White Silence, but he seeks a communion there. His heroes almost always have a human trailmate, reflecting not the "lone wolf" hero so often stereotyped as his but his sense of justice in socialism and belief in community. His trailmates in life were his family and friends. In an age when people still wrote long and thoughtful letters—or any letters at all—friendships were just as intense whether one had seen the recipient of a letter yesterday or not for a year. Writing among friends was different in those days, but letters could fly back and forth, as when London carried on a spat with Ambrose Bierce or when he wrote his love letters to Charmian Kittredge London (1871–1955), his second wife.

*Atlantic Monthly*'s publication of "An Odyssey of the North" in the January 1900 issue[1] was a fitting introduction for the East Coast literary establishment of Boston and New York, and then for the world, to its West Coast author, one of the newest, youngest, and most striking literary voices of the new century, the photogenic, masculine "adventure" writer of the Gold Rush, a San Francisco Bay Area intellectual and active socialist. *The Call of the Wild* (1903) did for London what Mark Twain's "Jumping Frog" story did for Twain.[2] From a modern critical point of view, he appears as one of several American writers influenced by Émile Zola's new post-Darwinian theory of literature known as naturalism,[3] the successor to literary realism, or in the American newspapers' parlance, "muck-raking." Many American writers have started as journalists, but from Twain on, this documentary orientation found a new home in exposés such as Stephen Crane's *Maggie: A Girl of the Streets* (1893) and Theodore Dreiser's *Sister Carrie* (1900), the latter censored upon publication. Naturalism's focus upon the poor was viewed askance by those who benefited from the onerous labor and immigration laws, namely, the robber barons of the Gilded Age. But among workers, London's books became dog-eared as they were passed around, translated into dozens upon dozens of languages in countries around the world. Like other famous socialist war correspondents of his day, including William English Walling and John Reed, London was globally admired for his written and photographic sense of war correspondence as well as adventure, but also as an artist of a very new kind of fiction. Especially if one tracks the order of composition of his short fiction, as the Stanford University Press edition of *The Complete Short Stories of Jack London* does, one can see his continual changes and experimentations even within the often-used settings of the Klondike and life at sea in the Pacific, how he takes one point of view in a tale, then takes an opposite one in the next story he writes that week, as well as how themes of class and race intersect on the factory floors of Oakland or the farms of Northern California. London advocated socialism, and he saw his writings as contributions to the cause. This is in line with how naturalism developed: naturalism can range from determinism to a type of Romanticism to social reform, but, as Donna M. Campbell formulates it, while naturalism offers startling views of social evils not usually presented in the literature of realism, it did not and does not offer solutions, as did progressive writers and activists such as Eugene V. Debs, Jane Addams, Lincoln Steffens, W. E. B. Du Bois, Charlotte Perkins Gilman, or even London's friend and correspondent, Upton Sinclair, many of whom lived into the 1960s.[4]

Naturalism, and especially London, were largely concerned with the lower classes and with race. Darwin follower Herbert Spencer felt social Darwinism revealed the natural hierarchy of the races, with the Anglo-Saxons on top and the rest left behind as "evolutionarily unfit" in some way, either by birth or by social forces destined to cast them aside on the road to success. London's mother, Flora Wellman London, was a thoroughgoing white supremacist, and her son, following the racialist thinking taught at Stanford and the University of California (the latter of which he attended for one semester), initially embraced Spencer but gave him up in favor of a more ethically based response to Darwin's questions about the future for the human race suggested in the ambiguous "entangled bank" metaphor for nature at the end of *On the Origin of Species* (1859). Unlike Spencer, Thomas Henry Huxley, another follower of Darwin, heard a call to virtue in that final paragraph:

even if nature constitutes a relentless and to us disorderly and simultaneously evolutionary determinism and we will one day lose the battle for survival, he argued, humankind must still maintain ethics. London turned to Huxley; though London's Klondike tales in particular make the competition for survival stark, nearly every one of them contains a very human moral, usually the essential call to community and not isolation. And the more London traveled, especially in racially mixed, exotic corners of the world, the more he came to embody Twain's famous observation that "[t]ravel is fatal to prejudice, bigotry, and narrow-mindedness, and many of our people need it sorely on these accounts. Broad, wholesome, charitable views of men and things cannot be acquired by vegetating in one little corner of the earth all one's lifetime."[5]

Though London's heroes in such socialist novels as *The Iron Heel* (1908) and *Martin Eden* (1909) struggle for survival in the Arctic or the South Seas, they share with the characters of other American naturalists—Crane (1871–1900), Dreiser (1871–1945), Frank Norris (1870–1902), and Edith Wharton (1862–1937)—resistance to the urban forces that can crush the naturalist hero.[6] The three "Sonoma" novels, beginning with *Burning Daylight* (1910), represent a big change in his work, agrarian and feminist novels wherein naturalism is replaced by romantic love and love of the land. Who was this writer of violent tales, mischaracterized as "man against nature" stories privileging the individual male conqueror—the stereotypical Nietzschean hero London discarded.? Most of the heroes and heroines in the short fiction are nonwhite and demonstrate the importance of real, as opposed to imperialistic, relationships. One thinks of a landmark story, his first Hawaiian tale, "The House of Pride" (1908).

Though London's image as a man of the frontier annoyed Theodore Roosevelt, who was perhaps jealous, it is one reason London has for many years remained one of the most popular American writers in the world, translated into dozens of languages, a writer with a mythic appeal to anyone who seeks a journey. It is also the case that despite his complex vocabulary and tendency toward allusions, his prose is readily readable and not difficult to translate, though what he saw as his deeper layers of meaning may be understood differently by different people. The California farms and ranches of *The Valley of the Moon* (1913) and *The Little Lady of the Big House* (1915) pastoralized and complicated the westward movement.

The autodidact London, with strikes against him for being too socialistic (*and* too individualistic), too Western, too masculine, lower class, and so forth, and an alcoholic and womanizer, remained an outlier as a "western writer" in a way Twain did not because of the Boston support of William Dean Howells for the latter. But he read everything, a facet of his life overlooked by most biographers: classics, myths, science, histories, economics, philosophy, authorities on sexuality, manuals and journals on agronomy, sailing logs, missionary books, and literary works ranging from Spenser to Milton to Conrad and Henry James.

Above almost anything else, London valued friendship, and if he did not have a high reputation among the literary elite, neither did Twain for a long period after his death. Like many notable people a hundred years ago, London maintained a gigantic correspondence and had a public presence growing in part because of increased literacy and the technology that made wide serial and book readership and celebrityhood possible. London was one of the most photographed people on the planet, as Twain was before him. Both men entertained constantly but established boundaries to protect their writing time, which was not always easy on their families. London sometimes wrote angry advice in replies to letters from people he did not know, often ending with a hearty invitation to the ranch: "The latch-string is always out."

In this book we will hear both from some of his oldest friends and from later acquaintances scattered around the globe, an astonishing variety of people who knew him and remembered him in their writings. For example, though he is not included in the book, Luther Burbank (1849–1926), the famous California horticulturalist and leading breeder of new plant varieties, was a neighbor and friend of London (*Letters*, 602–603n). Burbank convinced London to plant spineless cactus for animal feed, albeit later failed to warn him about eucalyptus trees. Burbank helped inspire London throughout his ranch life to pursue the breeding of champion bulls, pigs, and stallions:

It was in October of 1897 that I first met him—No other man has left so indelible an impression upon my memory as Jack London. He was but a boy then, in years, but he possessed the mental equipment of a mature man, and I have never thought of him as a boy except in the heart of him—the clean, joyous, tender unembittered heart of youth. His personality would challenge attention anywhere. Not only in his beauty—for he was a handsome lad—but there was about him that indefinable something that distinguishes genius from mediocrity, he displayed none of the insolent egotism of youth; he was an idealist who went after the unattainable, a dreamer who was a man amongst strongmen; a man who could face death serenely imperturbable. These were my first impressions which months of companionship confirmed.

Burbank also writes: "Jack London was a big healthy boy with a taste for serious things, but never cynical, never bitter, always good-humored and humorous, as I saw him, and with fingers and heart equally sensitive when he was in my gardens."[7]

There are many other important people in his life from whom we have no written testament—his mother and stepfather, for example—nor have we any from Mrs. Virginia Prentiss (1832?-1922), his wet nurse and neighbor, with whom he lived until he was weaned and then off and on as a teen, and who remained a lifelong friend and companion. She cared for his children and their mother, Bess Maddern London (1876-1948), his first wife; for his second wife, Charmian Kittredge London (1871-1955); and for Flora Wellman London (1843-1922), his mother; as well as for many other family members. London provided generous support for her and her family even as they aged. Mrs. Prentiss is said to have been the one to call him "Jack," her "jumping jack," while he was called "Johnny" at home. She also helped teach him to read, using the King James Bible, and staked him a loan of $300 for his first sailboat when he was 15, which he paid back with proceeds from his oyster-pirating. His book inscriptions to her are quite moving, like those from a son to a mother. On the other hand, Flora, according to Jack, was cold, unloving, and self-absorbed—she also forced him to work, which as a young child he resented—but she was one of the first people to encourage him in his writing, beginning with his $25 prize from the San Francisco *Morning Call* for "A Typhoon off the Coast of Japan" (1893). Her emotional and financial escapades kept the family moving (every year of Jack's first twenty-one years), but her example of hard work combined with her "other" side probably inspired London more than he knew.[8] Bess's keeping his daughters Joan (1901-1971) and Bess "Becky" (1903-1992) away from the ranch when Charmian was present went a long way toward deepening the many family rifts caused by the divorce and London's will.

There are virtually no letters from fellow sailors and just a few from tramps (many fictionalized), as well as several journals and diaries from the Klondike. There are mountains of letters from friends in Hawai'i and the South Seas, including Ernest Darling, Martin Johnson, missionaries, traders, and plantation owners—but not one word from the many indigenous people he knew in those places, not to mention the First Nation people in Canada.

Direct memories of Jack London tend to be vivid, whether from the recollections of his family, his boyhood friends, or his gang pals with whom he roamed the docks of Oakland and San Francisco. There are accounts from fellow Klondike gold miners, who describe the gregarious London reading *Paradise Lost* aloud to them in crowded, smoky cabins during the long winter nights; from socialists in the Bay Area; from fellow artists and writers; and from some of his extended epistolary relationships, especially with his near-career-long editor at Macmillan in New York, George Brett. Those back at home in Oakland have left a record of his boyhood and teen years, his marriage and family, and then his divorce and family complications, as well as how he engaged in endless debates on socialism as he ran for "Boy Mayor of Oakland." His Klondike diaries show his first attempts at recording his Klondike experiences, and a number of his fellow prospectors remembered him. Later come reminiscences from fellow war correspondents in the Russo-Japanese War of 1904, writing in such august papers as *The Times* of London.

Many letters come from people who knew him best (especially several women); his sense of himself as a writer and a man is captured intimately by Anna Strunsky, for example, and his daily life by Charmian London in her diaries. His political aspirations are recorded by friends such as Upton Sinclair. Letters from his best friend, George Sterling (1869–1926), a California poet, are signed "Greek," and London's to him "Wolf." George was perhaps the person London focused upon as his ideal reader; they often exchanged manuscripts and trusted each other's judgment. George edited proof of *The Sea-Wolf* when London was in Korea.

London knew or was in contact with many of the most famous people of the age: Mary Austin, Rex Beach, Ambrose Bierce, Howard Chandler Christy, Buffalo Bill Cody, Joseph Conrad, Max Eastman, Charlotte Perkins Gilman, Emma Goldman, Maxim Gorky, Jack Johnson, David Starr Jordan, Sinclair Lewis, Joaquin Miller, John Muir, and Upton Sinclair. He was part of the Bohemian Grove and the San Francisco–area young radicals, artists, and socialists who migrated south to Carmel. His was among the "Human

Documents" series of portraits begun in 1893 in *McClure's Magazine*, edited by Sarah Orne Jewett.

After abandoning the 1907–1909 voyage of the *Snark*, London entered a hospital in Sydney for the treatment of multiple ailments, including a peculiar peeling rash later determined to be from his liberal use of corrosive sublimate to treat his skin sores, "yaws" or "Solomon Island Sores." Two crew members also published their accounts of the voyage of the *Snark*, Charmian London and Martin Johnson (1884–1937).⁹ Out of the hospital by Boxing Day 1908, London covered the Jack Johnson–Tommy Burns world heavyweight fight in Sydney for *The New York Herald*, the first attempt at the title by an African American boxer. *The Cruise of the* Snark (1912) is his only other book, after *The People of the Abyss* (1903), his study of homeless life in the slums of the East End of London, England, to contain his own original photographs.¹⁰

London tended to self-document, as in *The Cruise of the* Snark and *John Barleycorn* (1913).¹¹ But two early descriptions, first of himself to a book reviewer and then to his second wife, Charmian, are especially telling. His first description of himself is a three-page typed letter, signed March 24, 1900, and sent to Maitland LeRoy Osborne of Boston's *National Magazine*, who had written to London asking for information, as he was to write a review of London's *The Son of the Wolf*, the latter's first collection of Klondike tales and first book, published in 1900 by Houghton Mifflin. London wrote:

I was born in San Francisco and am a Californian by birth as well as residence. . . . I lived on Californian ranches until my tenth year when my family removed to Oakland. . . . By fits and starts I acquired a grammar school education, but rough life always called to me, my whole ancestry was nomadic (Its destiny apparently to multiply and spread over the earth), so at fifteen, I, too, struck out into the world. I did not run away. My people knew the strain in my blood, so I went with consent. I first went faring amongst the scum marine population of San Francisco Bay, where I got down close to the naked facts of life. It was a most adventurous experience, and one (like all the rest), which I have never regretted. . . . I there learned the rudiments of seamanship, . . . til, the month I was seventeen, I was fitted to ship before the mast as an able seaman. Went to Japan, seal-hunting on the Russian side of the Bering Sea, etc. It was the longest voyage I ever took (seven month); life was to [*sic*] short to admit of more.

He admits his interest in economics and sociology but also emphasizes the tramping he did after he returned to California—"to the manor [*sic*] born," he says, continuing his casual tone:

> I dabbled at high school, took a brief fling at the State University . . . and hurried away with the first rush into the Klondike. Having mined and camped through the Sierras and other places . . . [n]ever having been unwise enough to learn a trade, I have worked at all sorts of hard labor. When [I was] in the Klondike my father died, and I returned to take charge of the family. . . . I resolved to make the fight of my life by making my living with my pen. This was precarious, for my assets were nil and my liabilities legion. I was also a beginner, knew nothing of markets, methods of editors, needs, or how to furnish those needs.

He is proud of his "nomadic ancestry" but says he lived among "scum." The account speaks to his need to demonstrate his worldliness ("a brief fling at the State University") at the same time as it confesses his naivete ("a beginner, knew nothing of markets, methods of editors"). London's duality is evident here as well as in so many other places. *The Son of the Wolf*, he says, was written out of a need for cash.[12] But of the North, he says solemnly, "It was in the Klondike that I found myself. There nobody talks. Everybody thinks. There you get your perspective. I got mine."[13]

In a letter dated June 18, 1903, to Charmian, at the beginning of their love affair, London confesses to having an inner and an outer self, not unlike Hawthorne's narrator behind his "Veil" in "The Custom House" preface to *The Scarlet Letter*. London writes to her:

> I wonder if I can make you understand. You see, in the objective facts of my life I have always been frankness personified. That I tramped or begged or festered in jail or slum meant nothing by the telling. But over the lips my inner self I had long since put a seal—a seal indeed rarely broken, in moments when one caught fleeting glimpses of the hermit who lived inside. How can I begin to explain? Perhaps this way. My child life was uncongenial. There was nothing responsive around me. I learned reticence, an inner reticence. I went into the world early, and I adventured among many different classes. A newcomer in any class, I naturally was reticent concerning my real self, which such a class could not understand, while I was superficially loquacious in order to make my entry into such a class popular and successful. And so it went, from class to class, from clique to clique. No

intimacies, a continuous hardening, a superficial loquacity so clever, and an inner reticence so secret, that the one was taken for real, the other never dreamed of. Ask people who know me today, what I am. A rough, savage fellow, they will say, who likes prizefights and brutalities, who has a clever turn of pen, a charlatan's smattering of art, and the inevitable deficiencies of the untrained, unrefined, self-made man which he strives with a fair measure of success to hide beneath an attitude of roughness and unconventionality. Do I endeavor to unconvince them? It's so much easier to leave their convictions alone. (*Letters*, 366)

He wrote to Charmian in other letters that it was her frankness and spontaneity that immediately drew him to her. He would go on to create many more versions of himself, but these two are among the most interesting.[14]

We hear London's voice and see through his eyes in the work he produced: the short story, novella, novel, essay, play, poetry, sports reportage, war correspondence, speech, photography, sociology, travel narrative, and so on. But he was also a man of the newly global newspaper, periodical, and wire service that had appeared. We can hear his voice today, literally, as his very few voice recordings via wax cylinders have been analyzed by the Lawrence Livermore Laboratory. His voice sounds very soft and well educated, without a trace of hoboing, sailoring, or the orator. Despite his celebrity, he, like many before and after him, does not necessarily match the public idea of celebrityhood, but in this volume a more intimate view is offered by those who actually knew him. For one thing, as I hope readers will discover, he and his friends and family were very funny people with a sometimes over-the-top devotion to humor. When he spoke of going wherever the zest of life took him, he was telling the truth, be it a picnic or the South Seas.

London's companions wrote accounts of him as being a very happy man, contrary to the notion that he spent his life in despair after his success, like his character Martin Eden. This good mood is evident in the memoir kept by London's valet and secretary, Yoshimatsu Nakata. The cook on board the *Snark* (the two-year Pacific voyage vessel, 1907–1909), Martin Johnson, penned his reminiscences *Through the South Seas with Jack London* (1912) and went on to be a world explorer. Charmian wrote four books on their life together. His daughters remember him differently: Joan London (1901–1971), who was his biographer, and her younger sister, Becky London (1902–1992), who does not seem to have shared her sister's conflicts with their father.[15]

London himself was interviewed by newspapers wherever he went and constantly appeared in magazines; at the Huntington Library in San Marino, California, home to most of his papers, there are vast troves of microfilm and dozens of giant ledger books documenting his tear sheets and international press—five thousand pages' worth. The second-largest collection is located at the Merrill-Cazier Library at Utah State University. Even those who know the extent of London's celebrity—or think they know it—are startled to find the sheer number of obituaries upon his death in newspapers and magazines the world around. There are hundreds at the Huntington. Throughout his life, but particularly upon his death, poems were composed for him and while he was alive sent to him. The following is a typical example from a male admirer:

JACK LONDON

I.

Here's to you, Jack, whose virile pen
Concerns itself with Man Size Men;
Here's to you, Jack, whose stories thrill
With savor of the western breeze,
With magic of the south—and chill
Shrill winds from icy floes and seas;
You have not wallowed in the mire
And muck of tales of foul desire,
For, though you've sung of fight and fraud,
Of love and hate—ashore, afloat—
You have not struck a ribald note
Nor made your art a common bawd.

II.

Here's to you, Jack, I've loved your best,
Your finest stories from the first,
Your sagas of the north and west—
But what is more—I've loved your worst!
For in the poorest work you do,
There's something clean and strong and true,
A tang of big and primal things,
A sweep of forces vast and free,
A touch of wizardry which brings
The glamour of the wild to me.

III.

So when I read a London tale
Forthwith I'm set upon a trail
Of great enchantment, and I track
Adventure round the world and back,
With you for guide—here's to you Jack.[16]

There's an odd lilt of Dr. Seuss here. Most of the poems, however, hundreds more, are from rather sentimental ladies. Because space is limited here, I include only one, by Grace Monroe Davis, which, for its remarkably different meter and its metaphorical surprises, deserves quotation:

"To Jack London"
We wrote of a world that had pretty grown and pale,
From lack of blood. From life well insulated
We went our way. Then, like the untamed gale
That tears the bay where Suisun is mated
Unto the lusty ocean, Jack London wrote.
He told of sinewy men with passions taut,
Whose fishing skiffs like gun gray sea gulls float,
But never in the riptide waves are caught,
And shattered. Pirates, too, of saurian shapes
Watch for the fish catch splashed with light, as dawn
Flings flamingo flames against the western capes;
And how to picture these Jack London knew,
For in his early youth he fought with life;
He met this Foe on the rough Suisun slough.
And cut His heart out with an oyster knife,
Though London's tales may reek with muck and mind,
And tell of men uncouth and roughly dressed;
Still racing through the drab is the red of blood.
His tales will live; they meet Time's sternest test.[17]

And then there are other posthumous tributes in fiction. The men's magazine cover story "Before I Die, I'll Have 1,000 Women" by Roger Weston, purporting to quote Jack London, outdoes the rest. It relates an imaginary forecastle fight over a prostitute on the *Sophie Sutherland* in which Jack saves the Caucasian girl from a Lascar man who "clamps a ham-handed hand on her breast." Jack, a "lithe, muscular figure catapults onto the huge lascar's neck" and bites (perhaps in a tribute to Norris's *McTeague*)! The narrator continues: "London's teeth, blackened with scurvy, closed upon gristle and flesh. He chewed relentlessly. A roar of pain began, low at first, then rising in a crescendo of agony until it filled the forecastle." In this tale London is a "roistering, wenching American novelist" who boasts, " 'I enjoyed my first woman when I was only 12 years old.' . . . Jack London could sweet-talk virtually any woman out of her dress or her virtue within five minutes." The leering gives way to a fairly conventional bio of London, even if it ends with him in a bar pouring morphine into a double scotch in 1913, with a "crumpled note from an unknown female admirer" in his pocket. The note reads, "I have read all your books and think you are magnificent. Will you sire a child for me? It will be the product of pure passion between a real Mate-Woman and American's peerless male, the incomparable Jack London." Its illustrations are as alarming as its text.[18]

The present volume offers a set of views from people who actually knew Jack London, the real person and not an outlandish stereotype. Each item is introduced by a brief account of its historical and cultural context and bibliographical reference. The volume's dozens of primary sources illustrate the continuing complexities of this dynamic personality and artist in a way that no single voice could. Jack London was, as Alfred Kazin so famously noted, "the story" of his own life.[19]

## NOTES

1. London, "An Odyssey of the North."

2. The first version of Twain's tale appeared in *The New York Saturday Press*, November 18, 1865 ("Jim Smiley and His Jumping Frog"). Twain's first book was *The Celebrated Jumping Frog of Calaveras County, and Other Sketches* (1867).

3. See especially Zola, preface to *Thérèse Raquin*.

4. Campbell, "American Literary Naturalism."

5. Twain, *Innocents Abroad*, 650.

6. Some of the best introductions to naturalism include Furst and Skrine's *Naturalism*; Don Pizer's *Realism and Naturalism in Nineteenth-Century American Literature* and *Twentieth-Century American Literary Naturalism*, not to mention his dozens of editions of naturalist writers; Link's *The Vast and Terrible Drama*; and Campbell's *Bitter Tastes*, in addition to her web sites on American realism and naturalism.

7. Burbank, *Harvest of Years*, 225.

8. For an account of Flora and several other important women in London's life, see Stasz,

*Jack London's Women*. Many biographers and critics are very harsh on Flora because London was, but Stasz helps portray Flora in a broader, more balanced and sensitive way.

9. See Charmian London, *The Log of the* Snark; and Johnson, *Through the South Seas with Jack London.*

10. It is fitting that his early and best photographic recorder was Arnold S. Genthe, fellow member of the so-called Crowd from the San Francisco area who gathered in Carmel at George and Carrie Sterling's cottage.

11. "John Barleycorn is frankly and truthfully autobiographical. There is no poetic license in it." Jack London to Mr. D. King, March 19, 1915, Jack London Collection, Huntington Library, JL 12281.

12. Letter in private collection.

13. "Jack London, by Himself."

14. It is not hard to understand that London had numerous doubles, popping up around the country and generally causing trouble. The *Battle Creek* (Michigan) *Journal* reported on April 8, 1915, that "[a]t last Jack London is to have an opportunity to show himself before a local audience" (Jack London Collection, Huntington Library, JLE). According to this paper, London was in Battle Creek "practically the entire winter" training to face a local boxing heavy, "Bull" Anderson, who did not show, and so he would fight someone named Barrett from Detroit. This must have amused London, who was then trying to recover his health in Hawai'i.

15. We have no account of him written by his first wife, Elizabeth "Bessie" Maddern London (1876–1948).

16. Berton Braley, Jack London Collection, Huntington Library, JLE 2435.

17. Davis, "To Jack London," 108.

18. Weston, "'Before I Die, I'll Have 1,000 Women,'" 44, 60–64.

19. Kazin, *On Native Grounds*, 88.

# Chronology

1821    JANUARY 13. William Henry Chaney born in a log cabin near Chesterville, Maine.

1828    JANUARY 11. John London born in Decatur Township, Clearfield County, Pennsylvania.

1848    AUGUST 17. Flora Wellman born in Massillon, Ohio.

1867    OCTOBER 13. Eliza London born on her parents' farm in Iowa.

1871    NOVEMBER 27. Charmian Kittredge born in Wilmington, California.

1873    OCTOBER. Flora Wellman leaves the Everhards, her relations in Alliance, Ohio, for Seattle, Washington.

1874    JUNE 12. Flora Wellman and W. H. Chaney begin a relationship and become common-law man and wife, living at 314 Rush St., San Francisco.

1875    FEBRUARY 11. Eliza and her sister Ida are left at the Protestant orphanage in Oakland, California, where John London has moved his surviving children after his wife's death.

1876    JANUARY 12. John Griffith Chaney born at 615 Third St. in San Francisco, California, to Flora Wellman, who names William Henry Chaney, an itinerant astrologer, as the father, who deserted her when she refused an abortion. Flora cannot produce milk, so the boy is taken in by Daphna Virginia Prentiss
        JULY 13. Elizabeth "Bessie" M. Maddern born.
        SEPTEMBER 7. Marriage of Flora Wellman and John London, a Civil War veteran and widower; the baby is now called John Griffith London, "Johnny" for short.

1877    FEBRUARY 19. John's daughters Ida and Eliza are brought home.

1878    Jack and Eliza suffer near-fatal attacks of diphtheria; to escape the epidemic, family relocates to Oakland, where John London goes into the produce business.

1879    MARCH 21. Anna Strunsky born in Babinotz, Russia.

1883    JANUARY 12. London family moves from a farm in Alameda to a farm in San Mateo County.

1885    Discovers books by reading a partial copy of Ouida's romantic tale *Signa* and Washington Irving's *Tales of the Alhambra*; the family moves to raise chickens in Livermore Valley.

1886    MARCH. John buys a boardinghouse in Oakland, but it fails; Flora loses on lottery tickets. Jack is often taken by John down to the Oakland waterfront to fish and look at its ships and boats.
SUMMER. Works as a newsboy and at loading ice wagons and setting up pins in bowling alleys; frequents Johnny Heinold's saloon and learns to sail a skiff; discovers the Oakland Free Public Library.

1887    FALL. Enrolls in Cole Grammar School in West Oakland.

1891    Graduates from eighth grade; works at Hickmott's Cannery; purchases sloop, the *Razzle-Dazzle*, with $300 loaned him by Mrs. Virginia Prentiss; joins oyster pirates and their heavy drinking; attempts suicide age 15.

1892    Joins, then deserts, the Shore Patrol, taking up with some Sacramento "Road-Kids" and "Gay Cats," riding train cars "over the hill" (the Sierra Nevada Mountains) to Reno; goes by moniker "Sailor Kid."

1893    JANUARY–AUGUST. Seven-month voyage as an able seaman on the *Sophia Sutherland*, a 150-ton, three-masted sealing schooner, crossing the North Pacific to the Bonin Islands, Japan, and the Bering Sea.
LATE AUGUST. Takes job in a jute mill at 10 cents an hour for ten-hour-plus workdays.
NOVEMBER 11. Encouraged by Flora, enters and wins the $25 first prize in a contest for "best descriptive article," published in the *San Francisco Examiner*, "Story of a Typhoon off the Coast of Japan"; beats out Stanford and Cal students and earns a month's factory wages.

1894 Works as a coal-heaver for the Oakland, San Leandro, and Hayward Electric Railway power plant; quits because he learns he has been cheated into doing the job of two men.

APRIL 6. Leaves Oakland for an extended tramping experience with Kelly's Army, the western contingent of Coxey's Industrial Army, a national march of unemployed men on Washington, under the moniker "Frisco Kid"; walks or rides in wagons or under trains, going east.

MAY 25. Abandons the army in Hannibal, Missouri, after the arrest of Coxey.

MAY 30. Visits the 1893 World's Columbian Exposition in Chicago and his mother's Everhard relatives there and in Michigan.

JUNE 29. Arrested for vagrancy in Buffalo, New York, where he had stopped to view Niagara Falls, and imprisoned at the Erie County Penitentiary for thirty days; becomes an ardent socialist.

JULY 29. Released from the penitentiary, tramps through New England and then across Canada to get home.

1895 Attends Oakland High School, earning his expenses by serving as school janitor; writes for the *Oakland High School Aegis* and participates in the Henry Clay Club, a debating society; falls in love with Mabel Applegarth, the Ruth Morse of his semi-autobiographical *Martin Eden* (1909); meets Herman "Jim" Whitaker, who teaches him boxing and fencing.

DECEMBER 25. "What Socialism Is" published in the *San Francisco Examiner*.

1896 Leaves high school for Belmont Academy in Belmont, California, to cram for his entrance exams for college; tutored by friends Bess Maddern, Fred Jacobs, and Ted Applegarth, Mabel's brother. Was a fellow alum with Frank Norris.

APRIL. Joins Socialist Labor Party.

SEPTEMBER. Attends the University of California; becomes known in newspapers as the "Boy Socialist of Oakland."

1897 Leaves university after one semester owing to lack of funds.

MARCH. Turns to hard labor back at the Belmont Academy laundry in punishing conditions.

JULY 14. S.S. *Excelsior* docks at San Francisco with riches brought home by men returning from the Klondike gold strikes.

JULY 25. Travels to Alaska for the Yukon Gold Rush partnered with Eliza's elderly husband, Capt. James H. Shepard, on the S.S.

*Umatilla* to Port Townsend, Washington, then on the *City of Topeka* to Juneau, Alaska.

AUGUST 5. In Juneau teams up with Merritt Sloper, "Big Jim" Goodman, and Fred C. Thompson.

AUGUST 8. Writes to Mabel Applegarth, "I have 1,000 lbs. in my outfit[, and] . . . I have to divide it from 10 to 15 loads according to the trail. I take a load a mile and come back empty. That makes two miles. 10 loads mean 19 miles, for I do not have to come back after the 11th load because there is none. If I have fifteen loads it means 29 miles. Am certain we will reach the lake in 30 days. Including Indians there are about 2,000 people here and half as many at Skagway Bay, 5 miles from here."

AUGUST 14. Shepard's rheumatism sends him home to recover, though he and Eliza mortgaged their house to stake the trip.

AUGUST 31. Arrives in Dawson City, after the unforgiving incline of the Chilkoot Trail and the building of boats and rafts to negotiate nearly frozen lakes and treacherous river rapids, before the creeping cold of deep winter begins. Later describes murderousness among many gold-seekers, especially partners using long two-handed saws to cut boards from trees.

OCTOBER 9. Arrives at the Stewart River and takes possession of a cabin on an island between the river and the mouth of Henderson Creek 80 miles from Dawson. As of December, he and his companions spend the rest of the winter in a few cabins. His reading out loud entertains them in the long nights.

OCTOBER 14. John London dies in Oakland.

1898    MAY–JUNE. Contracts scurvy; with friends constructs a raft, getting first to Dawson, then floating 5,000 miles north to the mouth of the Yukon River in the Bering Sea to St. Michael; makes many notes, especially on stories heard in the mining camps and saloons, observations of First Nation peoples encountered on the river, and the reminiscences of a French priest who accompanied him.

JUNE 11. Crosses the Arctic circle at 3:00 a.m., with 23 hours and 30 minutes of sunshine.

JUNE 30. Reaches St. Michael. Takes steamer to Seattle; upon returning to Oakland is now the sole support of an extended family that eventually consists of nearly a dozen members.

SEPTEMBER 13. Writes "The Mammon Worshippers," the introductory poem of "The Devil's Dicebox," his first Klondike story, submitting it to *McClure's* on September 23 (eventually published nearly one hundred years after its composition).

NOVEMBER 14. Bessie Maddern's fiancé, Fred Jacobs, is killed in the Philippines.

DECEMBER. Meets Anna Strunsky, Stanford graduate and Bay Area socialist intellectual, his eventual lover and coauthor (*The Kempton-Wace Letters*, 1903), later Anna Strunsky Walling, and a lifetime friend to him and his second wife, Charmian Kittredge London.

DECEMBER 25. "About the loneliest Christmas I ever faced," he writes Mabel Applegarth. "Guess I'll write to you. Nothing to speak of though—everything quiet. . . . Well the FIRST BATTLE has been fought. While I have not conquered, I'll not confess defeat." He writes of children and a wife at Christmas, earning income as a writer, but now having to give what he has to his mother: "DUTY—I turned every cent over"; keeps pawning his bicycle, coat, and typewriter. He ends with "[Y]ou just watch my smoke."

1899   JANUARY. First Klondike short story, "To the Man on Trail," published in *Overland Monthly*; turns down a job as a postal worker.

FEBRUARY. Begins correspondence with fellow writer Cloudesley Johns.

FEBRUARY 28. Writes to Ted Applegarth, "I am living hand to mouth."

SEPTEMBER 17. Sends "From Dawson to the Sea" to the San Francisco *Bulletin*; his Klondike material meets with little interest at first.

DECEMBER. Writes many, many letters to Anna Strunsky, which continues for many years.

1900   JANUARY. *The Atlantic* publishes "An Odyssey of the North"; Jack attains his position as a currently popular and important author, eventually introducing millions of readers worldwide to his naturalistic subject matter and style; begins coauthorship of *The Kempton-Wace Letters*; continues grueling pace of writing and circulating his work, with numerous speeches to socialist organizations; starts to receive better pay for his writing.

MARCH. Meets Charmian Kittredge when interviewed for *Overland Monthly* by her aunt, Ninetta Eames.

APRIL 7. Marries Bessie Maddern, his friend and former math tutor, within a week of being turned down by Anna Strunsky; on the same day, his first collection of stories, *The Son of the Wolf*, is published by Houghton Mifflin.

JUNE 2. Contracts with McClure, Phillips & Co. for $125 per month for five months to write his first novel, *A Daughter of the Snows* (1902).

1901    JANUARY 15. Joan London, his and Bessie's first daughter, is born.

JANUARY 21. Is nominated by the Social Democratic Party and runs unsuccessfully for mayor of Oakland.

SPRING. Meets George Sterling and many of the so-called Crowd of bohemian Bay Area artists and philosophers who often congregated at the Bohemian Grove and at Sterling's home on the beach in Carmel.

MAY. *The God of His Fathers and Other Stories* published by McClure, Phillips.

JUNE. Review of Frank Norris's *The Octopus* published in *Impressions*.

1902    First novel, *A Daughter of the Snows*, published by Lippincott; *The Cruise of the Dazzler* published by Century; and his second collection of Klondike tales, *Children of the Frost*, published by Macmillan, beginning his long association with George Brett and Macmillan Publishers.

MARCH 23. Meets up with Charmian, Emil Jensen from his Klondike days, Jim Whitaker from his school days, and George Sterling for fencing and other sports; Eliza and her son, Irving Shepard, are also present.

JULY 21. Asked by the American Press Association in New York City to go to South Africa to interview participants in the Boer War. Though the trip is canceled before he gets to New York, he goes anyway to London, England, arriving on August 6, and decides to live for six weeks among the poor and homeless of London's East End.

AUGUST 9. Watches festivities for the coronation of King Edward VII from Trafalgar Square.

AUGUST 17. Anna Strunsky, learning that Bessie is pregnant with his second child, breaks off their just-renewed affair. Jack finishes what he always called his favorite among his books, his sociological study *The People of the Abyss* (1903), illustrated by his documentary photographs.

OCTOBER 20. Second daughter, Bess, called Becky, is born.

DECEMBER 1. Starts writing *The Call of the Wild* as a short story, which grows to be a novella.

DECEMBER 11. Signs a contract with Macmillan for two years to write six books: *The Kempton-Wace Letters*, *The Call of the Wild*, *The People of the Abyss*, *The Faith of Men*, and *Tales of the Fish Patrol*.

1903     *The Call of the Wild*, *The People of the Abyss*, and *The Kempton-Wace Letters* published.

JANUARY 7. Having been injured on December 30, Jack is visited by George Brett, then also in London, one of the few times they actually saw each other.

JANUARY 8. William Henry Chaney dies in a Chicago hotel.

FEBRUARY 12. *The Saturday Evening Post* offers to buy *The Call of the Wild* if he will cut five thousand words and set a price; he agrees and sells it for 3 cents per word, or $750. London never earned much from his publication of one of the most widely read American novels in the world.

FEBRUARY 23. Jack and Bessie move to the Piedmont Bungalow.

MARCH. "Getting into Print" published in *The Editor* and "How I Became a Socialist" in *The Comrade*.

MARCH 10. Buys sloop named the *Spray*.

SUMMER. Alternates between time spent with George Sterling and bohemian friends in Carmel and time spent at home as a husband and father, without guests.

JUNE 16–18. Visits to Charmian at Glen Ellen result in their falling in love.

JULY. *The Call of the Wild* published by Macmillan.

JULY 14. Informs Bessie that he is leaving her; later moves out, mourning the "Poor, sad little bungalow" in a letter to Cloudesley Johns.

AUGUST 14. Writes in a letter to Fannie K. Hamilton: "At least believe this of me: that whatever I have done I have done with the sanction of my own conscience."

DECEMBER. *The Call of the Wild* is a best seller.

1904     *The Sea-Wolf* and *The Faith of Men* published.

JANUARY 7. Sails for Yokohama on the S.S. *Siberia* to serve as war correspondent attached to the Japanese army for the Hearst syndicate.

FEBRUARY 1. Arrested in Moji, Japan, for unknowingly making photographs of a military installation; tried the next day and his camera confiscated; it is restored on February 3.

FEBRUARY 3–16. Finally arrives after two punishing weeks aboard steamers, junks, and small boats in Chemulpo to meet Bobby Dunn of *Collier's Weekly*.

FEBRUARY 27. "How Jack London Got In and Out of Jail in Japan" appears on the front page of the *San Francisco Examiner*; most of his other dispatches from Korea are front page, above the fold.

MARCH 4. Enters Ping Yang (Pyongyong) with the Japanese army; frustrated after long and dangerous journey to be held back from the front lines by Japanese censorship; files dispatches and makes photographs behind the lines on the displacement of Koreans and other ruins of war; witnesses the Battle of the Yalu River; ordered back to Seoul.

APRIL 6. Reads from *The Call of the Wild* at a YMCA benefit with Japanese officers in dress uniform; wears a black stovepipe hat and a Prince Albert tie.

JUNE. Nearly court-martialed by the Japanese army for striking a Japanese groom he said he caught stealing from him; bailed out and brought home with the help of fellow correspondent Richard Harding Davis and a sometime fan, Theodore Roosevelt.

JUNE 28. Bessie sues for divorce, naming Anna Strunsky as correspondent.

JULY 25. Jack writes and asks Charmian to come to him.

AUGUST 18. Accompanies George Sterling to the Bohemian Grove summer High Jinks, as he will nearly every August.

SEPTEMBER 3. Charmian corrects final proofs of *The Sea-Wolf*.

SEPTEMBER 8. Begins yachting trip in the newly purchased *Spray* with friends including the Sterlings, Blanche and Dick Partington, Herman Whitaker, Herman (Toddy) Albrecht, Cloudesley Johns, and Ernest Matthews.

DECEMBER 19. *The Sea-Wolf* is a best seller.

1905     *War of the Classes*, *The Game*, and *Tales of the Fish Patrol* published.

MARCH. Riding back and forth over Nun's Canyon Road and other passes from Sonoma to Napa to visit Charmian; cruising on the *Spray*.

MARCH 20. Charmian spends evening with Jack at 1216 Telegraph Avenue in Oakland.

APRIL–MAY. Continues periods of intense writing and lecturing ("The Class Struggle," "The Rising Tide of Revolution," and then "Revolution"); is ill with major depressive disorder, what he calls "the Long

Sickness"; Charmian stays with him at Wake Robin Lodge through many weeks.

SUMMER. Begins to buy parcels of what would become his "Beauty Ranch" in Sonoma Valley.

SEPTEMBER 12. Intercollegiate Socialist Society founded at Peck's Restaurant on Fulton St. in New York City; new officers are Jack London, president, and Upton Sinclair, vice president; membership includes W. D. Howells, J. G. Phelps-Stokes, Clarence Darrow, Lincoln Steffens, Thorstein Veblen, and Edwin Markham. Later earns London an FBI file.

OCTOBER 18. Begins lecture trip throughout the East and Midwest on socialism.

NOVEMBER 17. Divorce from Bessie final.

NOVEMBER 18. Wires Charmian to come to Chicago.

NOVEMBER 19. Charmian and Jack London are married.

DECEMBER 27. Concludes lectures at Boston's Faneuil Hall on December 26. They spend their honeymoon in Jamaica; newspapers and magazines are critical of his divorce and immediate remarriage, yet Charmian is featured in hundreds of photo spreads, displaying her fashionable taste in clothing and millinery.

1906     *White Fang*, *Moon-Face & Other Stories*, and *Scorn of Women*, a play, published.

JANUARY 19. Resumes lecture tour, giving his speech "The Coming Crisis" at New York's Grand Central Palace and Carnegie Hall; speaks at Yale University, the University of Chicago, and the University of North Dakota.

APRIL 18. At 5:14 a.m. is awakened in Sonoma by an earthquake; with Charmian, saddles horses and rides to the top of Sonoma Mountain, where, even 50 miles south, San Francisco appears an immense tower of firestorm. They take the train and ferry over to the city from Sausalito, where they observe the flaming, melting, collapsing, horrifying disaster firsthand.

SUMMER. Begins building his sailboat, the *Snark*, for proposed round-the-world seven-year cruise; steadily writing and building the ranch.

JUNE 20. States in a letter to Frederick Irons Bamford that "[p]ersonally I like Nietzsche tremendously, but I cannot go all the way with him."

JULY 15. Tells Fannie K. Hamilton in a letter that "[t]hough I am not classed as a follower of his [Spencer] his thinking has profoundly affected my life."

JULY 17. Photo taken with George Sterling and Mexican painter Xavier Martinez blowing soap bubbles.

AUGUST 31. Goes on a boat trip with Charmian, Herman Whitaker, and other friends to see the *Snark* in progress.

SEPTEMBER. "The Apostate" published by the *Woman's Home Companion*, based on his childhood working in factories.

OCTOBER 16. Asks Macmillan for $5,000 advance, as *Snark* construction costs grow; these requests would multiply exponentially as he pursued other projects.

OCTOBER 20. Sells the rights to the *Snark* voyage to both *Cosmopolitan* and *Woman's Home Companion*; a series of misunderstandings ensues.

NOVEMBER 8. A jaunt with many friends up to Monterey to see George and Carrie Sterling, Xavier Martinez, Jimmy Hopper, and Arnold Genthe. Genthe makes several portraits of Jack on November 12; during this autumn the number of visitors to the Londons at the ranch begins to increase rapidly.

DECEMBER 7. Lectures on socialism at Equality Hall in Oakland. Martin Johnson arrives from Independence, Kansas, to join the crew of the *Snark*; they join Charmian and Sterling for dinner at Saddle Rock Restaurant.

DECEMBER 13. Writes Ina Coolbrith to thank her for her friendship and guidance when he was a boy.

MIDWINTER. Visits Nevada gold mines at Tonopah and Goldfield with Charmian.

1907    *The Road, Before Adam,* and *Love of Life and Other Stories* published; a year of many dinners, luncheons, theatre, friends, and visits to San Francisco, Oakland, and Carmel; working hard on writing and the ranch; buys up several adjacent ranches.

JANUARY 2. Complains to Brett in letter that "conditions in San Francisco after the earthquake have made me pay double [for the *Snark*] what I should have paid. When I increased the length from 40′ waterline to 45′ waterline I figured the boat would cost me $7,000. Already I have passed the $15,000 mark." The eventual cost of building the boat reached $22,000.

FEBRUARY. Borrows $5,000 against 490 27th St. house to pay off *Snark* bills before sailing. Neither his finances nor his health would ever improve after this voyage, life-altering as it was, but artistically second only in importance to the Klondike in terms of his four volumes of Pacific short stories.

APRIL 23. After seemingly endless delays, the *Snark* sails out of the Golden Gate, hounded at the dock by creditors.

MAY 20. Passage to Hawai'i in constant danger as the boat malfunctions in nearly every respect; though very sick for much of the crossing, Jack, Charmian, and four others of their amateur crew (Martin Johnson, Herbert Stoltz, Roscoe Eames, and Tochigi) arrive in Pearl Lochs on Oahu for a five-month stay in the Hawaiian Islands. Jack was proud he had taught himself celestial navigation, too busy to worry about it beforehand.

MAY 20–OCTOBER 14. In Hawai'i to complete building and repairing the *Snark*; Eames, Charmian's uncle, is fired as captain: he neither knew nor learned navigation.

MAY 18. Finishes second version of "To Build a Fire."

MAY 28. Dines with Charmian at the Royal Hawaiian Hotel and meets Alexander Hume Ford, a young promotor of Hawai'i; Ford tells Jack about surfing. Sees Theodore Roosevelt's article on "Nature-Faking" in *Everybody's Magazine*.

MAY 30. Staying in tent-cabin at Seaside Hotel on Waikiki Beach; original Outrigger Club was built at this spot.

JUNE 2. After a day of hiking Diamond Head, paddling an outrigger, and surfing, is confined to bed for four days with a severe sunburn.

JUNE 7. Ford arranges for Jack and Charmian to visit the "Ewa," or west side of Oahu, where sugarcane and pineapple plantations are staffed by migrant labor under sometimes harsh employment contracts from Japan, China, Portugal, South America, and elsewhere. His socialist sensibilities inflamed, Jack starts on a course of criticizing the U.S. annexation of Hawai'i, with the descendants of white missionaries living on stolen land and using wage slaves to do the work, in his first book of Hawaiian stories, *The House of Pride* (1908). His new friend, *Honolulu Advertiser* editor Lorrin Thurston, writes angry editorials when the title story appears.

JULY 1. Leaves with Charmian to spend the Fourth of July rodeo and festival at the leper colony at Kalaupapa on Molokai, with the help of two prominent physicians, Dr. Lucius Pinkham and Dr. E. S. Goodhue; makes sensitive photographs and narratives of the lepers as people who are not very different from anyone else; mentioning leprosy further incenses his *haole kama'aina* friends in Honolulu.

JULY 12. He and Charmian spend time on the Haleakala ranch managed by the Louis von Tempsky family; meets budding writer Armine von Tempsky; rides cane flumes down the mountain.

AUGUST 15. The *Snark* arrives on the Big Island; on August 25 they visit Kealakekua Bay, where Captain Cook and his crew were massacred in 1779.

SEPTEMBER 8. They visit Kilauea; in the Volcano House register, Jack calls the volcano "the pit of Hell," then writes, "Let us go down. Jack London"; Charmian writes: "And where Jack goes, there go I; so I followed along. Mrs. Jack."

SEPTEMBER 28. Hires Yoshimatsu Nakata, who speaks very little English; another new crew member is Herman de Visser.

OCTOBER 7. They sail for the Marquesas, making south by southeast, a crossing they were warned was not possible.

NOVEMBER 4. Discovers new flaws in the planking and then the beams of the boat—the "oak" is actually pine; the winds and tides are against them: they are too far west and south.

NOVEMBER 20. Discovers that someone left a water tank faucet open; they now have only twenty days of water; in the doldrums.

NOVEMBER 21. Charmian drinks less than a pint of water per day; crew is rationed to three quarts per day for drinking and two for cooking; thirst afflicts them all.

NOVEMBER 23. Rainfall saves them.

DECEMBER 6. After sixty-three days at sea with no sight of another vessel, they slip with difficulty into Taiohae Bay on the southern coast of Nuku Hiva at 10:00 p.m. and wake up, as Charmian put it, "in fairyland."

DECEMBER 7. They engage a cottage with Mrs. Fisher, who formerly hosted Robert Louis Stevenson; for the next few days there is feasting and enjoying their Victrola.

DECEMBER 18. Departing Taoihae, they sail to the Paumotus (as they called it; now Paumotu), the "dangerous archipelago" with its squalls and reefs; storms drive them on toward Tahiti.

DECEMBER 25. Christmas dinner at sea: tinned soup, shrimp fritters, fried taro, tinned corn, salad of tinned French beans and mayonnaise, sliced oranges and bananas garnished with grated coconut, all accompanied by champagne.

DECEMBER 27. Arrive at Papeete at noon.

1908     *The Iron Heel* published.

JANUARY. Brief trip with Charmian from Papeete back to California on the steamship *Mariposa* to settle financial affairs; both fall ill.

MARCH 16. Mails *Martin Eden* to Macmillan.

MARCH 28. Arrive back in Papeete.

APRIL 4. *Snark* journey resumed, sailing for Raiatea; meets Tehei of the village of Tahaa and sails with him in his canoe; the crew are feasted, as he writes in "The High Seat of Abundance" (in *The Cruise of the* Snark); Tehei becomes their pilot.

APRIL 9. Arrive in Bora Bora.

MAY 7. Arrive in American Samoa, hosted by the governor. Joan and Bess London are baptized at Trinity Episcopal Church in Oakland.

MAY 8. At Apia, Upolu, German Samoa; visit to Robert Louis Stevenson's grave at his home, Vailima.

MAY 20-27. Sail to Suva, Fiji Islands; main boom tackle is carried away.

JUNE 6-11. Sail to New Hebrides, Port Resolution, Tanna, and Vila Harbor, Erromangga.

JUNE 20-28. Sail to Solomon Islands, Santa Anna, Port Mary; Jack is quite ill. After drifting among the "Cannibal Islands," the *Snark* anchors at the Pendyffryn plantation on Guadalcanal, owned by George Darbishire and Tom Harding. *Adventure* (1911) relates the cruelty of life on the coconut plantations for the enslaved native workers.

JULY 22. Jack and Charmian go aboard "blackbirding" ship the *Minota*.

AUGUST 8. Leave Guadalcanal aboard the *Minota*, a slaver under the command of Captain Jansen, which, having survived an August 19 attack by outraged islanders as it is "recruiting," goes onto a reef. The Londons and crew are rescued by the local missionary and the ship *Eugenie*. The Londons take the terrier, Peggy, as a pet, from the late slaver Captain MacKenzie of the *Minota*, Captain Jansen's predecessor. Captain MacKenzie was killed and eaten six months earlier on Malaita.

AUGUST 23. Finally back on the *Snark*, sailing to Gubutu, Florida Island, and Lord Howe Atoll; more illness, now *ngari-ngari*, an intensely itchy rash.

SEPTEMBER. Everyone very sick: a new cabin boy, Wada, seems to have lost his mind; Nakata Yoshimatsu, a new assistant they hired in Hawai'i, has malaria; Jack has several illnesses; Wada deserts; even Peggy and the cockatoo get sick.

SEPTEMBER 5. Jack's retort to Theodore Roosevelt's charge of "Nature-Faking" in *White Fang*, an essay called "The Other Animals," one of the first "animal rights" essays, is published in *Collier's*.

SEPTEMBER 17. The *Snark* makes Lord Howe Atoll. On September 28, the Londons hear the story of "Mauki" and meet him. Jack's hands are swollen, as he, Charmian, and the crew are starting to suffer from malaria; yaws, or Solomon Island sores; and ngari ngari, an itching affliction of the skin.

OCTOBER 16. Back to Pendyffryn, to find Darbishire drunk and having lost their mail.

OCTOBER 26. Wada returns.

OCTOBER 28. Notorious alcohol and hashish costume party at Pendyffryn; Charmian starts her book manuscript for *The Log of the Snark*.

NOVEMBER 4–14. Jack and Charmian sail to Australia on the *Makambo*; Martin Johnson is left in charge of the *Snark;* several crew members fired, mostly for drunkenness.

NOVEMBER 20. Surgery in Sydney hospital for double fistula; treated for Solomon Island sores and malaria; doctors are puzzled by his paralyzed and peeling hands, diagnosing pellagra, but more likely a result of using corrosive sublimate mercury, stored in the *Snark*'s medicine chest, on his sores.

DECEMBER 8. Announces end of the *Snark* voyage owing to illness; Charmian writes, "We are heartbroken."

DECEMBER 17. Editor of *The Australian Star* asks him to report the Jack Johnson–Tommy Burns world heavyweight fight.

DECEMBER 26. His health improved, Jack covers the fight for the *New York Herald* syndicate itself; Charmian attends dressed as a man. Johnson's is a historic victory in front of thirty thousand fans, which Jack celebrates; but Jack Johnson, the winner, is refused service in any hotel or restaurant and asked to leave the country immediately.

1909   *Martin Eden* published.

FEBRUARY 13–APRIL 8. Recovering, tours Sydney and enjoys the theatre, the zoo, cave exploring, and swimming at Bondi Beach.

MARCH. "The Lepers of Molokai," one of the first accounts of sufferers of Hansen's disease that is both scientific and sympathetic, published in *Woman's Home Companion*.

MARCH 3. Martin Johnson and the *Snark* arrive, weeks late, having sailed for thirty-five days from Guadalcanal to Sydney.

MARCH 29. Advances Martin Johnson money for his round-the-world trip; Johnson sails March 31 for Italy.

APRIL 5. Signs papers to return via Guayaquil, Ecuador, on the *Tymeric*, a coal steamer, with Charmian as stewardess at $11 a month, Jack as purser, and Nakata as cabin boy.

APRIL 8–JULY 21. Returns to Oakland via Ecuador, Panama, New Orleans, and the Grand Canyon; seas are rough and the Londons suffer from fever, but Jack boxes regularly with the crew.

APRIL 19. Londons arrive at Guayaquil; travel by train to Quito.

MAY 30. Attend bullfight in Quito, which Jack condemns.

JUNE 25. Arrive in Panama and are quarantined; they read five months of mail.

JULY 6. Plans to leave on 6:45 a.m. train to Colon but gets left behind watching baggage; Nakata is thrown off train; more missed connections and confusion. When they reunite, they haven't enough money for passage.

JULY 12. Arrive in Louisiana and are quarantined; Nakata is held by Immigration and Customs. Jack writes to the secretary of commerce and labor in Washington, DC; reporters descend; Jack pays $500 bond for Nakata on July 13.

JULY 15. Depart New Orleans on Texas-Pacific and switch to the Santa Fe line.

JULY 21. Arrive in Oakland; take Eliza to dinner.

JULY 24. Return home to Glen Ellen.

AUGUST 21–29. Sees daughters and Flora; begins his lectures on *Snark* voyage.

SEPTEMBER 4. More and more guests, including Finn Froelich, the sculptor; Cloudesley Johns and his wife; George Sterling; and even A No. 1, the "Famous Tramp" otherwise known as Leon Ray Livingston, the author of many books on tramping.

SEPTEMBER–NOVEMBER. Both Londons are ill on and off; Charmian very depressed, enters Burke's Sanitarium and recovers.

OCTOBER 17–NOVEMBER 9. Sails the *Spray* in the San Joaquin and Sacramento Rivers; visits friends in Carmel.

DECEMBER. Many visits and outings in Oakland with daughters; buys them furs for Christmas.

DECEMBER 31. Orders the *Snark*, which by now has been stripped of much of its accouterments and is listing in Sydney Harbor, sold for £700.

1910     First Sonoma ranch novel, *Burning Daylight*, published, as well as *Lost Face, Revolution and Other Essays*, and *Theft: A Play in Four Acts*. Devotes most of his energy to building the Beauty Ranch; begins construction of Wolf House; numerous visits with friends at the ranch and with daughters.

JANUARY 15. Orders fifteen thousand eucalyptus trees for ranch and plans for more.

JANUARY 16. Attends Rev. Charles R. Brown's sermon against *Martin Eden* with Charmian in Oakland; attacked for having two wives; writes rebuttal to San Francisco *Bulletin*.

JANUARY 27. Visits Bessie, who tells him she has ended her marriage to Charles Milner, her second husband; relations between the ex-spouses worsen as they bicker over what Milner should have paid for.

FEBRUARY 12. Hires Eliza as his business manager and superintendent of the ranch.

JUNE 19. A baby daughter, Joy, is born and dies shortly thereafter, her neck having been broken by forceps; Charmian suffers alone in a hospital. Jack is away covering the Jack Johnson–Jim Jeffries world heavyweight match, considered the leading story in the world at the time, the black fighter challenging and beating the "Great White Hope"; Charmian writes in her diary, "The pity of it. Our own baby, our little daughter gone at four in the morning. Only 38 hours old — in the twilight of the morning."

JUNE 21. Takes part in a brawl at Muldowney's Saloon in San Francisco.

JUNE 24–JULY 5. Writes article on the fight every day for the *San Francisco Examiner*, the *San Francisco Chronicle*, and *The New York Herald*.

JULY 4. Jack Johnson–Jim Jeffries world heavyweight fight, Reno, Nevada; Jack, initially thinking the white man would win, is converted to admiration for Johnson; in the coming days and weeks. Johnson's victory sparks white-incited race riots across the country.

AUGUST 3. Charmian returns from her convalescence in Oakland and surprises Jack at Wake Robin.

OCTOBER 11. Buys the *Roamer* in Alameda.

OCTOBER 17–NOVEMBER 14. With Charmian, sails aboard the *Roamer* in the San Joaquin River Delta; she writes in her diary, "We Snark again"; they sail regularly each season.

NOVEMBER 16. Discovers he owes $2,400 and has only $1,200 in his bank account.

NOVEMBER 20. Architect Albert Farr visits the ranch to discuss plans for Wolf House.

NOVEMBER 28. Travels with Charmian to quarries to look at volcanic stone for Wolf House.

DECEMBER 2. Now has $500 in the bank; the Rev. Charles R. Brown resigns as pastor of the Congregational Church in Oakland, accused by his wife of having an affair.

DECEMBER 31. Big redwoods cut for Wolf House.

1911    *The Cruise of the* Snark, *Adventure, South Sea Tales,* and *When God Laughs and Other Stories* published.

JANUARY–FEBRUARY. With Charmian, visits Los Angeles and environs; their visits to Los Angeles grow more frequent owing to film contracts.

FEBRUARY 3. American newspapers mistakenly report that Jack London is riding with Pancho Villa on a raid on Mexicali, California; on February 5 the *Los Angeles Times* runs the story, which is picked up by the syndicates; Flora calls one of the papers and says that Jack is at her home having supper.

FEBRUARY–MARCH. Travels to San Francisco and Oakland; many friends visit at the ranch; Sterling is drinking heavily, and Jack's own alcoholism is starting to cause more and more trouble.

MARCH 17. Hires Eliza to oversee the building of Wolf House for $50 a month.

APRIL 11–MAY 3. Sailing trips with Charmian aboard the *Roamer* on the Napa River and San Pablo Bay to the Oakland estuary, and also through Benicia, Suisun Bay, and the delta of the San Joaquin River.

MAY 30. Mails "The Mexican" to *The Saturday Evening Post*.

JUNE 12–SEPTEMBER 5. Drives four-horse carriage with Charmian and Nakata through Northern California and Oregon.

SEPTEMBER 5. Arrives home; guests begin to appear: Ninetta and Edward Payne, George Wharton James, Jimmy Hopper, Spiro Orphans, Albert Farr, Ernest Matthews, Blanche Partington, and Allan Dunn; there are often fourteen for dinner; Charmian notes in her diary the very special and rare evenings when they are alone on the ranch together.

DECEMBER 24. Jack, Charmian, and Nakata leave by rail from Oakland for New York City.

1912    *The House of Pride and Other Tales of Hawaii, A Son of the Sun*, and *Smoke Bellew* published.

JANUARY 2. Arrive in New York City; move into apartment at 40 Morningside Park East.

JANUARY 27. Jack and Charmian attend a reception at the Liberal Club where Mary Austin as well as the Strunksy family are present; visit with many friends such as Arnold Genthe; Jack spends many nights at the theatre, many contract negotiations, honorary dinners; his drinking and late nights increasingly upset Charmian.

JANUARY 30. Signs publishing contract with the Century Company, abruptly abandoning Macmillan.

FEBRUARY 28. Signs papers for *Dirigo* voyage as third mate, Charmian as stewardess, and Nakata as assistant steward.

FEBRUARY 29. Returns to hotel at noon with his head shaved; Charmian hacks off eight inches of her own hair in retaliation and cries for two hours. They attend a ceremony at Edgar Allan Poe's gravesite in Baltimore and their photograph is taken, in which Jack's hat appears a few sizes too big; they buy another pet, Possum, a two-month-old fox terrier.

MARCH 1. Depart as crew aboard the *Dirigo*, bound from Baltimore around Cape Horn to Seattle. Charmian throws Jack's cigarettes and liquor overboard; he objects but begins to exercise vigorously, like Charmian; Nakata takes over many of Charmian's typing duties.

MAY 10. Cape Horn sighted off starboard bow.

MAY 20. The *Dirigo* rounds Cape Horn at 50 degrees after being blown backwards again and again in the frozen and treacherous South Ocean. Jack and Charmian have a talk about alcohol: he claims that he is not an alcoholic and says he will do better, but that he can still safely drink when they return home; Charmian writes in her diary, "I knew he would fail of the perfection of such a plan."

JULY 26. They arrive in Seattle; *Dirigo* captain Omar Chapman, whom Charmian has been nursing for many weeks, dies shortly thereafter of stomach cancer.

JULY 27. On the steamer home to Oakland, they read out loud to each other Henry James's *The Ambassadors*.

AUGUST 10. Martin and Osa Johnson visit the ranch.

AUGUST 12. Charmian miscarries their child conceived on the *Dirigo* and is nursed by Virginia Prentiss.

AUGUST 22. Attend Martin Johnson's South Seas show at the Orpheum in Oakland; Jack is introduced on-stage.

OCTOBER 2. Copy of *Smoke Bellew* arrives; Jack writes in Charmian's copy: "Dearest Mate-Woman: I am still filled with the joy of your voice that was mine last night when you sang. Sometimes, more than any clearly wrought concept of you, there are fine sounds in your throat that tell me the lovableness of you, and that I love as madly as I have always madly loved all the rest of you. Oct. 12, 1912, Wolf-man."

1913    *The Abysmal Brute, The Night-Born, John Barleycorn*, and *The Valley of the Moon* published; several films of works are made by Bosworth Inc. and the Balboa Amusement Producing Company; Martin Johnson publishes *Through the South Seas with Jack London*.

JANUARY 1. Sends remainder of *John Barleycorn* manuscript to Century Co.

FEBRUARY 1. Begins work on his "pig palace" at the ranch; begins building a home for Bessie.

FEBRUARY 9. Is sold a Dictaphone, on which he can record himself on reusable cylinders for his assistants.

FEBRUARY 15. Decides to buy imported Shire stallion, Neuadd Hillside, the 1912 California State Fair champion.

MARCH 7. Frolich makes medallion of Jack.

MARCH 9. Charmian drives Allan Dunn, who has been visiting the ranch, to the train station; that evening, Jack and Charmian have a marital discussion. She writes in her diary, "The Dear Mate, I love him so," but she adds, on March 11, "Feel very much of a battle ground. But what men. I can't help pouting out my chest!"

APRIL 13. Charmian notes in diary, "Still no word from Allan. Rather expected to hear from him. Guess he's keeping 'sober counsel' with himself."

APRIL 24–30. Visits Los Angeles to discuss movie contract with Sidney Ayers and Herbert M. Horkheimer of the Balboa Amusement Producing Company.

MAY 3. James Shepard appears on the ranch with a gun; Irving, Eliza and her estranged husband's son, runs for Jack: "Come quick, Papa's trying to hurt Mama. Papa's got a pistol"; Jack disarms him and throws him off the ranch; Shepard tries to have Jack arrested.

MAY 10. Writes in a letter, "If I should die at this precise moment I would die owing $100,000."

MAY 12. States he is for Prohibition.

MAY 20. Starts planning an autobiographical book called "Sailor on Horseback."

JUNE. Resumes publishing with Macmillan and George Brett; Macmillan asks him to slow down his book production to keep his market strong.

JULY 8. Undergoes appendectomy; is warned by personal physician, Dr. William S. Porter, that kidneys are deteriorating.

JULY 17. Rescinds movie rights from the Balboa Amusement Producing Company; travels to Los Angeles and signs with Hobart Bosworth and Frank E. Garbutt for movie rights; numerous lawsuits ensue.

AUGUST 22. Wolf House, nearly finished, burns down in an accidental fire, likely caused by spontaneous combustion of rags soaked in linseed oil left lying about by workers after wiping down the redwood interior; the temperature that day in Sonoma was over 100 degrees. The couple mourn but vow to rebuild. This event may have been a turning point from which his personal health begins to descend sharply; as he wrote, after the Wolf House fire, "My face changed."

SEPTEMBER 28. Writes in a letter, "The only trouble, I may say, about *John Barleycorn*," his alcoholic memoir, "is that I did not put in all of the truth. All that is in it is true; but I did not dare put in the whole truth."

OCTOBER 5. With Charmian attends premier of Bosworth Inc.'s film of *The Sea-Wolf* at Grauman's Chinese Theatre; it is the first feature-length film produced in America.

NOVEMBER 9. Receives ultimatum from Joan in a letter defending Bessie.

DECEMBER 10. Meets Ed Morrell at the Saddle Rock Restaurant in Oakland to get the story of his prison experiences for *The Star Rover* (1915).

DECEMBER 14–16. Visits Los Angeles for copyright trial arising from dealings with the Balboa Amusement Producing Company; ruling is in Jack's favor.

DECEMBER 17. Despite enormous royalties has only $10.60 in his bank account.

1914    *The Strength of the Strong* and *The Mutiny of the* Elsinore are published. *John Barleycorn, The Valley of the Moon,* and *Martin Eden* are filmed by Bosworth Inc.; by the end of 1914, Macmillan has sold one million books by Jack London.

JANUARY 8–FEBRUARY 20. Travels to New York to discuss business affairs.

JANUARY 9. Charmian has so little to live on she has to borrow $107 from Martin Johnson.

JANUARY 25–29. Visits with Anna Strunsky Walling at Cortland Hotel on 49th St.; they see each other often in New York.

JANUARY 30. Loses lawsuit against Joseph Noel for movie rights to *The Sea-Wolf.*

FEBRUARY 24. Sends Joan $4.50 and has $3.40 left in his account; still paying off Wolf House; writes her in a bitter vein.

MARCH. Earns approximately $10,000 in new royalties; hosts Ed Morrell at the ranch; learns that the governor has signed a bill passed by the California Assembly prohibiting the use of straitjackets in prisons; has finished about one hundred thousand words of *The Star Rover*; plans trip to Japan.

APRIL 3. Begins writing *The Little Lady of the Big House*; Charmian writes up descriptive pieces for it, as she did for *The Valley of the Moon.*

APRIL 15. Contracts with *Collier's Weekly* to report the Mexican Revolution instead of Far East trip.

APRIL 21. U.S. military invades Mexico, and navy seizes custom house in Veracruz; casualties ensue, and the naval college there is bombed.

APRIL 23. Old war-correspondent friend Richard Harding Davis arrives at the same time in Galveston.

APRIL 24–25. Refused credentials by U.S. Army general Frederick R. Funston because of a hoax in which someone distributed pamphlets printed by "the I.W.W.," with an article attributed to Jack, "The Good Soldier," a wild socialist attack on the military. Once Davis, with influential political friends, points out that Jack could not have written it, as it contains numerous grammatical errors, the matter is cleared up, and Jack sails on the S.S. *Kilpatrick* for Veracruz, while Charmian and Nakata sail aboard the S.S. *Atlantic*.

MAY. Sees correspondents Bobby Dunn, Jimmy Hare, and others; dinners aboard other ships, bullfights, riding, and other social diversions. Meanwhile, writes about and photographs U.S. and Mexican troops in the revolution, as well as prisoners, *soldaderas* (camp followers), trials, and a raid on American oil interests in Tampico.

MAY 30. Suffers severe dysentery and rheumatism; heavily criticized back home by socialists for supporting the side of U.S. oil interests and demeaning *mestizos* in racist terms.

JUNE 18. Returns to Glen Ellen.

JUNE 25. Writes in letter, "I am a hopeless materialist. I see the soul as nothing else than the sum of the organism plus personal habits, memories, experiences of the organism. I believe that when I am dead, I am just as much obliterated as the last mosquito you or I smashed."

JUNE 26. Offers "testimonial" for Corona Folding Typewriters; asks for two of them in July.

JULY 28–AUGUST 4. War is declared by Austria and Hungary against Serbia; Germany and Russia declare war against each other; the British Empire declares war on Germany; Jack thinks of traveling to Europe as a correspondent.

SEPTEMBER. Installs electricity at the ranch; silo, costing $5,000, is finished, as is dam at the lake.

1915    *The Star Rover* and *The Scarlet Plague* published; Charmian's *The Log of the* Snark published by Macmillan.

JANUARY 15–17. Attends Winter Carnival in Truckee, California.

FEBRUARY 12. Suffers acute attack of rheumatism.

FEBRUARY 19. Mabel Applegarth dies of tuberculosis, age 41.

FEBRUARY 22. Attends Panama-Pacific International Exposition in San Francisco.

FEBRUARY 24. Sails on the S.S. *Matsonia* with Charmian and Nakata for five months in Hawai'i, hoping to improve his health; tries to avoid alcohol; arrives in Honolulu to stay at 216 Beach Walk.

MARCH–JUNE. Tours, balls, dinners, and lectures given to various groups; they tour Pearl Harbor with the admiral and are asked to attend Queen Liliuokalani at 9:00 a.m. on March 11; invited to parties by the royal family. Jack sees old friends; much exercise, especially swimming; joins congressional junket to Kauai, the setting of his story

"Koolau the Leper"; once again they visit the leper settlement on Molokai, and visit friends in Pahoa, Puna, and Hilo.

MAY 5. Gives speech, "The Patriotism of the Pacific," later given as "The Language of the Tribe," to the Pan-Pacific Dinner, including the congressional delegation; theme is world peace and racial, ethnic, and national coexistence; argues that Americans should learn Japanese and vice-versa.

JULY 23. Return to Glen Ellen. Nakata plans to leave the Londons' service and settle in Honolulu, becoming a dentist and writing a personal memoir of Jack.

NOVEMBER 3. Writes letter to J. F. Connor listing the most important factors in his literary success: "1. Vast good luck. 2. Good health. 3. Good brain. 4. Good mental and muscular correlation. 5. Poverty. 6. Reading Ouida's *Signa* when I was eight years old. 7. Herbert Spencer's *Philosophy of Style.*"

NOVEMBER 25. The Londons see Houdini's performance at the vaudeville theatre in Oakland; afterwards they take him to Saddle Rock.

DECEMBER 16. Sails with Charmian on the S.S. *Great Northern* to Hawai'i; in Honolulu they live at 2201 Kalia Road in Waikiki, now the site of the Halekulani Hotel. They attend the grand reception for the queen, who sits in her throne room for the first time in thirty years, as well as numerous military and local dinners and receptions, luaus, poker games, balls, races and picnics at Kapiolani Park, and carnivals and fireworks. Lectures and impromptu readings and interviews, honorary membership in the Outrigger Club, Charlie Chaplin films, and friends occupy many days and nights. A favorite spot is the roof garden at the old Alexander Young Hotel at Bishop and Hotel Streets (demolished in the 1980s) for dinner and dancing.

1916  *The Little Lady of the Big House*, as well as his Bohemian Grove play, *The Acorn Planter: A California Forest Play*, and *The Turtles of Tasman* published.

APRIL 4. Londons sail with friend Mary Low for the Big Island, with Sekine, a new valet, to visit her Puuwaawaa Ranch; Low tells many local stories during this visit.

APRIL 17. Visit the Parker Ranch, see other friends, and head for Hilo to see Lorrin Thurston, editor of the *Honolulu Advertiser*—first a foe but then a close friend.

APRIL 28. Crossing Waipio Valley, Jack begins "The Hussy," finished at Kohala.

MAY 13. Back to Honolulu; "Most wonderful of love days with Mate," Charmian writes in her diary.

JUNE 6. With Mary Low, the Londons are given a luau attended by Princess Kalanianaole; on July 22 they give a big luau at their home for their friends.

JUNE 25. Mary Low hosts a luau with forty people, including royalty and the mayor; a "Jack London Hula" is chanted by Ernest Kaai and his singers and players, a *mele* written by Mary Low; at each stanza, Jack's progress is sung: "*Hainaie mai ana ka puna / No keaka lakana neia inoa /* The song is then echoed, / Tis in honor of Jack London."

JUNE 13. Mails "On the Makaloa Mat" to *Cosmopolitan*.

JULY 26. Londons sail from Honolulu to San Francisco on the S.S. *Matsonia*.

AUGUST 1. Arrive in Oakland; by August 9 Jack joins Jimmy Hopper and George Sterling at the Bohemian Grove; is disappointed his *The Acorn Planter* is turned down for production.

SEPTEMBER 3. Attends California State Fair in Sacramento; Neuadd Hillside wins another Grand Champion; Jack is stricken with rheumatism in left foot.

SEPTEMBER 21. Resigns by letter from the Socialist Party on behalf of himself and Charmian.

OCTOBER 2. Finishes "The Water Baby," his last story.

OCTOBER 22. Neuadd Hillside dies of a rupture; Jack quits work on "Cherry" or "Eyes of Asia" to write a story about the horse, but never does.

NOVEMBER 8–14. Second trial in Santa Rosa over water rights dispute settled in Jack's favor; on November 10 he suffers what he thinks is a slight attack of ptomaine poisoning.

NOVEMBER 16. Newsreel of Jack made at the ranch by Gaumont Company; film shown December 16.

NOVEMBER 21. Writes letter to daughters to arrange a meeting at Lake Merritt and lunch at Saddle Rock for the next Friday; suffers from stomach pain and nausea, vomits his breakfast, and cannot rest. He tells Charmian, "You're all I've got in this world"; talks excitedly with Eliza about building a post office on the ranch for the hired help.

NOVEMBER 22. Is found unconscious by Sekine; attempts are made to revive him, physicians arrive, and Charmian shouts "Fire!" to try to wake him, but Jack dies at 7:45 p.m. in his sleeping porch in the cottage at the ranch. While they try to make him get up and walk in the cottage, he is found to be paralyzed on one side; though he was taking morphine for kidney pain, an overdose of morphine is ruled out; death is attributed by four attending physicians to a "gastro-intestinal type of uraemia," causing a stroke; his kidney failure, probably caused by the doses of corrosive sublimate of mercury he self-administered for his "Solomon Island sores," is now widely thought to be the cause of death. For sixteen years of his life, he was one of the most famous writers and travelers in the world, partly inspired by his boyhood reading of Herman Melville's *Typee* (1846). It is a terrible and sad irony that his greatest adventure, the *Snark*, took only eight years to kill him.

### POSTHUMOUS PUBLICATIONS

1917     *The Human Drift, Jerry of the Islands, Michael, Brother of Jerry, The Red One, On the Makaloa Mat*

1920     *Hearts of Three*

1922     *Dutch Courage and Other Stories*

1963     *The Assassination Bureau*

1971     *Daughters of the Rich: A One-Act Play* (curtain-raiser written by Hilda Gilbert under Jack's name with his permission)

1972     *Gold* (with Herbert Herron)

1999     *Cherry*, unfinished last novel, published as "Eyes of Asia"

# Eliza London Shepard

## Letter to Jack London (March 12, 1904)

One of Jack London's first correspondents was the person he trusted above everyone else, Eliza London Shepard (1867–1939), his older stepsister. London's stepfather was John London, who had moved to California from Moscow, Iowa, after he mustered out of the Union Army in 1865 on a small pension owing to his injury in the war. In Iowa, he married and ran a small construction company. Widowed in 1870, John placed six of his children with a local family before he moved west with Eliza and her sister Ida, as well as an ailing son, Charles. In 1874 John enrolled them in the Protestant Orphanage in Marysville, California, where Charles died at the age of 5.[1] On February 19, 1877, London married Flora Wellman (1843–1922), the former common-law wife of itinerant astrologer William H. Chaney, Jack's probable father. Flora, originally from a well-to-do Massillon, Ohio, family, stunted by typhoid at age 12 and unhappy, fled for the bohemian life of the West Coast, appearing in Seattle in the 1870s and then San Francisco. She was by Jack's and others' accounts a small, intense, and driven woman, given both to working hard but also to gambling and get-rich-quick schemes, as well as to bizarre bursts of anger and what today we might call borderline personality disorder, and then dementia as she aged. She tried hard, but in her discontent she made others suffer too. For example, one wonders if it occurred to her that running through the house shrieking as her "spirit guide," Plume, and giving seances might possibly be damaging to her son. Eliza and Ida were not brought home from the orphanage until February 1877. But from the moment Eliza arrived, she, along with Mrs. Virginia Prentiss (1832–1922), London's African American foster mother, provided maternal love to young Johnny. She was the person on whom her little brother could rely. Yet by age 16, Eliza had had enough of Flora. At age 17 she impulsively married Capt. James H. Shepard (1843–1917), a 43-year-old two-time widower and Army veteran, with three children, and they moved to Oakland (Jack London, *Letters*, 26n3). For Jack, this was heartbreaking. Yet Shepard was Jack's grubstake and his Klondike partner, until he turned back home at Dyea owing to physical exhaustion.

Eliza's marriage did not go well. James was an attorney, and Eliza earned her law degree and license to practice law in California, proud to join J. H. Shepard and Co.; she enjoyed, as she often said, being "the Co." But in 1910, when Jack was traveling more and had acquired much more of his Beauty Ranch in Glen Ellen, Eliza left James Shepard to become Jack's ranch foreman, managing very large agricultural, animal husbandry, and maintenance projects on the land, a combination of seven former ranches totaling 1,400 acres, as well as overseeing the construction of Wolf House. London actually had to throw Shepard off the ranch when he appeared, brandishing a gun at Eliza.[2] Eliza, rather than Charmian's inept aunt Netta ("Ninetta") Wiley Eames (1852–1944), handled all his affairs, including mail, telegrams, books, stories, purchases, and payments, when he and Charmian were gone.

In fact, Eliza and Charmian saved the ranch after his death: during the Depression they rented out guest cottages, with Charmian doing most of the work on copyrights and Eliza most of the work on the ranch. Eliza's legal training helped save the property and London's finances, as disputes occurred in court over water rights and other issues, as well as with publication contracts and the film industry. Eliza had her own life, however: she served as national president of the American Legion Auxiliary, formed to aid the American Legion in providing service to American veterans after World War I.[3]

Though she was very patient, Eliza did not suffer fools, and she had little time or interest in writing about herself, being photographed, or generally promoting herself.[4] These traits could also be seen in her son Washington Irving Shepard (1899–1975), whom she brought with her when she became ranch foreman in 1910, and her son Irving Milo Shepard (1925–2010), both of whom handled London's ranch and his copyrights. Like her, they were committed to the ranch, pragmatic and direct, and like her, they had a deep understanding of the land and the family, and of Jack London's legacy.[5] As the Paris Times put it in its "The Woman of the Day" feature story, "[A] forceful person, her slate-blue eyes sparkle when she smiles and fairly blaze when she talks. . . . Capability is written in her tanned, rugged looking hands and face." She was a "War Mother" who counted her son Irving and ten of her "'ranch boys'" as vets, flying a service flag with eleven stars in 1917.[6] The following letter, on her impressive letterhead as president of the Woman's Relief Corps in California and Nevada, not only demonstrates the loyalty and good sense Jack treasured in her but offers an uncharacteristically long and loving personal passage at the end.

Headquarters
Department of California and Nevada
Office of the President
Feb. 12th, 1904

Dear Old Boy,

It seems so strange to write to you and feel you are so far away, and yet may be on the road home before you get this or rather before this letter reaches the place where you were when it was written. We are all well on this side of the stream and most sincerely hope you are in good health. Bess left for Los Angeles last Friday. Dr. Crawford told her, she said, to go there on account of Joan's bad cold, he thought the change would do her some good. I helped her get off. Fixed up the childrens [*sic*] clothes and made Bess two suits & a waist so she would look all right. . . . Don't worry about Joan. She is all right as far as I can see, only somehow always has a cold. But looks fine, eats well, & sleeps well, so you see there is nothing to worry about. Little Bess is . . . getting so fat she can hardly see, walks all over and is learning to talk, is in fine health. Grandma is the same old story. And now to business, Frank tells me he is going to leave in a few weeks. I spoke to Grandma, she is willing to go out to the flat for a few months—as a matter of duty? I said duty be darned, go if you want, or stay where you are. Now old boy can you give me any idea how long you will be gone. If only for a short time say 3 or four months—I will have Grandma go out, she will not die of lonesomeness in that time. If you think you will be gone as long as a year, why I will go out there myself and take care of the place until you do get back, as I think it will be almost as cheap for you to keep the place, as it would to pack & store the things, as rates and insurance are so high on stored goods. Now be dear old Jack & tell me honestly—just how you feel about this. If you want me to go out I will gladly go. Mr J is willing, just express yourself and it will be all right. In any event I will see that the mail & place is taken care of. And if there is anything else you want me to do just say so. For you know to me there is only one person who is always right & that one, Dear Old Jack.

I saw of your arrest but I tried not to worry and do not worry for I know you can take care of your self. But don't take too many chances, as you have many things to live for and the world needs you.

Well Jack let me know as soon as you can about the House & I will do whatever you think is best.

With lots — lots — of love & good wishes.

Your sister — Eliza.

Don't forget to bring me a *real* pretty cup & saucer for my collection. Just think how proud I will feel to have one brought all the way from Japan by you.[7]

## NOTES

1. Kingman, *Jack London*, 3-4.

2. A contemporary account of Shepard's courtroom shenanigans in front of Superior Court Judge Seawell on November 23, 1915, notes that it was Eliza who was thrown out of court first for shouting Shepard down as he accused her. When both were readmitted to the courtroom, Eliza, who unlike her husband had amassed evidence, especially about his shooting up the ranch, apologized to the Court for her outbursts, and the trial was ended on November 24. "Lie Passed at Trial of Divorce Suit Yesterday: Defendant Is Sent From Courtroom by Judge — Sensational Evidence Given in Action Brought by James H. Shepard against Mrs. Eliza Shepard in This County," *Santa Rosa Press Democrat*, November 24, 1915, Jack London Collection, Huntington Library, JLE 2292. The Shepard Family Papers at the Huntington reveal that the divorce gave custody and all the land they owned to Eliza. The final divorce decree was not issued until December 19, 1916, nearly a month after Jack's death.

3. A 1925 press release by the American Legion Press Association in Indianapolis praises Eliza for her "Londonian virility" through the auxiliary in giving "much of her life to women's patriotic organizations." Mrs. Shepard "unwinds red tape as readily as most of her sex unwind a skein of years." Jack London Collection, Huntington Library, JLE 2289.

4. London did have a way of springing surprises on her, such as writing to her to give a convict a job by hand, directly on a letter to him from the warden of Sing Sing. Jack scrawled to her, "Dear Eliza — If we never do anything more for another convict, we must do something for this one & give him a place on the ranch. If we get him out, I think, like Stryker, he will soon find a place more to his liking and transfer out of our hands. Ten years ago I paid fifty dollars for typewriting transcripts of evidence for his appeal to Supreme Court. He is serving fifty years, & I have always been confident that he was 'railroaded.' Jack London." Under Jack's pencil is the letter from Donald Lowrie, on letterhead from the State of New York Sing Sing Prison, dated April 9, 1915: "My dear Mr. London: Thanks for your kind response regarding Joe King. I have written several letters to the court, in an effort to get Joe out before he really superannuates. I have asked Dr. Foster (you remember her, I presume) to see Fremont Older, and several others, and I have a hunch that this is Joe's year, at last. Again, thanking you, and with best wishes to Jack and yourself." Jack London Collection, Huntington Library.

5. As London declared on the evening of the great 1916 fire at the stock exhibition in Sacramento, when Charmian demanded to know whether or not he was going to see to his prize

horses, cattle, sheep, and hogs that would fulfill his dream of showing his fellow Californians "the ultimate perfection in stock production," he yawned that he was tired and that "Eliza's there or will get there; Eliza will do all anyone can do." Carter Johnson, "'Eliza Will Do All Anyone Can Do,'" *American Legion Weekly*, September 22, 1916.

6. *Paris Times*, no. 564, undated clipping, Jack London Collection, Huntington Library, JLE 2289.

7. London was in Korea covering the Russo-Japanese War when Eliza wrote him about Flora.

# Eliza London Shepard

## Letter to Jack London (March 1904)

> Jack trusted Eliza to be able to handle anything and everything regarding family, the ranch, and his complicated business arrangements. Her brother inscribed her copy of *The Valley of the Moon* (1913): "Dearest Sister Eliza: We know where lies the Valley of the Moon, you and I; and the Valley of the Moon, in our small way, yours and mine, will be a better valley for our having been." When London was away in Korea covering the Russo-Japanese War for the Hearst syndicate, or in Mexico during the revolution, on many occasions her status as an attorney helped him out of lawsuits and contract disputes, such as his extrication from the short-lived Jack London Grape Juice Co. in 1914.

Oakland March 4—[1904]

Dear Old Boy,

Imagine my surprise when I received a Phone message from Bess, saying she had returned from Los Angeles, & that she had my letter I had written you in her trunk, as the Examiner had forwarded theirs to her. I do not know whether you approve but I did as I would like you to have done under the circumstances. . . . I wrote the Examiner & asked to have your mail sent to me, if they were not going to forward same to you, & I will forward to you until I hear from you. Now about the house . . . , if you are going to be gone any length of time say a year or for nine months; I will move in if you would like me to—& see that everything is taken care of if not then I will have grandma go out. She does not want to go out of town but is willing to go out for a few months. I would willingly go if you do not object. I think it will be as cheap for you to keep the flat as it would be to pay storage for goods. I wish it did not cost so much to cable, so I could get your answer soon, one word, yes, would be all that is necessary. Bess & the children are well, but Joan's throat still bothers her, just swollen. Bess phoned me she had of us 8 letters from Charmian for you which she would hold, but I am going to get them from her & forward. If I am going to have charge of your things I am going to do it, &

not have part go one place & part another. I am just a little mad about a few things (now I hear you say, "just like a woman["]) but I am not rowing with anyone & you are my Confessor, so no one else knows, but if I give Bess a good raking over one of these days it will be simply because well, I love you, that is all and now Dear Boy don't be rash but take care of your self & send me word about the House as soon as you can. Shall I go or send Grandma or lock up until you get back.

With dearest love,
Your sister,
Eliza

# Frank Irving Atherton

## From *Jack London in Boyhood Adventures* (1997)

Frank Atherton (1875–1953) was London's favorite childhood friend; they attended Cole Grammar School in Oakland together beginning in 1887. In his posthumously published account of their friendship, Atherton describes Jack's bookishness, but also his ability to fight. In other sections of the memoir, Atherton takes exception to the idea that his friend was poor by describing a steak dinner at Flora and John London's home, but he also notes the tension between London and his mother. Their friendship continued until London's death in 1916, including visiting each other numerous times in their respective homes in the hills on the Bay Area's eastern and western sides; Atherton's last visit to the ranch was in 1914. His is an intimate portrait with valuable insights into London's boyhood.

It was recess at Cole School, and the pupils marched out into the school yard to the rhythmic beats of a snare drum. Upon reaching the yard they broke ranks, running helter-skelter about the grounds, shouting boisterously as they began their various games.

On the boys' side of the yard the youngsters became quite obstreperous, their vivacity busting forth in animated excitement as they gave free rein to their youthful proclivities.

In spite of the confusion however, one boy hurried across the school yard to a wooden bench, where he sat down and began to read a book. This being his usual custom during the recess and the noon hour, other pupils paid little attention to him. If he preferred to occupy his recreation time with his face buried in some stupid, old book, rather than to enjoy playing games with his schoolmates; well, that was unimportant to them.

Still, there were a few meddlesome boys who seemed to find pleasure in concerning themselves with the affairs of others. If however, a pupil saw fit to keep aloof from his classmates, he would be considered "high-hatted," and would consequently be subjected to annoyance.

On the day our story begins, one "Mike Panella," a leader of young gang-sters, took occasion to start trouble. Mike had noticed the lad who sat apart from his school mates, and leaving his companions he approached him with a belligerent grin. "Hey, kid, w'y don'cha ever play wid us guys? Don'ch get 'nough books in de school room, widout readin' at recess like a sissy?"

Being thus interrupted, the lad glanced up momentarily, but immedi-ately resumed reading, ignoring the young gangster. But Mike was not to be thwarted; he was itching for a fight.

"Huh, don't wanta talk t' me. Think yer somebody; better'n us guys, sneakin' off by yersef t' read a crazy ol' book. Yuh better git on to yersef an' git yer mug outta dat book, an' be a sport like us guys."

Closing the book over one finger, the lad glanced up into the ugly face of the young gangster. Instantly he became aware of impending trouble. "I'm not bothering you, Mike; why don't you go on and play with your gang and leave me alone? I want to read."

"Aw, yuh wanta read, do yuh?" Mike's lip curled up sarcastically. "Yer jus' a damn sissy; don't wanta mix wid us guys. Go on an' read yer damn head off, sissy, an' now les see yuh run an' git yer ol' book."

Snatching the book from the lad's hands, Mike threw it far out on the dusty ground. Then with another insulting remark he turned toward his com-panions.

"Look out Mike," warned one of the gang. But the warning came too late. With the agility of a cat the lad had sprung from his seat to attack the arro-gant bully. His square jaws were set in firm determination, his gray eyes blaz-ing from indignation. "I'll make you pay for this, you dirty low-lived dago." Mike had whirled about to face the lad, eager himself for a fight. He launched a swinging blow, but his opponent ducked, and delivered a stinging blow to Mike's ear, stunning him momentarily, thus gaining time to plan another blow.

Mike now rushed into the fray like a whirlwind, feinting with his left [while] planning a fierce blow with the right. Again, the lad eluded him, and as Mike struck the air he lost his balance, regaining his poise just in time to meet a terrific blow on the point of his chin. Then as he reeled backward, the lad socked him in the nose, knocking him completely off his feet.

Groaning in pain, cursing this fate, Mike lay groveling in the dust while the "Sissy" stood wiping the blood from his lacerated knuckles.

# James Hopper

## "Jack London on the Campus" (1916)

> When London set sail on the *Snark* on April 23, 1907, he hoisted his college friend Jimmy Hopper's blue-and-gold Cal football sweater up the mast. Hopper had known London as far back as Cole Grammar School in Oakland and met him again during London's one semester at the University of California in fall 1897, when London was a wide-eyed freshman hungry for knowledge and Hopper a seasoned junior. Though London was forced to drop out after that semester owing to lack of funds, Hopper graduated with the class of 1898. London had found himself disillusioned with what he thought of as merely canned thought on the part of his professors, especially disgusted with professors of English literature. Hopper was editor of *The Occident*, the campus literary magazine, and he greatly admired London the artist. Hopper finished law school and was admitted to the bar, but after a stint as head football coach at Nevada State University he chose to be a writer and reporter. When he and his wife moved to Carmel, he became part of the so-called Bohemian Crowd and friends with London, George Sterling, Mary Austin, Sinclair Lewis, and Arnold Genthe. The following article was written the day after London died and was published a few days later in the campus alumni magazine, the *California Alumni Fortnightly*.

It was on campus of the University of California, right at the bottom of the North Hall steps, on the side facing the bay, that I first met Jack London—one morning in the fall term of 1897, I think. He had just entered the University; under his arm were about sixteen books, and his eyes were full of a gay fever.

Our trails had crossed before. We had been to Cole Grammar School, in Oakland, together. And at the same time—this I discovered much later—Elmer Harris, the playwright, and Ed Boreen, since illustrator and artist, were also going to Cole School—all of us pretty tough kids, I think, who would have shied a brick at any long-nose who might have suggested we write or draw.

That day on the campus, though, was the first time I came upon Jack knowingly. He possessed already then a certain vague reputation among us boys as one who had done man things and wild things and romantic things. It was rumored that he had been a tramp, a sealer, an oyster pirate, and that he spoke at night in the socialistic meetings of City Hall Square. His latest exploit—that of passing the University entrance examinations after three months vigorous cramming while stoking the furnace of the Oakland High School—was in many mouths. His already was a colorful personality, and when the boy who had been telling me about him said suddenly, "There he is, see? Coming down the steps," I moved up and "braced" for him.

But—but—well, I hate to say it. Perhaps if I explain carefully people will understand. You see, he was a newly-entered freshman, and I was a full-fledged junior. I was a junior, and on the football team and editor of the Occident. Also holding a well-defined place in a very regular organization—a bit of a bourgeois prig, in fact. So that when I went to Jack London, I did so—God forgive me—thinking consciously how nice and democratic this was of me!

If he felt my condescension—and he must have, for under his sturdiness ran a fine net of fine nerves—he did not show it. I may say right here that the dominating quality of Jack London's character was bigness. "Attend to the big things and let the little things go"—if ever he made for himself a motto, it must have been that. He let the little thing go that time and met my advance with an open frankness which was like a flood of sunshine.

Sunshine—the word leaped of itself to the end of my pen, and it is the word which best describes him as I saw him that day nearly twenty years ago. He had a curly mop of hair which seemed spun of its gold; his strong neck, within a loose, low, soft shirt was bronzed with it; and his eyes were like a sunlit sea. His clothes were flappy and careless; the forecastle had left a suspicion of a roll in his broad shoulders; and he was a strange combination of Scandinavian sailor and Greek god, made altogether boyish and loveable by the lack of two front teeth, lost cheerfully somewhere in a fight.

He had just entered the University—as I have said. And he was a-thrill with enthusiasm over the new venture—this adventuring into the ideal seas of learning—and full of gigantic plans—just as, indeed, I was to find him always whenever I came upon him later in life. He told me what he meant to do. He was going to take all the courses in English, all of them, nothing less. Also of course he meant to take most of the natural sciences, many in history, bite a respectable chunk out of the philosophies. But as to English, this was simple: he was going to take all of the courses in English—all of them.

And as he thus unfolded his intentions to me, there in the sun in front of North Hall, radiating himself at least as much light and warmth as the sun, I, junior, end on the football team and editor of the Occident, all of twenty years old and hence disillusioned, frozen (lightly frozen) in a gentle pessimism, polished with a worldly skepticism, I listened to him and smiled, and tried to make my smile just a bit ironical and withal kindly. You see, I had taken some of the courses of which he was going to take all, and I had found there—well, not all that I had sought. Three or four times I came near to telling him that. But his enthusiasm was so intrepid, so young and touching, so pure and vibrant—that I didn't have the heart. So I let him go; meaning, however, to watch him and see what he thought of it all later.

Well, with this in my mind I looked him up some few weeks afterward, and I found him gone! Bag and baggage gone, with the enterprise, of which he had spoken to me so glowingly, unfinished, hardly begun. He had gone to the Klondike, on the crest wave of the gold rush.

From the Klondike he returned a year later. And in the folds of his brain, all ready for the settling down, were The Son of the Wolf and his wonderful stories, and the immortal Call of the Wild. And it was only much later that I realized how true and unerring had been the instinct—heeded and obeyed with such splendid bravery—which had led him from the adventuring among the dead books to the adventuring among the live men, from stagnant alcoves to the wind-swept snows. And just this morning, when there came to me the brutal news, and I knew with heart-sickness I should never see Jack London again, I wondered if this time also it had been his true instinct which had plucked at his sleeve and told him to leave us; I wondered—ah, I wondered—whither his true instinct—heeded once more by his eternal courage—had taken him; to what new and wondrous and tremendous adventure.

—James Hopper
Carmel, Cal
November 23, 1916

# Ina Coolbrith

## Letter to Jack London (1907)

Ina Coolbrith (1841–1928) was a prominent Bay Area poet and librarian who was California's first poet laureate and the first state laureate in the country. Over the course of her career she was an honorary member of the Bohemian Club and knew Mark Twain, Bret Harte, John Muir, Joaquin Miller, Charles Warren Stoddard, and Ambrose Bierce. She, like many of them, published in the *Overland Monthly*. As her poetry sales flagged and her responsibilities in caring for loved ones increased, she served as head of the Oakland Public Library from 1874 to 1893. In a letter he wrote to her, partly in celebration of a sonnet George Sterling had published about her, "To Ina Coolbrith," in his *A Wine of Wizardry and Other Poems* (1909), London fondly recalled:

> The old Oakland Library days! Do you know, you were the first one who ever complimented me on my choice of reading matter. Nobody at home bothered their heads over what I read. I was an eager, thirsty, hungry little kid— and one day at the Library, I drew out a volume on Pizzaro in Peru (I was ten years old). You got the book & stamped it for me. And as you handed it to me you praised me for reading books of that nature. Proud! If you only knew how proud your words made me. For I thought a great deal of you. You were a goddess to me. I didn't know you were a poet, or that you'd ever done so wonderful a thing as to write a line. I was raw from a ranch, you see. But I stood greatly in awe of you—worshipful awe. In those days I named by adjectives. And I named you "Noble." That is what you were to me—noble. . . . [I]n all the years that have passed I have met no other woman so "noble" as you. (*Letters*, 650).

In response, she wrote back to him, which connected the brainy little boy to the great writer that he became, with the influence of the local public library.

15 Lincoln St.
San Francisco,
January 2, 1907

Dear Jack London:

Mrs. Radclyffe did not wish to give up the manuscript. It is all right.

Your autobiographical photographed book came to me on Christmas day, and your letter somedays before.

Dear lad! Great man! It was worth my twenty years in the Oakland Public Library to receive such a tribute. Would that I were worthy of it.

Ina Coolbrith.

# [Anonymous]

## "London Honest and Straight as Boy — Johnny Heinold Mourns Author Friend"
### (*San Francisco Chronicle*, 1916)

> Heinold's First and Last Chance Saloon on the Oakland waterfront, on what is now called Jack London Square, to be precise, is a building made of remnants of an old whaling ship and was once used as a bunkhouse for workers in the nearby oyster beds. Johnny Heinold bought and renovated it in 1883 as a pub for seamen. London first came there in 1891 and after a time borrowed money from Johnny. Returned from the Klondike, London would do homework for his high school diploma at the bar and perhaps gather ideas for stories, according to Johnny. There were other writers who drank there before heading to sea or coming back, including Melville, Stevenson, Bierce, and others. Its floor still leans sharply, and its clock is still stopped at 5:18 a.m., the time of the April 18, 1906, earthquake. In chapters 8–10 of *John Barleycorn*, the narrator describes his entering the saloon as a rite of passage, particularly drinking prodigiously and buying drinks: "And so I won my manhood's spurs" (*John Barleycorn*, 97). Saloons were one of the only places working-class men could easily gather and enjoy their friends.

"I can't realize that Jack is dead," said Johnny Heinold, of the "First and Last Saloon," at the Oakland approach of the Webster street bridge, on Oakland estuary. "Jack was in here about two months ago and a heartier fellow you never could find. And now he is dead. Too bad."

It was in Heinold's establishment that Jack London secured most of his material for his "John Barleycorn," and Johnny Heinold is mentioned in the book in several places. Heinold knew London from his early childhood and was always an admirer of his talk.

"It was nearly thirty-three years ago that Jack first came into my place," said Heinold. "He was then a little dirty-faced, half naked boy, but he had the 'stuff' in him. This place has not changed a particle, with the exception of

[55]

that icebox, since the day he first came in here. He wasn't big enough to get up to the bar, and he used to stand up on the footrail to see over.

"He was always honest and straight and paid his bills promptly. When his father died, Jack came in and leaned over the bar, whispering to me, 'Did papa owe you any money?' He didn't owe me a cent, and I told him so. And Jack went all over the water front, looked up all his father's debts and paid them. Not many boys in Jack's circumstances would do that.

## Worked on Water Front

"When he was a little shaver we had real men on the water front here. He did quite a junk business. He was always determined and when he went after anything he usually got it. Those were the halcyon days. They were the days when we had real men on the water front. They would work hard all day and drink all night, and the next morning would come back to work, just as fit as ever. Jack held his own with them all.

"Jack came in one day and I knew he was thinking about something. I asked him what it was and he said, 'I have decided that education is the only thing to make a man out of me.' I told him he was right, but he must be careful not to make a plaster out of it."

"'What do you mean?' asked Jack. I told him I meant an education that improved inner man without making a snob out of him. And Jack always remembered that. His education was not a plaster. Jack treated everybody alike. In later years, when he came in here, he laid his money on the bar and invited everybody to drink, strangers and friends alike. And nobody else could buy until the money was gone.

## Always Repaid Loan

"When Jack started to the University High School I loaned him money. Time and time again I loaned him what he asked for. He never wanted it for foolish purposes. But he paid back every cent of it, and I never had to ask him for it, either.

"Every time Jack came to Oakland he came down here to see me. He always wanted me to come up to Glen Ellen and see him, but I never could get away. I am all alone here and I had to attend to my business. My bartender, the only one I could ever trust, died several years ago, and I couldn't leave. Besides I knew if I went up there Jack wouldn't let me leave for a month. Jack was just that way."

# Johnny Heinold

"Heinold Tells Early Life—Was 'Barleycorn' Character:
'Saloonman Says Friend Was Determined Finisher'" (1916)

> It is not really surprising that the floor of Heinold's First and Last Chance
> Saloon leans precariously, as it suffered several earthquakes, yet there one
> will also find the original gas lamps and pot-bellied stove in use. Interestingly,
> though London praises Heinold for helping him out in his younger days, by
> 1913, when he published *John Barleycorn*, his looking back on those saloon
> days feels savagely ironic: "Ah!—and I say it now, after the years—could John
> Barleycorn keep one at such a height, I should never draw a sober breath
> again. But this is not a world of free freights. One pays according to an iron
> schedule—for every strength the balanced weakness; for every high a corre-
> sponding low; for every fictitious god-like moment an equivalent time in rep-
> tilian slime. For every feat of telescoping long days and weeks of life into mad
> magnificent instants, one must pay with shortened life, and, oft-times, with
> savage usury added." Alcohol came to play an increasingly dark role in Lon-
> don's life. Yet Johnny Heinold captured something essential in London, his
> love of friendship. As Heinold puts it below, "I never knew a man to enjoy
> company more than he."

So Jack London is dead. Too bad, too bad. Just forty years of age and in the
prime of his manhood and useful and at the height of his fame.

He was one of a million men to rise the way he did from a poor, half-naked
kid in spite of the things that went against him in the start.

But there was one thing that could not be downed in Jack London. That
was his determination in finishing anything he started. He was a great finisher, Jack. When he set his mind upon accomplishing anything it was as
good as done.

Don't I remember him as a little fellow? He was ambitious then, full of gin-
ger and eager to get an education.

*

When Jack started to high school I loaned him money to buy books. My, but he was a great reader. Again I loaned him money when he went to the University. He always paid me back, for Jack was a square shooter.

As a boy he used to pick up rope and other junk from around the whalers in the estuary and sell the stuff. He would always weigh it himself, and if he had a hundred pounds he would get paid for a hundred.

### Sailed with Sea Wolf

He knew all of the rough waterfront characters of the whaling days that now about gone around here. He sailed with Captain Alexander McLean on the "Sophie Sutherland," a sealer. Captain McLean was the original of the "Sea Wolf," one of the toughest old mariners that ever sailed out of a port. He flatly boasted that everything north of 45 degrees belonged to him.

When Jack got a little older he went around with the gang known as the oyster pirates. I loaned him $10 and made out the bill of sale for the "Razzle Dazzle," a thirty-foot, flat-bottomed skiff in which they cruised down to the oyster beds with a makeshift mutton-leg sail."[1]

I remembered one day Jack came in here with $23 in his pocket. He told me that he was going to buy a suit of clothes. I told him to run along and get the suit before he spent the money. He went out, met the gang and they all went to Josie Harper's saloon. He came back later dead broke, but that did not bother him.

### Writers Came, Too

Jack was a great fellow to eat candy as well as read books. He always had a pocket-full.

Since he became wealthy he has made many visits here. He never came to Oakland but what he called upon me. Also he sent dozens of writers from all over the world who visited him at his home to see me here. One man he thought a lot of was Richard Harding Davis.[2]

I could tell Jack blocks away. He would come along with that swinging gait of his, never wearing a vest, always with a black tie flowing from his shirt front. He would come in and lay two or three dollars on the bar and no one could buy while he stayed. I never knew a man to enjoy company more than he.

How he would laugh when we sat around talking about old days. Those were some days all right. There will never be any more like them around here. The old crew is gone.

I could not but help admire his ambition. When Kelly's Army started from Oakland in the old Elmira and got dumped near Sacramento Jack came in here one day and said that he had joined Kelly's gang. I thought he was crazy, but on the quiet he told me was going along to write articles for a San Francisco newspaper.

When he got to Sacramento he was pinched and thrown into the cooler by a cop who caught him crawling out from under the brake beams where he had ridden from a small town down the line.

### Heart Was Right

Jack London's life was an early struggle. He loved rough ways and he sought to understand what they meant, to know the men he associated with. They were all characters for his study. While on the outside he was rough and ready, innermost he maintained high ideals that carried him through and which ultimately gave him the success of his desire.

And now he's gone. Somehow they always get the fellows the world needs most, don't they?

#### NOTES

1. A mutton-leg sail is a simple triangular sail set on a long spar boom mounted horizontally on the mast, running in a fore-and-aft direction.

2. Richard Harding Davis (1864–1916), journalist, editor, and war correspondent, was the son of fiction writer Rebecca Harding Davis and a friend of Theodore Roosevelt's; Davis helped create the Rough Riders myth during the Spanish-American War. He, like London, was sent to Korea to cover the Russo-Japanese War in 1904. He helped extricate London from court martial by the Japanese army by using his leverage with Roosevelt.

# Del Bishop

## Letter to Jack London (early 1900s)

> Del Bishop was a sourdough London met in the Klondike who wrote letters
> and descriptions of London. He figures as a character in some of London's
> Northland tales. In *A Daughter of the Snows* (1902) "Del Bishop" is a pocket-
> miner who welcomes Frona Welse, the heroine, upon her return to the North-
> land, and he travels with her over the Chilkoot Pass.

Friend Jack I don't know if you will remember me or not on a short time I
know you I met you at Stewart river in 97 + 98 and if you remember if things
were as they should be—but no satisfaction Jack I have been up and down
several times but I am in the wrong country for my like there is no pockets
here that is it is not a pocket country like old Cal now, Jack I saw a article in
the Examiner and your name to it so I take a chance on you getting this what
I want is for you to write to me and tell me what the possibilities are for pan-
ning in the [illegible] . . . I am thinking of going out that way this fall Jack if
you will answer this I will appreciate it.

Address Del Bishop Dawson N.W.F.

# Emil Jensen

## From "With Jack London at the Stewart River" (1926)

Emil Jensen was a Klondike friend whom London admired greatly, making him into the character called "the Malemute Kid" in six stories, including "The White Silence," "An Odyssey of the North," and "The Sun Dog Trail," who exemplifies London's Northland code, specifically the sharing of food and trail with others in a brother- and sisterhood of the North, caring for the injured, making clear the wisdom of the trail: "Never travel alone." Though these stories focus upon the deeds of white "Anglo Saxon" Americans in the Klondike, London never gives the "Kid" a name, thus perhaps offering a broader point of view. It is interesting that the Kid is named for a dog, adumbrating the two great anthropomorphic dog heroes, Buck and White Fang. Jensen admired London as well, typing and sending to Charmian a glowing tribute in 1926. Here he speaks of their meeting and of Jack's lending him *Paradise Lost*.

" 'How do you do?' he greeted me, as I stood before him on the snow-covered river-bank. "Where from, friend?"

"San Francisco," I replied rather tersely as I tried to dislodge a heavy chunk of ice from my moustache, where it had grown beyond all comfortable proportions until it threatened a combination with the week-old stubbles on my lower lip.

"Bay man, I'll bet!" ventured the youth, nothing daunted as he drew his right from his mitt; "and a sailor in the bargain," he added as I shook the proffered hand. "I can tell a boatman," he continued, "as far as I can see him, and I had my eyes on you as you 'came to' out there on the ice. In spite of the current and drift ice you landed without a jar."

The curly-haired, blue-eyed boy—he was little more than a lad—certainly pleased me by this remark, for I was rather proud of the way I had handled our boat on this turbulent and most trying of rivers. Besides, the smile on his lips was boyishly friendly and his eyes sparkled as they gazed straight into mine. His were the first words of welcome I had heard on the cold, inhospitable river front, and the feel of his hand sent a current of warmth through my numbed body.

"What a likeable youth," I thought, as my eyes took in the lithe, strong young figure before me, and perhaps my face reflected the thoughts that flitted through my mind, as a responsive light came into his eyes and his smile broadened into a happy, comrade-like grin.

"My name is Jack London," he volunteered in a soft, pleasing voice, and, with what I thought at the time, the suspicion of a lisp. "I, too, come from San Francisco Bay; my home is in Oakland."

Such was my first meeting with the lad who, within a few short years, was destined to become one of the world's famous authors. Not often, in the past, had I been deceived by first impressions, but seldom had my heart gone out so readily as to this boy with the soft, almost caressing voice which but spoke the words I could read in the smiling blue eyes. It was enough; I would gamble on my judgment. Thus far in life, eyes had never misled me nor was I to be disappointed this time. Jack London proved to be all that I thought him in those first few moments on the banks of the Yukon in far Alaska, and each day I grew to like him better and become more and more interested in him. He was never quite the same, always developing new traits though consistently cheerful, always likeable, and, always, he was my friend. Although fifteen years his senior, I was still young in the days of the Klondyke Gold Rush and experienced no difficulty in entering into the spirit of London's youthfully refreshing outlook upon things in general.

I derived not a little enjoyment in following the trend of his various arguments, most of them bearing upon the economic and social conditions of the workers. This vital topic was, I learned, Jack London's hobby. At that early date, I pronounced it a hobby, destined to voice the wrongs that early and frequent injustice had burned into his soul and which he could not forget.

*

One unwritten law of the camp was that at night all regular visitors must bring their own candles. With candles worth a dollar and a half each, this rule was nothing more than just. Another thing well understood was that books must be kept no longer than was absolutely necessary. Few of us had brought more than one, although some had brought as many as three. It was from Jack I borrowed the first book. Anywhere else, I would have passed that thing up without a second thought, but, in the Yukon, a book was a book and

I read it—Darwin's "Origin of Species." I confess I did not like Jack so well that week.

Of course I had heard and read of the Darwin theory, but this was my first tussle with the thing itself. Once having started the book I could not lay it down, but, God, how it punished me! To hand me that book was, I thought, not fair of Jack, for its language was far beyond me, and my small, gold-ornamented dictionary was of little use in that wilderness of academic verbiage. In addition, day or night, our light was bad and the air was over-charged with a mixture of wood smoke, resin—forced by the fumes from strong tobacco and stronger pipes.

While it might have been Darwin, it might have been the smoke through the long hours, or perhaps it was the disappointment I experienced each time I opened my pretty little dictionary that sent me to bed in the early morning, day after day, with a pounding headache and the firm conviction that I had not been fairly dealt with. Being in doubt, I laid the blame at Jack's door. "An unfriendly act," I said to him, "foisting such absorbingly interesting stuff on an untutored, simple mind." Furthermore, its contents savored of rank heresy, which, in my homeland beyond the North Sea, could bring but one reward—a full measure of undisguised, unqualified horror.

"Try Huxley," suggested Jack, grinning gleefully at my evident distress. I shook my head sadly. "How about Spencer?" came with a whimsical smile. "Too serious," I replied. "I am loaded down with weighty matters right now." "Well, then," remarked Jack with finality, "here is your last bet;" saying which he resurrected from among the blankets in his bunk a book and placed it on the table before me. A book of poetry this was—portly and awe-inspiring. "You have read every scrap of paper in camp but this," he continued, sliding a loving hand gently over the upturned pages as though this thing beneath his fingers were the very embodiment of all that is beautiful and joy-giving.

# Marshall Latham Bond

## "An Eulogy" (1916)

> Marshall Latham Bond (1867–1941) and his brother Louis Whitford Bond knew Jack London in the Klondike and owned a dog, Jack, a St. Bernard/collie mix, on whom Buck of *The Call of the Wild* is based. The Bond brothers owned a cabin and storehouse near Dawson City; London was for a time one of their tenants. The brothers were the sons of well-to-do Hiram Bond, a mining investor. The family owned a beautiful house and grounds for fruit orchards in Santa Clara Valley, California; it is closely described in the novella as Buck's original home, "Judge Miller's place." Marshall Bond authored an account of his adventurous life in his book *Gold Hunter: The Adventures of Marshall Bond* (1969).

Shortly after our arrival in Dawson when Pearce and I stood in front of the Dominion Bar to get a drink, our reflections in the mirror resembled a couple of hobos. Two men who looked just as unkempt and forbidding as these reflections of ourselves set up a tent near our cabin until they could arrange for more permanent winter quarters. They asked to be allowed to put up their provisions in our cache for the time being, to keep them from the depredations of predatory Malamoot dogs, whose underfed condition kept them constantly on the lookout for an opportunity for theft, and from light-fingered marauders of our own breed. This led to an acquaintanceship which an occasional evening in our cabin ripened into friendship. One of these men was of medium height with very square broad shoulders. His face was marked by a thick stubbly beard. A cap pulled down low on the forehead was the one touch necessary to complete the concealment of head and features, so that that part of the anatomy one looks to for an index of character was covered with beard and cap. He looked as tough and as uninviting to us as we doubtless looked to him. On a box, out of the circle of light from the lamp, he sat in silence one night (November 17, 1897) as a confusing blur of cap, mackinaw, and moccasins. Conversation turned to the subject of Socialism. Some of those present confused it with anarchism. One of our number, who at least knew more of the subject than the rest of us, clarified it somewhat with his greater knowledge, but this was soon exhausted. Then from out of the shadow of the lamp, from the blur of beard and cap, came a quick-speaking, sympathetic voice. He took up the subject from its earliest history, carried it on through a rapid survey of its most important points and held us thrilled by the hypnotic effect which a profound knowledge of a subject expounded by an exalted believer always exerts. Intellectually he was incomparably the most alert man in the room, and we felt it. Some of us had minds as dull as putty, and some of us had been educated and drilled into a goose step of conventionalism. Here was a man whose life and his thoughts were his own. He was refreshing. This was my first introduction to Jack London.

*

## II

The two dogs we took into the Klondike with us were fine specimens. One of them in particular had characteristics of such fine excellence as to be called character. He had a courage that, though unaggressive, was unyielding; a kindness and good nature that the most urbane man in the world might have observed with profit, and a willingness to do his work, and an untiring energy in carrying it out. I have had too much loyalty and affection from dogs to doubt that they have souls if men have them. London liked these dogs, and particularly this one which I called Jack. His manner of dealing with dogs was different from anyone I knew, and I remarked it at the time with interest. Most people, including myself, pet, caress, and talk in more or less affectionate terms to a dog. London did none of this. He always spoke and acted towards the dog as if he recognized its noble qualities, respected them, but took them as a matter of course. It always seemed to me that he gave more to the dog than we did, for he gave understanding. He had an appreciative and instant eye and he honored them in a dog as he would in a man.

*

## IV

His home at that time was but a small affair and scantily furnished. The room in which he worked contained a desk, a typewriter, and behind his chair in

[65]

easy reach were the works of Herbert Spencer, Huxley, Darwin, and other authors. "I had to first read all these," he explained "to get a basic knowledge for writing." "Does writing pay, Jack?" I asked with the frankness of friendship. He answered, "I came out of the Klondike broke, found that my father had died and left some debts. I have paid up everything and am supporting three families. The first year I never got a thing accepted, and I began to get morbid and believe that I got turned down because I was a socialist. I now wonder how the first stuff that was finally accepted ever got by. But it is hard work. He who waits for the muse to move him will never get anywhere. I write five thousand words a day to discipline and command myself. Much of it has to be torn up, but I make myself write it. Robert Louis Stevenson said that there eventually comes a feeling of great exaltation when a man realizes that he is the master of his tools. I hope for that moment." System and precision characterized his work. Newspaper clippings, articles from magazines and all data he wished to preserve were neatly bound in folders, labelled and filed handy for use. He was a tremendous worker, and an orderly one. He also visited me at my home in Santa Clara, and his description of the place is the beginning of "The Call of the Wild."

*

V

Later when he had become recognized as an author of distinction he was sought after by many people of social prominence in and around San Francisco. Once I chaffed him about being a social butterfly. He replied: "That side of life had been denied me, and when I began to be asked to the houses of prominent people I went to broaden my experience, and because I believed it a complement to my efforts as an author. I was soon disillusioned by the discovery that I was merely being used as an advertising medium or possible feature of interest for other people's social functions. My last hostess held almost no conversation with me, her time being entirely taken up with another woman in mutual recitation of the notables they had met abroad. I think I have learned all that is necessary from such experiences and have cut them out." During the last years of his life, after he had become a worldwide author, I regret that I never saw him. I should like to have as personal recollections the man in his maturity with all the added wealth to his virile mind that came from work, rich experiences and notable success. During his period of development the man was leonine in courage, brilliant in speech, loyal, and independent. The impression lasts over all these years that "Here was a man."

# Elizabeth "Bess" Maddern London

## Letter to Jack London (1905)

Elizabeth "Bess" Maddern (1876–1948) was Jack London's first wife and mother of his two daughters, Joan and Becky. She and London met during his 1896 rush to get tutored for university entrance, when he relied on her for math tutoring. A neighbor of London's, she lost her fiancé in the Spanish-American War in the Philippines. Bess was intelligent, loving, and lonely. She enjoyed bicycling with Jack, and she taught him how to take and develop photographs. But she accepted a loveless marriage, which London explained to her was only for the purpose of settling down and raising good "Anglo Saxon" stock. They should both have known better. Though she was lively and athletic, Bess was first of all a devoted mother, and she did not feel comfortable with his evenings with artist and writer friends. When Bess filed for divorce in 1904, she suspected Anna Strunsky (1879–1964) as being the other woman, but she was a former lover; in fact it was Bess's friend Charmian Kittredge. Bess constantly had to beg him for money. Unfortunately, he squandered a lot of it on such adventures as the *Snark*, though he supported his first family and several others adequately. Bess's refusal to allow their daughters to visit their father at his Glen Ellen ranch when Charmian, whom she called "the Beauty," was there created great distance between him and his surviving children and stoked his resentment of Bess, as well as, in turn, Joan's deep resentment of him. Sadly, in Bess's letters written just post-separation she takes on a desperately jolly tone with "Daddy-Boy," despite her humiliation and anger; perhaps she thought that he would one day come back to her and their girls. The girls, poignantly, believed he would for many years.

Dear Daddy-Boy:

I got your letter this afternoon. . . . Babies are all well. They make a great deal of "Lass." How do you like the name? She is so gentle as a lamb. I know you will like her. Ernest got me a fine harness for fifteen dollars. The brushes etc. came to about five dollars. Eighty-five dollars. This includes the complete rainy outfit new. I will need two robes and a horse blanket and whip. I would like to have rubber tires put on, they will cost twenty-five dollars more, but

I can do nicely without them now. Maybe later on you might be able to get them put on for us.

I used ten dollars of your money. When I pay for the harness there will be about one dollar left. Goodness Boy, it costs money to have things — don't it? I've lots to tell you when you come down. . . .

Joan and Bess had [whooping cough] very lightly, oh I don't know. You saw the winding up of it and I had two at once, where she has just the one and two grown ones to help him. Well it's the same old story, you understand.

In case Ernest did not write you about the surrey ($60+$25) and you think it's too much let me know immediately but if not let me have the check the first of the week at the latest will you Boy?

Do you know anything about the robes? I'll go down tomorrow and get the different prices.

Did I tell you Genthe[1] (how do you spell his name?) wants me to bring the children over and let him take some pictures? I'm going to take them next week if all goes well. How do you like the idea? I hope they will be as good as yours.

Joan and Baby B and mother-girl send their love to Daddy.

Yours as ever,
Mother-girl.

**NOTE**

1. Arnold Genthe (1869–1942) was a widely praised San Francisco photographer and ethnographer. He made numerous studio portraits of Jack London and described him in his 1936 autobiography, *As I Remember*.

# Elizabeth "Bess" Maddern London

## Letter to Jack London (1908)

Dear Daddy Boy:

I received your letter of Feb. 16th, and was glad to hear of your safe arrival.

Your letter surprised me very much especially when I thought over our last conversations together.

You spoke then of this place being worth more than $4000. Do you remember telling me about your surf board. How you said it was the only time you ever made anything and that you were not a business man. I agreed with you in regard to this house being worth more, but of your own free will you said I might have it for $4000 cash. I said then it was to be understood, that I should have it unconditionally and you said yes.

I had you draw up the agreement so there would be no misunderstanding and Jack your agreement is legal—and I shall keep my part of it and I look to you to do yours also. I sign no document.

You say you do not want Charlie[1] and I to make a profit from you. How about you making on our advertisement?

You will get $4000 cash.

We expect to make many changes in this house. About $2000. It would then stand us $6000.

Suppose you invest your $4000, you will get your profit upon that. Then you want the profit upon our $6000 or in other words you want the profit on $11,000 for the use of $4000. What do you think of that?

Now Jack I'm not buying this place for investment. I want a home. We madams have always had a home. I want mine.

Now another thing I do not think you have thought about. When I marry your little girls will have their share of Charlie's estate just the same as they have of yours. Do be just Jack.

The next day after you left, I went to see an attorney to see if this agreement was legal. It was all right Jack. . . . I did consult an attorney and found that I was right you were wrong.

Jack, I signed away my rights to your royalties etc. (which was community property) with the understanding I was to have the insurance instead. You offered to build me the house for myself unrestricted which you afterward changed but you did not change the life insurance and here are your own words.

"And the said second party further agrees that he will at all times keep in full force and effect all life insurance policies now in force upon life of said second party and by their terms made payable to said first party and to the said minor children of the parties hereto: that he will pay the premiums upon same as they fall due and will not suffer said policies to date or become forfeited by reason of the non-payment of said premiums."

Do you see your words?

Jack, I worked hand in hand with you from the very beginning doing my very best to keep you and surely I deserve something besides a little household furniture. Don't you think so?

If you would rather take up my first offer wherein I shall give up all claims upon life insurance for a life interest in this house I could not sell. I am willing to put $1000 cash with it, making it life insurance $4000 + 1000 cash, $5000.

If you do not wish to take this offer, I still shall stand by my $4000 cash offer.

Jack treat me right. I have lived up to the letter of our agreement between us, why can't you. It was your own drawing up.

I have not been writing this in anger but Jack I wish you to be just by me.

Mrs. Eames has not sent me the money yet. She wished me to pay second installment so as to avoid interest. How about my money losing interest ever since last October. She does not think about that.

Your book "The Iron Heel" came today. Thank you kindly.

The children are well and full of life and mischief. Joan is writing to you and it is funny to watch her looking up the words in the dictionary.

She wants you to see her arithmetic. She is the youngest in her class. The next to her is nine. She and two others were the only ones perfect in arithmetic today. I feel quite proud of my work with her! I shall prepare Bess just the same. Joan has gained three pounds since you left. Evidently school agrees with her.

Bess wants me to tell you she sends you a big hug and thousands of kisses. We all join in sending love and good wishes to you.

Mother-girl.

## NOTE

1. Charles Milner was Bess's second husband.

# Elizabeth "Bess" Maddern London

## Letter to Jack London (1916)

Piedmont, Oct. 9, 1916.

Dear Jack,

Pardon my writing in pencil as my wrist is still very weak.

In reply to your letter to Joan in regard to the change in the allowance. The amounts, as you have arranged are perfectly satisfactory, also the idea of the girls handling their own money and rendering you their monthly statements.

Now Jack; will you please explain to me, the reason of my signing the policy, which you refer to in your letter, over to you.

In the agreement, which you drew up twelve years ago, adjusting our community property, among the things mentioned were the policies you were carrying in my name.

Equity Life No. 1025963 Aetna Life 330212 New York Life "3410981" Pacific.

You gave me the above list.

These policies, you explained to me were to take the place of the claim I had upon the royalties of your books etc., then written, if I would consent, which I did.

Also in the same Agreement, you mention the fact that you would meet the increased care and education of the children but nowhere is there a word about my having then to sign over one of the policies to you.

You also stated in your letter to Joan, you have paid the premium out of your pocket.

I also, Jack, have had to pay numerous extra bills out of my own pocket, doctor bills which your allowance never could cover.

The girls were very unfortunate in being susceptible to all disease, and they took them very hard.

You know Joan had pneumonia five times. I wrote you each time. Twice out of the five times I had to have a nurse, as she was so ill I could not care for her and Bess also.

Bess had a very hard case of enlarged glands. I had her under the doctor's care for nine months.

Joan's last attack of pneumonia, Doctor Wright advised me to take Joan away as her left lung was in a very bad condition.

This was at the time you were leaving in your trip on the Snark, and you told me you were unable to let me have any extra money. I borrowed the money, which I paid back later out of the money left me by my father.

I took the girls South, and for ten months traveled from place to place with them.

In my return, Joan was strong enough to have her throat and nose operated upon.

Also, last summer, I had to have Bess' throat operated upon.

For the past three years I have paid twelve dollars a month for music lessons.

This increase in care and education I have met, not out of your seventy-five dollars a month, but out of the money left me by my father, and all the money I could earn by my teaching.

Now Jack, I have not overlooked the fact that you have given the children, especially the last three years, extra clothes, paid for school books, car far [*sic*] and luncheon money, also an allowance for spending money. Also you paid for the nurse in Joan's typhoid, and Joan's dentist bill, besides paying the balance due on Joan's and Bess' bill, my own operation and Joan's typhoid coming so close together I had been unable to meet the dentist bill.

For the past twelve years I have done my best for the girls. Living and working wholly for them, as was a mother's duty, but now my health is breaking. Since my operation my heart has not been right; and my last spell in June doctor told me I had to give up all outside work. My home and care of the girls was all I should do.

The extra care and education mentioned afore I have met, but I cannot do it any longer on account of my health, neither can I see why I should sign over to you my rights according to agreement in the community property.

Yours sincerely,
Bessie London

# Cloudesley Johns

From "Who the Hell *Is* Cloudesley Johns?" (1994, 1995, 1996)

Cloudesley Johns (1874–1948) was, like London, a beginning writer, a fellow journalist, and a socialist. The two exchanged numerous letters over London's lifetime, but were especially important to each other as they launched their writing careers. As a reporter at the San Francisco *Post*, Johns mailed London a note of encouragement in 1899 about his short stories, and they were soon very close pen pals and friends. The letters they exchanged about writing could serve as a course of study for would-be authors, as they traded stylistic and philosophical elements of their craft.[1] Johns introduced London to Charles Warren Stoddard (1843–1909), the famous author of *South-Sea Idyls* (1873), who settled in Monterey and was a member of the Bohemian Club. London introduced Johns to George Sterling (1869–1926), London's closest friend and resident leader of the "Bohemians" of Carmel-by-the-Sea. If Stoddard made Carmel known, Sterling made it famous as an artists' colony. In 1929 Johns wrote his autobiography, "Who the Hell *Is* Cloudesley Johns?" It became a part of the Jack London Collection at the Huntington Library.

### From *Boy Jack and George*[2]

Coming together after three years, except for the brief meeting in New York, Jack and I had much to talk of, about what each of us had done and hoped to do; what we had read and planned to read; whom we had met and how and to what end; and a host of other matters. As our conversation darted and weaved its way through a hundred various occurrences and ideas, Bessie came into the library to inform us it was past 2 a.m. and to remind Jack that there was to be a party at the bungalow in the evening. We talked for a little longer and then went to bed. I was up before 8 o'clock and after breakfast found Jack already at work in his study, trying to get out his thousand-word daily stint despite any and all distractions. He handed me a carbon copy of "The Call of the Wild," which had been accepted for serial publication in *The Saturday Evening Post*. I was fascinated by what I felt then and still believe to be Jack London's greatest long story when the author, with no more than 300 words done as his morning's work, came into the library with a chessboard and a box of pieces under one arm and a book in the other hand, hurling questions at me. Had I been playing much chess while I was in New York? Had I found Joseph Conrad? I had played some chess at the Press Club; I had not really found Conrad, having read with delight only some excerpts of his work in book reviews. To these questions and answers I was giving only part of my attention, as I continued to read "The Call of the Wild," laying aside each sheet of the copy, face down, as I finished it. Presently Jack lifted the sheets, to see what part I was reading, and out of the corner of my eye I could see his interest centering on my impressions of his own work as he watched my changing expression while I read on. From time to time I commented upon the story, sometimes critically but more often in sheer admiration. Yet now and again he would glance at the chessboard or the volume he still held in his hand.

"Listen to *this*!" Jack exclaimed suddenly, taking away from me the copy of his own great story and waving the book he had brought. Then, his expressive and melodic voice caressing the living sentences of the Master, he read to me Joseph Conrad's "Youth," with boyish delight in sharing with kindred spirits his own joy of life.

*

### Other Days at Piedmont [3]

[E]arly enough to break into Jack's morning writing period, George with his promised "coach-and-four" and assorted Partingtons, Bierces [4] and others drove up to the bungalow. Jack and I squeezed into the already pretty well filled wagon and away we went at a brisk pace. For awhile George drove at random through the *semper virens* redwood groves of the Berkeley Hills. "We're near the Heights," he said. "Let's stop and see Joaquin."

We were in sight of the place by then and could see the tip of a tall pyramid of stone which the aging Poet of the Sierras had reared as a monument to Adam. . . .

"What time is it?" George asked as he reined in the four horses at the gateway of The Heights, where we could see the monument to Moses as well as the memorial pyramid for Adam.

Wondering what that could have to do with it, we waited as Jack glanced at his wristwatch, worn for convenience years before other he-men dared risk derision thereby.

"Eleven-twenty," he announced.

George shook his head. "After eleven," he remarked regretfully. "We won't go in. Joaquin will be drunk by now."

So near as that I came to meeting Joaquin Miller, but no nearer. From what I had known of him indirectly, however, good, bad, and just erratic, I was inclined to question the verity of George's remark. He admitted that it had been unduly harsh, and that the worst he had meant was that after his first two or three morning drinks the Poet of the Sierras was likely to be exceptionally uncivil. There came a time, not many years later, a physician having convinced Joaquin Miller that he should stop drinking, then George Sterling, who always had cherished real affection for the grouchy old genius, begged him to take an ounce or two of prime brandy he had brought, deeming it unsafe for a two-bottle man through many years to become suddenly a teetotaler when well past eighty. Whether or not a little stimulant would have helped prolong his life cannot be known, for he refused it, which was characteristic of Joaquin Miller when he made up his mind not to do what somebody wanted him to. A few days later he reached the end of his amazing trail.

"Where are we going now?" asked Kate as George drove on past The Heights.

"Let's have the picnic at Toddy's place," Carlt Bierce suggested thoughtlessly, and then flushed as he realized the faux-pas he had made.

"Toddy" winced, and then heartily seconded Carlt's suggestion, making everything all right for all of us. "Toddy," so dubbed in our circle for his skill in concocting a certain beverage referred to almost reverently in Jack London's "John Barley-Corn," was an Austrian baron by birth; by character, intelligence and geniality he was one of nature's own noblemen. The place spoken of by Carlt was in no sense Toddy's, but belonged to his divorced wife. Once magnificent among distinguished country seats in the San Francisco Bay region, it had been deserted and neglected for years, yet still was beautiful despite the state of decay into which it had fallen. Beside a pool where once a fountain had played over a group of marble fauns and nymphs, and now green rushes grew profusely, we spread rugs and ate our picnic lunch, a gay repast. George arose, produced a fancily fabricated stag-handled Bowie knife, replicas of which he had presented to Jack and me and which we were carrying out of regard for the donor, and slashed off one of the rushes. Hold-ing it in his left hand he clipped off bits of it with the big knife, trying to flick them as far as he could. Jack and I joined him, making a game of it. In a mo-ment more we could have been betting nickels or dimes, but suddenly Jack uttered a smothering outcry. He had slashed too close to his hand, clipping off about a third of the first joint of his left thumb, taking nearly half of the nail but missing the bone. From gaiety we were plunged into consternation, the girls especially, Jack alone making light of the accident.

"Under the law of averages," he remarked, "considering the chances I take, I had worse than this coming. It's my left thumb any how. It won't interfere with my writing."

*

## From *Changing Plans*

The *Spray* was a thirty-eight-foot sloop, nearly all of the space taken up by the large house, in which we could stand almost erect, and the cockpit. On either side of the cabin was a bunk long enough for two persons to sleep in end to end. The space between the bunks was taken up mostly by a table which was split by the centerboard slot. Heavily ballasted, the little boat drew over five feet of water, more than the big ferryboats plying across San Francisco Bay.

*

### First Cruise with Jack London

We started our cruise on an almost windless day, drifting out of Oakland Estuary on the ebb tide, our sails only partly filling now and then to enable Jack, master steersman that he was, to maneuver the sullenly moving sloop out of danger on one side and then the other. Along the southern bank of the creek, which was all it was despite the Oakland Chamber of Commerce des-ignation of the greasy inlet as an "estuary," lay a dozen or more rusty hulks of iron sailing vessels, against one of which we came near to crashing as the wind failed us utterly. Almost too late Jack shouted to me to get out one of the long sweeps kept aboard for such emergencies, and then managed with a twist of the helm to swing the unwilling boat out of the way of destruction. Jack sighed as he glanced back at the row of old ships destined apparently to lie forever sinking into the mud of Oakland Creek unless sold for scrap.

"Old whalers, Cloudesley," Jack explained. "They've been laid up there for years, and of course they'll never go out to sea again. But, God! What life they've seen in their day."

The guess was wrong. Some of those old whaling ships, all that would float or might float, were refitted years later while the World War raged, and sent out to defy the torpedos of undersea craft.

Scarcely had the stodgy *Spray* wallowed its way out of the creek to the comparatively safe waters of the open bay than the breeze, such as it had been, sighed and died, and we drifted on, sidewise a good deal of the way, much to the annoyance of captains and owners of various power craft, from launches to ferry boats and sea going freighters, which had to give us the right of way to our leisurely and erratic course as the falling tide dragged us along toward the Golden Gate and Pacific Ocean. If printed and bound, the profanity we caused that morning would have filled several large volumes.

Approaching the Gate, swirled along faster in tide rips piled up by millions of gallons of water a minute trying to rush through the narrow channel, we shipped the two sweeps and rowed with all our strength to win our way across the current and escape being carried out to sea. We made it, though only because the time of slack water was near and the current subsiding. We anchored near Sausalito, hoping for a sailing breeze on the morrow. There was a little wind in the morning, barely enough to give us steerage way, so we had to wait for the flooding tide to get under way. The same ill luck in this respect attended us for days, and it was more than a week before we got the sloop across San Pablo Bay and into the Sacramento River, a distance we were to traverse two months later, homeward bound, in a single day, tearing along in the grip of a half gale.

*

## Tule Fog

There is no living thing on the face of the earth so stealthy as a tule fog. It hides through the night in the vast expanses of twelve-foot-tall rushes in the slough region of the Sacramento and San Joaquin valleys, to come creeping out at dawn and spread itself over the face of the waters. There is nothing more ghostly than the movement of the wraithlike mass, a creeping advance that is almost imperceptible until the shore line dims and disappears, the sloop's mast becomes a vague gray line in a smother of white and the riding light fades into faint and shapeless glow. The perceptive senses become distorted in the midst of this weird phenomenon until one seems to see grotesque, moving shapes at a distance to which vision could not possibly penetrate through the thickening mist, and to hear sounds in directions from which no sounds could come.

It was in sounds just then that Jack and I were most interested, specifically the whistle of some river steamboat or the blare of a fog-horn from some unseen scow schooner or motor boat. We were anchored well away from the channel, but that gave no great assurance of safety in fog so dense as this. Presently we heard the chugging of a motor boat engine, like the beating of a giant heart somewhere, shattering the fleecy silence. Jack caught up the horn and blew long blasts into the mist. The sound of the motor ceased and answering horn blasts filled the invisible space about us, seeming to come from close by, yet without enabling us to determine the direction. We tried shouting, and there came an answering hail. This worked better. In a moment the throbbing of the engine was resumed, became fainter in the distance and died away. Jack and I began discussing what might follow if some craft should crash into the *Spray*. The 500 pounds of scrap iron clamped as ballast inside the hull would take the boat to bottom in a few seconds. We might swim to shallow water in the tules, even fully dressed, but after that the chances of our making our way out, through miles of swamp studded with quicksand pools and tules towering everywhere above our heads, would be slight indeed. . . . Then, dimly in the thinning edge of the retreating fog, we saw a ponderous mass bearing down on us. It was a scow schooner, without even a steerage way in the moveless air but borne along in the grip of the flooding tide. As the hulk drifted clear of the fog we saw an animated figure on the deck, and a minute later, seconds before the weird-looking craft could have crashed into the helpless sloop, the mudhook went overside with a splash and the vessel rode harmlessly at anchor. . . . He was tall and ungainly, this captain of a scow schooner. His face and hands were seamed and looked like seasoned leather.

"You're Jack London, aren't you?" he asked in a casual manner. "I read in the paper about how you were on the river. Good thing the fog lifted when it did," he added reflectively, measuring with his practiced eye the short distance between the sloop and his own peculiar vessel. We agreed that it was good indeed.

"Quite an old boat you've got," Jack remarked. "Own her?"

"Owned her and sailed her for forty year."

"Doesn't she need repairs?" Jack asked.

"Needs 'em but can't git 'em," chuckled the captain of the *Annee*. "I wouldn't dare have her lifted out of the water. She'd fall apart. It's only her shape and the water pressure holds her together. I did have to have a new rudder post. . . . I bored through four feet of rotten timbers before I found solid wood to bolt to it. But there's some good wood in her; and there's her shape and the water pressure."

"I hope you're a good swimmer," said Jack.

"Never seemed to git time to learn. Fell overboard two–three times, but made out to grab something and climb aboard."

. . . A light breeze sprang up, and the captain of the *Annee*—comprising the entire crew as well in the person of one remarkable man—prepared to depart.

"How is the water at the mouth of False Bay?" Jack asked. "Has it been shoaling up much lately? This sloop draws more than five feet of water."

"There's water to burn," the old riverman assured us as he shoved off.

*

### Memories and Mudhens

Peering through Carquinez Strait on our way upstream, Jack London gazed wistfully at the town of Benicia and adjacent tule swamps, as memories of some of the wonderful wild days of his youth went through his mind. Somewhere in that mile-wide expanse of tall rushes, he had learned by diligent inquiry in various places, dwelt three survivors of the reckless band of oyster pirates with whom, as a boy of sixteen, he had been associated. Others had been shot to death by officers of the law, were killed in waterfront saloon brawls or died of hardship, accident or disease, while a few still lived as long-term prisoners of state penitentiaries. . . . "I regret none of it," Jack mused, gazing at the waste of tall tules above which rooftops and chimney caps of a hundred arks were visible. . . .

Among the letters awaiting us at Walnut Grove when at last we arrived was one from George Sterling. Our poet friend reminded us jeeringly of our promise to send him some wild ducks. Had we turned too soft-hearted to kill the dear little birds? Had our marksmanship failed utterly, or had we become gluttons, avidly devouring all the game we slew. Or had we forgotten that we had friends or ever had made any promises?

[81]

George must have forgotten who he was writing to when he penned that derisive missive, nor did he remember it in time to save himself heavy expense. As we read the letter in the cockpit of the anchored *Spray*, at the heart of Georgina Slough, we could see and hear a hundred or more chattering mudhens feeding less than forty yards away. I think Jack and I got the idea at the same moment, as I saw him look up from the letter he had just finished reading aloud, turning toward the noisy birds and then glance at the 22-caliber rifle in a corner of the cockpit, which already I was reaching for. I potted a dozen or so and handed the rifle to Jack, who went on with the work until there enough dead mudhens to fill a gunny sack. This we expressed to George with our compliments and finest regards. Our joke worked better, or worse, than we had expected. Without opening the sack George sent it to the manager of the Gas Kitchen, then Oakland's most famous and expensive eating place, with instructions to have the game prepared for a special occasion and engaging a private dining room. He invited Kate, "Toddy," Blanche,[5] Dick and half a dozen others to the feast, and was looking forward proudly to the event when a troubled message came from the Gas Kitchen manager. He did not like to ask any of his chefs to cook mudhens he wrote, and was Mr. Sterling really serious? If it was a joke on some of Mr. Sterling's friends, would Mr. Sterling please play it elsewhere rather than at the Gas Kitchen?

The joke was on George, of course, and a joke Jack and I never would have perpetrated had we thought how harsh it might turn out to be. Game guy that he was, George changed his order to a wild duck dinner for all his invited guests, which ran into money, and did not tell anybody about it. Until the story leaked out, doubtless through Gas Kitchen connections, George's guests of the evening were permitted to believe the ducks had been supplied by us aboard the *Spray*.

\*

### There Had Been Pirates

For days we loafed along through some of the thousand miles of watercourses stemming out of the San Joaquin and Sacramento rivers and their chief tributaries, writing, playing chess, arguing, reading, sometimes aloud to each other or commenting upon what we were reading. Often we went overside for swimming, usually when the sloop was at anchor but sometimes when she was moving with the tides or even in a light breeze, in the latter case always swimming ahead so we could catch her if she should try to dash away from us in some sudden gust of wind. We lived lazily, in a way, through those pleasant days, though doing at least as much writing as we would have done ashore, Jack turning out an average of nearly a thousand words a day of the last chapters of "The Sea Wolf." We slept at least six hours each night and sometimes more, for which Jack, who generally had limited himself rigidly to five hours, sometimes reproached himself. . . .

At the mouth of False Bay we ran the *Spray* aground three times, despite the assurance of the captain of the *Annee* that there was "water to burn," and had a tough time carrying out the anchor in the skiff and hauling on the cable to pull the sloop clear of mudbanks. So we came again to Carquinez Strait, one of the most extraordinary short stretches of water in the world, and early one afternoon anchored off the tule swamp south of the town. We rowed in the skiff to a ramshackle wharf which apparently had been built and maintained after a fashion by the ark community of some 200 members, predominantly male though there were a few families. Landing, we walked along narrow plank footpaths which at low tide were six or seven feet above the water, two or three feet above at high tide. At ark after ark Jack asked for information, receiving sullen and evasive answers from men who had been through experiences which made them suspicious of all strangers. A few, however, responsive to Jack's genial manner, told us what they knew, that the three we sought were living in an ark "over there somewhere," the general direction indicated by a more or less vague wave of the hand. On we went, over the maze of branching and crossing footingways. We saw three men coming toward us, walking single file of necessity yet all visible to us at once as they rounded a curve. Two were nearing middle age, lined and worn by hard living, the third being still youthful in appearance. The one in the lead, tall and rawboned, halted his shambling advance twenty feet from us, stared steadily for a few seconds with widening eyes and then uttered a joyous shout:

"Jack London! Why, you old —," a nominally insulting epithet not uncommonly employed as a term of affectionate regard in certain social circles. The other older man echoed the cry, while the younger of the trio whooped in gladness:

"By God! The Prince!"

As "Prince of the Oyster Pirates" Jack had been known when, at the age of 16, he sailed his *Razzle Dazzle* in forays on planted oyster beds along the shores of San Francisco Bay.

[83]

"Well, Jack!" they babbled on delightedly, the younger one adding eagerly: "Say, Jack, did you write those pieces in the paper with the name 'Jack London' to them? I always said our Jack London was smart enough to do it, but these mudhens wouldn't believe it."

"We thought you might be smart enough, Jack," the accused pair hastened to defend themselves, "but we weren't right out certain."

Jack assured them that he really had written those pieces in the paper (what he called potboilers, by-line stories for the San Francisco *Examiner* done to meet financial emergencies), and then chuckled to me under his breath:

"Cloudesley, such a fame!"

"The Call of the Wild," sixth of Jack's books to be published, was then at the height of its stupendous popularity, and others had won a place among the current "Six Best Sellers." But books rarely found their way into that colony of arks.

Jack was obviously pleased at meeting his former associates, yet there was a suggestion of regret in his manner which I am sure only I perceived— something remaining in his memory in regard to them. These were men who had exchanged gunfire with police patrol boats; who had raided private oyster beds guarded by armed men, escaping by masterly sailing, with buckshot and bullets singing past their ears, when sudden gusts of wind tore the concealing fog; who by inches and minutes had evaded arrest on charges which would have sent them to spend the rest of their lives behind prison bars. Now they paid for their bread and beer by ferrying passengers across Carquinez Strait in their skiffs between trips of the railroad ferryboat, selling wild ducks shot in season and out, and petty thefts from unguarded tramp freighters anchored in the straits. When we met them they were on their way to some small gainful enterprise, but abandoned it with enthusiasm to give a duck stew and steam beer party to Jack London and his friend.

### NOTES

1. Many of London's letters to Johns and writings about writing are collected in Walker and Reesman, *No Mentor but Myself*.

2. "Boy Jack and George" takes place in early spring 1903; Johns has returned to California for his health. *Jack London Journal* 2 (1995): 51–53.

3. "Other Days at Piedmont" occurs just after the previous section. The remainder of Johns's record of sailing with London takes place after London's purchase of the *Spray* on March 10. *Jack London Journal* 2 (1995): 56–59.

4. Blanche and Dick Partington, brother and sister, and Carlt and Lora Bierce, niece and nephew of Ambrose Bierce. Blanche (1866–1951) was a Bay Area journalist who wrote for the San Francisco *Morning Call* and enjoyed close relationships with California writers George Sterling, Ambrose Bierce, and Jack London, as well as being a sometime rival of Charmian's. Cincinnatus Heine Miller (1837–1913), known by his pen name Joaquin Miller, was a California nature writer called the "Poet of the Sierras." Bierce was called "Bitter Bierce" for his early scathing reviews in various publications, but he was producing searing naturalistic tales of the Civil War, his "Weird Fiction," and his satire *The Devil's Dictionary* (1906, 1911). He, London, and Sterling really were a group of forward-thinking critics. It was two-against-one for years, though, in person and in letters. London's furious letters to George Sterling about Bierce are housed at the Jack and Charmian Collection at Utah State University's Merrill Library and make an entertaining read, along with Sterling's responses. At the Bohemian Grove, one late afternoon, London and Bierce went fist to fist, but, drunk, landed themselves in the Russian River and had to be pulled out.

5. Blanche Partington (1866–1951) was a journalist and member of the San Francisco literary scene. She was one of London's lovers and an early rival of Charmian's.

# Anna Strunsky Walling

## From "Memoirs of Jack London" (1917)

Anna Strunsky, later Anna Strunsky Walling (1879–1964), was born in Babinotz, Russia, to a leftist Jewish family who left what is now Belarus; they emigrated to New York in 1886, then San Francisco in 1893, enjoying a prosperous life. She was a Stanford graduate and a socialist activist, intellectual, and writer, an early part of the so-called Crowd or bohemian set, including George Sterling, Jack London, and Herman "Jim" Whitaker. She met London in December 1899 at a Socialist Labor Party meeting commemorating the Paris Commune of 1871 at San Francisco's Turk Street Temple. Having joined as a teenager, Anna was, unlike Jack, a lifelong member. As she recalled later, "[We] had climbed the dusty stairs and had sat in the garish hall lighted by gas-jets. [We] looked about . . . at the red-draped speaker's stand, the pictures on the walls of Marx, Engels, Liebknecht, Lassalle, at the black letters on white stretched across the platform: 'Workers unite! You have only your chains to lose, you have a world to gain.'"[1] She noticed London as they both approached speaker Austin Lewis afterwards, likely introduced by Frank Strawn-Hamilton, "a tousled socialist philosopher" who was a friend of London's. He asked her, "Do you want to meet him?"[2] She was 22 and he 23, and they had quite a conversation. They became very close friends, exchanging hundreds of letters, his beginning on December 19, "My Dear Miss Strunsky," but soon "Dear, dear You." He immediately pictured her as a very special sort of writer-friend, "[a] woman to whom it is given to feel the deeps and the heights of emotion in an extraordinary degree; who can grasp the intensity of transcendental feeling, the dramatic force of situation as few women, or men either, can" (Jack London, *Letters*, 133). He wrote her: "Take me this way: a stray guest, a bird of passage, splashing with salt-rimed wings through a brief moment of your life—a rude and blundering bird, used to large airs and great spaces, unaccustomed to the amenities of confined existence" (135). He was invited for dinner that weekend. They loved to discuss philosophy and enjoyed bicycling in the Berkeley hills. They were lovers (he was "the Sahib") and coauthors (*Kempton-Wace Letters*, 1903). As Russ Kingman has described it, "Jack, as Herbert Wace, would discuss love from the biological point of view; and Anna, as Dane Kempton, would take the idealistic and emotional viewpoint. *The Kempton-Wace Letters*

. . . constitute one of the most interesting and curious books in the whole literature of love."[3] London proposed to her in 1900 but was confused when she genteelly deflected him; for her to accept immediately would to her have been improper, and things were made worse by mentioning that she might need to go cover the growing revolutionary fervor in Russia. Angry, he married Bess Maddern within a week. They maintained their friendship and worked on their book, though Bessie was troubled at Jack's insistence that Anna live with him, Bessie, and Joan in the Piedmont cottage; Anna soon sensed the problem and moved out, but their attraction only grew. There arose another chance for their love: unhappy in his marriage to Bess, acknowledging that he married her for all the wrong reasons, London confessed his misery, and he proposed again on May 3, 1902, this time saying they could run away to Australia or New Zealand and begin a new life. She answered him this time in the affirmative: "Yes, darling, with all my heart."[4] In her account, Anna hesitated over marrying a divorced man with a child; nevertheless, "there was a tumult of joy in her heart and she promised to marry him."[5] He left for his assignment in South Africa via New York and London following the Boer War; when his assignment was canceled, he went to London to research and write *The People of the Abyss* (1903). But he had heard nothing from her; Anna had discovered that Bess was pregnant with Becky. Anna and Jack, by mail, argued it out, but the affair was over. Anna's memoirs of London reveal not only that she was in love with him all of his life but also that she was perhaps his most truly insightful friend.[6] Her eulogy "Memoirs of Jack London," from which the selections below are taken, may be the best word-portrait of Jack London written by anyone. Anna was devastated when she learned of his death and published an obituary using part of her "Memoirs of Jack London" in *The Masses* in 1917. Her full and complete "Memoirs of Jack London" was never published.[7] She and Walling divorced in 1932.

"Who that ever knew him can forget him, and how will life ever forget one who was so indissolubly a part of her? He was youth, adventure, romance. He was a poet and a social revolutionist. He had a genius for friendship. He loved greatly and was greatly beloved. But how fix in words that quality of personality that made him different from everyone else in the world? How convey an idea of his magnetism and of the poetic quality of his nature? He is the outgrowth of the struggle and the suffering of the Old Order, and he is the strength and the virtue of all its terrible and criminal vices. He came out of the Abyss in which millions of his generation and the generation preceding him throughout time have been hopelessly lost. He rose out of the Abyss, and he escaped from the Abyss to become as large as the race and to be identified with the forces that shape the future of mankind.

His standard of life was high. He for one would have the happiness of power, of genius, of love, and the vast comforts and ease of wealth. Napoleon and Nietzsche had a part in him, but his Nietzschean philosophy became transmuted into Socialism—the movement of his time—and it was by the force of his Napoleonic temperament that he conceived the idea of an incredible success and had the will to achieve it. Sensitive and emotional as his nature was, he forbade himself any deviation from the course that would lead him to his goal. He systematized his life. Such colossal energy, and yet he could not trust himself! He lived by rule. Law, Order and Restraint was the creed of this vital, passionate youth. His stint was a thousand words a day revised and typed. He allowed himself only four and one-half hours of sleep and began his work regularly at dawn for years. The nights were devoted to extensive reading of science, history and sociology. He called it getting his scientific basis. One day a week he devoted to the work of a struggling friend. For recreation he boxed and fenced and swam—he was a great swimmer—and he sailed—he was a sailor before the mast—and he spent much time flying kites, of which he had a large collection. Like Zola's, his first efforts were poetry. This no doubt was the secret of the Miltonic simplicity of his prose which made him the accepted model for pure English and for style in the universities of this country and at the Sorbonne. He had always wanted to write poetry, but poets proverbially starved—unless they or theirs had independent incomes—so poetry was postponed until that time when his fame and fortune were to have been made. Fame and fortune were made and enjoyed for over a decade, but yet the writing of poetry was postponed, and death came before he had remembered his promise to himself. Death came before he had remembered many other things. He was so hard at work—so pitifully, tragically hard at work, and it was a fixed habit by now. . . .

The time came when he had the bank account of $1,000 and an assured income of over $60,000 a year in addition, but he did not return to the simple and beautiful existence of the poet and the student of which he had dreamt. He paid the ultimate price for what he received. His success was the tragedy of his life. He mortgaged his brain in order to meet the market demands, and fatigue and over-stimulation led him to John Barleycorn and to the consequent torture of what he called the White Logic. He had written forty-four books. Sometimes a vertigo seized him. What had a strong, normal man to do with labor that involved so puny a tool as the pen? He longed for man's work. He conceived the idea of cultivating his Valley of the Moon. He would put the money he earned by his pen into a vast agricultural experiment; he would make arid land fertile. He would grow eucalyptus trees and raise horses. That was creative work in a sense that the stories he was writing so prolifically (four books a year) were not creative; he had not time to remember that the same pen that wrote these pot-boilers had written short stories of immortal beauty like "The Odyssey of the North" and "The White Silence," and books of such greatness as "Martin Eden" and "Call of the Wild," and essays of unparalleled brilliance like those in "The Kempton-Wace Letters," the book we wrote together.

His was not a vulgar quest for riches. In his book "The Game" he explains the psychology of the prize fighter to whom the ring is symbolic of the plan and the purpose of life itself. To become inordinately rich through the efforts of his pen was his way of "playing the game." It appealed to his sense of humor and his sense of the dramatic to house members of the I.W.W., Comrades of the Road, or Mexican Revolutionists in a palace. The best was none too good for them or for any man. Not only had the Abyss not been able to swallow him up; the Abyss had risen with him.

Here is a letter written from Oakland, Cal., January 21, 1900:

"Do you know, I have the fatal faculty of making friends, and lack the blessed trait of being able to quarrel with them. And they are constantly turning up. My home is the Mecca of every returned Klondiker, sailor or soldier of fortune I ever met. Some day I shall build an establishment, invite them all, and turn them loose upon each other. Such a mingling of castes and creeds and characters could not be duplicated. The destruction would be great. The sanctity of my fireside shall be inviolate. Or should my heart fail me, I'll run way to the other side of the world" [*Letters*, 144–146].

This is exactly what he did in Glen Ellen, in beautiful Sonoma Valley, California. He built a mansion, surrounded by fifteen hundred acres, where he kept open house, and when his heart failed him he did run away to the other side of the world. He went to the South Sea Islands and to Hawaii. He made the memorable and extraordinary cruise of the Snark, purporting to be away from the world for seven years.

Only a youth as intense as his could feel as deeply as he did the flight of time, and so eagerly hoard the hours. Life was very short. One should have no time to dally. It was his working creed. It has been given to him to see so much of life. Child of the people that he was, he had never had a childhood. He had early seen struggle and been forced to struggle. He thought himself "harsh, stern, uncompromising." Of course he was not. It is only that he had few illusions, and the sensitive nature of childhood and youth had suffered at what he had beheld in the Abyss and beyond. This suffering and this reaction against what is called organized society, but is in reality a chaotic jungle, became the basis of his world philosophy.

The following is from a letter written in December 21, 1899:

"Life is very short. . . . I , too, was a dreamer, on a farm, nay, a California ranch. But early, at only nine, the hard hand of the world was laid upon me. It has never relaxed. It has left me sentiment, but destroyed sentimentalism. It has made me practical, so that I am known as harsh, stern, uncompromising. It has taught me that reason is mightier than imagination; that the scientific man is superior to the emotional man. It has also given me a truer and a deeper romance of things, an idealism which is an inner sanctuary and which must be resolutely throttled in dealings with my kind, but which yet remains within the holy of holies, like an oracle, to be cherished always but to be made manifest or to be consulted not on every occasion I go to market" [Letters, 136].

Sincerity was the greatest trait of his character. He never made pretensions and he built neither his work nor his life of sophisms and evasions. If literature is marketable and had a price and he put the products of his brain for sale, then he could not stoop to pretend that he was following art for art's sake and was not writing for money. But it would not be seemly and according to "the eternal fitness of things" to offer wares for which society would not pay him lavishly. If you make yourself marketable at all, you must also be indispensable. With cold-bloodedness of the "economic man" which he claimed to be, he set work to achieve this. . . .

From overwork and from turning artwork into a toilsome trade, the natural reaction set in, and he, the most generous of natures, was obsessed by a kind of cynicism. His soul was sick with all the adulation which his success brought him. Why had these people, now eager to flatter him, not seen what was in him before he was "discovered"? A story from which he had received five dollars from the *Overland Monthly* and which had not brought him a word of praise from anybody, suddenly became great when it was found between the stiff covers of a book. So he held lightly the praise and kindness of people, and he suffered from a melancholy which made him question not only the worth of the world but of life itself. He had achieved so much, only to find it was not worth having. There was no intrinsic value in anything. He suffered from melancholia. He was obsessed by suicidal ideas. As with Tolstoy, there was a time when he kept a loaded revolver in his desk ready to use it against himself at any time. . . .[8]

It was in his twenty-sixth year that he began to sign all his letters "Yours for the Revolution" and thousands in this country and in the countries across the sea took up the phrase. He had served the revolutionary cause from his earliest youth. He had talked Socialism on street corners and he had addressed this regular Sunday night meeting at the "Locals." He had let his name stand on the Socialist political ticket for school director and for mayor, and when he became famous he came East and lectured, choosing socialist subjects.

In a letter dated February 12, 1908, he says: "The imposing edifice of society above my head holds no delight for me. It is the foundation of the edifice that interests me. There I am content to labor, crowbar in hand, shoulder to shoulder with intellectuals, idealists, and class-conscious workingmen, getting a solid pry now and again and setting the whole edifice rocking. Some day, when we get a few more hands and crowbars to work, we'll topple it over, along with all its rotten life and unburied dead, its monstrous selfishness and sodden materialism. Then we'll cleanse the cellar and build new habitation for mankind, in which all the rooms will be bright and airy, and where the air that is breathed will be clean, noble and alive."[9]

They have toppled it over in Russia, and how sad it is that Jack London should have passed into the silence, out of the sight of the red banners waving over a free people and out of the reach of the voices of millions singing the International!

He wrote "The People of the Abyss," a story of the London slums. It was on the occasion of his first visit to Europe. He did not even go see his publishers. He dropped out of sight and lost himself in the abyss of human misery, and the results was the strongest indictment against modern society written in our time, a "Les Miserables" in sociological form. To do this he compelled himself to live as a slum dweller. He cut himself off from his money and walked the streets seeking employment, starving and homeless.

London, August 25, 1902

"Saturday night I was out all night with the homeless ones, walking the streets in the bitter rain, and drenched to the skin, wondering when dawn would come. Sunday I spent with the homeless ones, in the fierce struggle for something to eat. I returned to my rooms Sunday evening, after thirty-six hours continuous work and short one night's sleep. To-day I have composed, typed and revised 4,000 words and over. I have just finished. It is one in the morning. I am worn out and exhausted and my nerves are blunted with what I have seen and the suffering it has cost me. . . . I am made sick by this human hellhole called London Town" [*Letters*, 306–308].

He had social wisdom. He understood the class struggle and he believed in the international organization of the people. He understood that international humanity in our present evolution had only one enemy, which was international capitalism, and that economic and social forces in society were clarifying the minds of the people and strengthening their hearts and investing them with weapons with which to give successful combat to their enemy. Society was a battlefield upon which were ranged in conflict the forces of the people against the oppressors and exploiters of the people. His place was in the ranks of the people. His success and his genius did not exempt him from bearing revolutionary arms. They were only proof of the basic truth of his social democracy, of the force of environment, of the fiction of blood and aristocracy. He had faith and vision and the courage not be overawed by the mighty of this world.

R. M. S. "Majestic,"
July 31 '02.

"I sailed yesterday from New York at noon. . . . I meet the men of the world in Pullman coaches, New York clubs, and Atlantic liner smoking rooms, and truth to say, I am made more hopeful for the Cause by their total ignorance and non-understanding of the forces at work. They are blissfully ignorant of the coming upheaval, while they have grown bitterer and bitterer towards the workers. You see, the growing power of the workers is hurting them and making them bitter while it does not open their eyes" [*Letters*, 303–304].

He wrote an essay called "What Life Means to Me" which takes its place with Kropotkin's "Appeal to the Young" and Oscar Wilde's "The Soul of Man Under Socialism," and its closing sentence rings with his faith in the rise of the common man. "The stairway of time is ever echoing with the wooden shoe going up, the polished boot descending."

He flaunted his physical bases. He was an idealist without any illusions. He was avid for truth, for justice, and he found little of it at hand. He was an individualist who was consecrated to the cause of mankind. As long as he lived he would strip the veils from truth and be a living protest against all the evils and injustices of society. . . .

What was this "physical basis" which he flaunted in those days? He justified war. He said that as long as we accepted the aid of policemen and the light of a street lamp from a society that legalized capital punishment, we had no right to attack capital punishment. He believed in the inferiority of certain races and talked of the Anglo-Saxon people as the salt of the earth. He inclined to believe in the biological inferiority of woman to man, for had he not watched women and men at the Piedmont Baths and had the woman not shivered at the brink of the swimming pool, "not standing up straight under God!" He believed that right made might. He fled from civilization and systematically avoided it. He had a barbarian's attitude toward death, holding himself ready to go at any time, with total indifference to his fate. He held that love is only a trap set by nature for the individual. One must not marry for love but for certain qualities discerned by the mind. This he argued in "The Kempton-Wace Letters," brilliantly and passionately; so passionately as to again make one suspect that he was not as certain of his position as he claimed to be. Later, Jack became the most mellow of thinkers, as passionately promulgating his new ideas as he had then assailed them. He now believed in romantic love, he had helped in the agitation for woman suffrage and was jubilant over its success in California. He was now an absolute internationalist and anti-militarist. He now laughed at himself when he recalled how in the Russian-Japanese War he had been on the Russian side although all Socialists wanted Russia beaten for the sake of the revolutionary movement. The Russians were white men and the Japanese were not. He had looked on a wounded Russian foot and had felt the thrill of "consciousness of kind." It was a white foot, a foot like his own. He made loathing of capital punishment the theme of his most ambitious book, "The Star Rover." And his former belief in sensation for the sake of sensation, leading him to experiment with drugs and drink, he repudiated in his classic, "John Barleycorn." He had come far—he had come out on the other side of everything he had before adhered to, as all who knew were convinced he would.

I see him in pictures, steering his bicycle with one hand and with the other clasping a great bunch of yellow roses which he had just gathered out of his own garden, a cap moved back on his thick brown hair, the large blue eyes with their long lashes looking out star-like upon the world—an indescribably virile and beautiful boy, the kindness and wisdom of his expression somehow belying his youth.

I see him lying face down among the poppies and following with his eyes his kites soaring against the high blue of the California skies, past the tops of the giant sequoias and eucalyptus which he so dearly loved.

I see him becalmed, on "The Spray," the moon rising behind us, and hear him rehearse his generalizations made from his studies in the watches of the night before of Spencer and Darwin. His personality invested his every movement and every detail of his life with an alluring charm. One took his genius for granted, even in those early years when he was struggling with all his unequalled energies to impress himself upon the world.

I see him seated at his work when the night is hardly over, and it seems to me that the dawn greets and embraces him, and that he is part of the elements as other less generic natures are not. I see him on a May morning leaning from the balustrade of a veranda sweet with honeysuckle, to watch two humming birds circling around each other in their love ecstasy. He was captive of beauty—the beauty of bird and Bower, of sea and sky and the icy vastness of the Arctic world. No one could echo more truthfully the "Behold, I have lived" of Richard Hovey, with which he closed the essay which sums up his world philosophy, "Human Drift."

"Behold, I have lived!"

He lived not only in the wide spaces of the earth, under her tropic suns and in her white frozen silences, with her children of happiness and with her miserable ones, but he lived in the thought always of life and death, and in the timeless and boundaryless struggle of international socialism.

## NOTES

1. Anna Strunsky Walling Papers, Yale University, folders 392 and 393. See also Manuscript Writings by Anna Strunsky Walling, Jack London Collection, Huntington Library; quoted in Boylan, *Revolutionary Lives*, 12.

2. Boylan, *Revolutionary Lives*, 12. Anna left her description of the evening in her memoir of January 17, 1919, folder 81, Anna Strunsky Walling Papers, Yale University Library. These memoirs were partially republished by Charmian London in her *Book of Jack London*, 1:319–322, and partly published in *The Masses*.

3. Kingman, *Pictorial Life*, 27.

4. Anna Strunsky Walling quoted in Labor, *Jack London*, 163. Labor traces her answer to Waters, "Anna Strunsky and Jack London," 30.

5. Anna Strunsky Walling Manuscripts, Jack London Collection, Huntington Library; quoted in Boylan, *Revolutionary Lives*, 23-24.

6. Anna's devotion to Jack was documented by Earle Labor, who, in his *Jack London: An American Life*, recalls his interview of Anna Walling Hamburger, Anna's daughter, on July 11, 1995. Mrs. Hamburger confirmed that her mother carried a miniature portrait of Jack in her wallet for the rest of her life: "Mother never stopped loving him" (167). She also corresponded with London scholar Russ Kingman; those letters are stored at the Jack London Foundation Research Center in Glen Ellen. Finally, in the guide to the Anna Strunsky Walling Papers at Yale's Sterling Library, MS 1111, the biographical section concludes: "She returned to California on short visits to old friends and helped dedicate a California state park built around the ruins of Jack London's home. She participated in Quaker social action projects and followed the activities of the War Resisters League, the League for Mutual Aid, the American League to Abolish Capital Punishment, the League for Industrial Democracy, and the National Association for the Advancement of Colored People which English (Walling, her husband) had helped found. Living in Greenwich Village, she had contact with some young bohemian writers, but by the time she died the sensational, enthralling Anna Strunsky had been long forgotten. Perhaps Jack London was shrewd in his observation that Anna's ability to carry forth her life with purpose would be thwarted by her self-abnegating attachments to others and her emotions. Hers was a life made interesting by the people she loved rather than by the work she produced" (7). Anna published only one novel, *Violette of Père Lachaise* (New York: Frederick A. Stokes, 1915), but numerous socialist essays.

7. Her full "Memoir" resides in the Anna Strunsky Walling Papers at Yale University; other diaries, letters, and memoirs are to be found at the Huntington Library and the Bancroft Library.

8. See Jack London, *Letters*, 269-270.

9. Anna Strunsky Walling Manuscripts, Huntington Library.

# George Sterling

## Letter to Jack London (1906)

George Ansel Sterling III (1869–1926), London's best friend, was a well-known California poet of the late Victorian style, à la Algernon Swinburne. London called Sterling "Greek" (Sterling was proud of his fine profile) and Sterling called London "Wolf." Together with their friends, they were at the center of the so-called San Francisco area's "Crowd" of young intellectuals of the day, or "Bohemians." Sterling was raised in Sag Harbor, Long Island, New York; he moved west to work for his uncle, a real estate tycoon in Oakland. He was befriended by Ambrose Bierce and probably met London at Coppa's Restaurant, a favorite hangout of both. Bierce first published Sterling in his "Prattle" column in the *San Francisco Examiner*. They loved and supported each other and their art, and they shared a wild sense of fun: practical jokes, drinking contests, hashish, visits to brothels. Probably one of the only things London's two wives could have agreed upon is that neither always liked George. Yet each gamely joined in the fun—up to a point. The Crowd would gather at George and his wife Carrie's cabin in Carmel-by-the-Sea, built by George and his friends, a rustic retreat on a knoll overlooking the pine forest, the Carmel Mission, and the sea, the whole beach home to an artist's colony first begun by Charles Warren Stoddard. A favorite romp with George was at the Bohemian Grove Hijinks, where London and Bierce could compete for George's attention in settling their ongoing personal feud. His long poem "A Wine of Wizardry" was lauded by Bierce in *Cosmopolitan* in 1907 and his dramatic poem *Lilith* (1919) earned him praise, but his poetry quickly seemed dated and his career fizzled. He and London were constant correspondents.

With considerable sangfroid, George Sterling dashed off a letter to London from Carmel on the date of the San Francisco earthquake, using his father's company stationery emblazoned with "The Realty Syndicate." His descriptions of the quake in Carmel tend to the comic, and he has the leisure to gossip and tell his friend that he finally sold one of his major poems and note his reading Wharton and plans to read Sinclair. Ambrose Bierce, Sterling's mentor, helped him sell the long poem. Bierce was a frequent topic of disagreement between London and Sterling. London had written the year before (June 24, 1905) that Bierce is "rudderless, compassless" in terms of science and socialism: "He's

best at long range slinging into it. He was groggy at the drop of a hat, and before it got done with him was looking anxiously around and wondering. . . .
All he did was to back and fill and potter around, dogmatize and contradict
himself.[1] (As was her habit in preparing London's biography, Charmian made
a few annotations on letters.)

Carmel, Apr. 18/06

Dearest Wolf:

We had a hell of an earthquake in Carmel (and assumably everywhere else
in America) this morning. You should have seen Carrie getting from her bed
to the front veranda in 1½ seconds! Mr. and Mrs. Gladys Maxwell were here,
and we made an *interesting* group. The dog was so scared that her heart
hasn't stopped thumping yet, and all the hens yelled "bloody murder." It
shattered both my chalk-rock chimneys, which will cost me about $50 to
fix, and knocked down and smashed lots of bric-a-brac, including most of
Carrie's Indian stuff. And my small statue (the one *you* have a sample of) was
broken. Thank God, the wood-pile is intact. [Here Charmian annotates: "He
*cut* it!"]. . . .

All's well in Carmel, but I still owe dear Charm. A letter. . . . Ambrose
[Charmian inserts "Bierce"] finally sold "A Wine of Wizardry" to a new
magazine that the Neale Pub. Co. is about to start. It took greenhorns to
bit. I'm not writing anything, but exercise a good deal: Chas. Warren Stoddard now addresses me "O Poem made flesh!" which is flattering but fear-
inspiring. Is he a good old man? [Charmian annotates: "!!!"]. I've just read
"The House of Mirth"—there's fine work in the book, and some bum English. "The Jungle" comes next. Love to you both, from Greek.

**NOTE**

1. Jack London to George Sterling, June 24, 1905, Jack and Charmian London Collection,
Merrill-Cazier Library, Utah State University.

# George Sterling

## "In Tribute" (1916)

When London left for Korea in 1904, he entrusted the manuscript of *The Sea-Wolf* (1904) to George and Charmian for copyediting and proofing. Writing was the glue that held these friends together. Sterling inspired the poet-socialist character Russ Brissenden in *Martin Eden* (1909). George was the only friend of London's present at the private graveside ceremony held after London's death. Sadly, George and his wife Carrie suffered from severe alcoholism and drug abuse, including opium. As their friends feared, both committed suicide, Carrie first, and a few years later George, in a guest room at the Bohemian Club in downtown San Francisco, with a tablet of cyanide he always carried. In 1913, in happier times, London inscribed George's copy of *The Night-Born*:

BLESSED, BELOVED GREEK:

> The seasons
> change, but I
> change not
> toward you; the
> years pass, but
> I pass not for
> you, as you
> pass not for
> me. Ours is
> some friendship,
> and greater than
> that, it is *love*.

> Thine,
> "The Wolf"
> Alias Jack London

Glen Ellen, Calif.

Under a sky of rain-washed turquoise, broken by white cloud-masses swept eastward from the ocean, the ashes of Jack London were laid to rest in the heart of his Sonoma County ranch of the afternoon of November 26th.

Aside from his thirteen workmen of the ranch, only the family relatives, by blood or marriage, attended, with a sole exception.

The spot selected by Mrs. London for the last resting place of her husband was a knoll, not far from one of the roads threading the region, and covered with white oaks, manzanita and madrona. Over their fallen leaves the funeral cortege ascended the steep hillside, to pause at the burial spot prepared by the workmen on the ranch.

No word was said. George Parslow, the senior member of the toilers on the ranch, received the small copper cylinder, which had been wreathed by Mrs. London with untimely-sprung primroses from the garden adjoining London's writing den, and with an Ilima lei worn by the late Frank Unger at a reception given by the Londons in Honolulu.

Parslow deposited the cylinder in the cement receptacle already prepared for it, and amid the profound silence of the onlookers, encased it in several gallons of fresh cement. This done, a huge boulder was urged by roller and crowbar above the sepulcher—a great block of red lava long-pitted by time and enriched by the moss of uncounted years.

The party dispersed as quietly as it had gathered, the stillness making it a funeral impressive beyond all memories of those in attendance.

No word, aside from a brief whisper, had been said. The thirteen strong men of the ranch faced the bearers of the remains in silence, and as silently departed.

The levels and ascents of Sonoma mountain, roamed over by London on horseback only two days previous to his death, shone green and yellow through the skirts of the drooping clouds. All nature seemed at hush, as if in realization of the great power that has turned from life to have endless peace on her bosom.

Jack London had gone—a stupefying and incredible departure. He, who had seemed almost immortal to all who knew him personally, and even to those who caught his quality from the written word, had turned his back on mortality with much of the splendid and dramatic quality of his accustomed life, going forth to the supreme adventure with a smile on his lips, the one instance of consciousness that had been awaked in him by the efforts of his physicians on the day of his demise.

Jack London had gone—and he died smiling triumphantly, as one who, finding himself on the summit of existence, and freed from the unhappiness of descending the nightward slopes, had kissed his hand in farewell as he sank lifeless on the lonely crest. . . .

If anything is certain, it is that Jack London is to be, and must be, represented in every library of the world that is to urge the slightest claim to Reason and the arts that cling to her knees. He [was] the sweet-hearted friend of all men. . . . And of the end of these things, who shall say?

# George Sterling, Jack London, Ambrose Bierce, and Gelett Burgess

## "The Abalone Song" (1930)

The Crowd, known also as the Bohemians, comprised Jack London, George Sterling, and Anna Strunsky, but also many others over time: Bierce's nephew and niece, Carlton and Lora; Jimmy Hopper, a successful journalist and old school friend of London's; Mary Austin, writer of the California Southwest and its Native peoples; Xavier Martinez, a Mexican painter trained in Paris—he painted London, but the portrait is lost—and his wife Elsie; and Arnold Genthe, a renowned photographer in San Francisco. Wednesday evenings at the Londons' home started with his marriage in 1900, but then there were more and more longer visits to the Sterlings in Carmel. Dropping by might also be the "Poet of the Sierras," Joaquin Miller; Jim Whitaker, a writer and boxing coach; the Partington siblings; Upton Sinclair; Sinclair Lewis; and Robinson Jeffers. The mood when they met on Carmel's beach was especially jolly: the conversation and ablutions sparkled, the waves rolled in and out, and the party went on. Abalone they had collected, pounded, and roasted over an open fire was a special pleasure. As the stars came up and the evening took hold, they could not but sing to the abalone—not unlike the greedy Walrus and the Carpenter. It is a tribute to their tune that it was eventually published and paid for by the Works Progress Administration. London reveled in company, good spirits, good food, and long conversations.

Oh! some folks boast of quail on toast
Because they think it's tony
But I'm content to owe my rent
And live on abalone.
Oh! Mission Point's a friendly joint,
Where ev'ry crab's a crony,
And true and kind you'll ever find
The clinging abalone.

He wanders free beside the sea,
Where'er the coast is stony;
He flaps his wings and madly sings—
The plaintive abalone.
By Carmel Bay, the people say,
We feed the lazzaroni
On Boston beans and fresh sardines,
And toothsome abalone.

Some live on hope, and some on dope
And some on alimony;
But my tom-cat, he lives on fat
And tender abalone.
Oh! some drink rain and some champagne,
Or brandy by the pony;
But I will try a little rye
With a dash of abalone.

Oh! some like jam, and some like ham,
And some like macaroni;
But bring me in a pail of gin
And a tub of abalone.
He hides in caves beneath the waves,—
His ancient patrimony;
And so 'tis shown that faith alone
Reveals the abalone.

The more we take, the more they make
In deep-sea matrimony;
Race suicide cannot betide
The fertile abalone.
I telegraph my better half
By Morse or by Marconi
But if the need arise for speed,
I send an abalone.

# Ambrose Bierce

## Letter to George Sterling (1905)

Ambrose Gwinnett Bierce (1842–1916?), was author of some of the most realistic and naturalistic fiction of his era, including his prolific short fiction based
on his experiences as a soldier in the Civil War. He became one of the greatest of American short story writers, satirists, social critics, and journalists. His
*Devil's Dictionary* (1906–1912) and his startling range of works, from short fiction to horror fiction, "weird fiction," and science fiction, display his insight
into an America he saw as dystopian. Bierce was a difficult man who left a
string of controversies behind him, even falling under suspicion in the assassination of President William McKinley while he was writing attacks upon him
for Hearst. He married and had three children; one son committed suicide,
and another died of alcoholism. He divorced his wife for infidelity in 1904. He
disappeared in late 1916 while attempting to travel with rebel troops during
the Mexican Revolution. Bierce also had trouble in his friendships with other
writers such as London and Sterling. He was sometimes mocked as "Bitter
Bierce," but bitter or not, Bierce was highly praised by H. L. Mencken and William Dean Howells. He has had a tremendous influence upon later writers,
especially his *Tales of Soldiers and Civilians* (1891–1892). He inspired H. P. Love-
craft, Ray Bradbury, and Robert Heinlein, among many others. Indeed, his
short story titled "An Inhabitant of Carcosa" (1886), as well as the work of one
of his protégés, Robert Chambers's *The King In Yellow* (1895), formed the central plot line for the hit HBO series *True Detective*, season 1 (2014).

Yes you sent me *The Sea-Wolf*. My opinion of it? Certainly—or a part of it.
It is a most disagreeable book, as a whole. London has a pretty style and no
sense of proportion. The story is a perfect welter of disagreeable incidents.
Two or three (of the kind) would have sufficed to show the character of the
man Larsen; and his own self-revealings by word of mouth would have "done
the rest." Many of these incidents, too, are impossible—such as that of a man
mounting a ladder with a dozen other men—more or less—hanging to his
leg, and the hero's work of rerigging a wreck and getting it off a beach where
it had stuck for weeks, and so forth. The "love" element, with its absurd sup-

pressions and impossible proprieties, is awful. I confess to an overwhelming contempt for both sexless lovers.

Now as to the merits. It is a rattling good story in one way; something is "going on" all the time—not always what one would wish, but something. One does not go to sleep over the book. But the great thing—and it is among the greatest of things—is that tremendous creation, Wolf Larsen. He will be with you to the end. So it does not really matter how London has hammered him into you. You may quarrel with the methods, but the result is almost incomparable. The hewing out and setting up of such a figure is enough for a man to do in one life-time. I have hardly words to impart my good judgment of that work.

# Ambrose Bierce

## "Small Contributions" (*Cosmopolitan*, 1908)

> Just as Bierce's contempt for London's "two sexless lovers" in *The Sea-Wolf* rang true for many readers, so does Bierce's assessment of London's *The Iron Heel* (1908), in which he hears a hero myth of bombast and violence, and much worse, a sentimental tale instead of a serious depiction of the attempted overthrow of a long-ruling capitalist "iron heel" of fascism by a workers' revolt. Though it was, like Bierce's own work, an early example of modern dystopian fiction and a powerful example of socialist fiction, Bierce's insights would have benefited London's plot development and perhaps helped him avoid some of the structural flaws of the novel. Mostly Bierce is showing the tyro London his greater expertise.

Jack London's titanic exaggeration may be obvious enough when he writes of social and industrial conditions, but mark his accuracy and moderation in relating (in *The Iron Heel*) the things that he knows about:

> The mob came on, but it could not advance. It piled up in a heap, a mound, a huge and growing wave of dead and dying. Those behind urged on, and the column, from gutter to gutter, telescoped upon itself. Wounded creatures, men and women, were vomited over the top of that awful wave and fell squirming down the face of it till they thrashed about under the automobiles and against the legs of the soldiers.

As an authority on the effects of gun-fire Colonel London stands foremost among the military men of his period.

Colonel London's book is supposed to be written in the year 419 B.O.M. (Brotherhood of Man), and following the cheerful incident related above come three centuries of similar controversy between people and their oppressors, the mound-builders and wave-makers. Then—a natural and inevitable result of tempers and dispositions softened by slaughter—behind this frowning providence the Brotherhood of Man reveals its smiling face and the book "ends happily," its gallant author is in receipt of a comfortable pension.

# Upton Sinclair

## "Upton Sinclair Pays Tribute to Jack London" (1916)

> Upton Beall Sinclair, Jr. (1878–1968), was a prolific American novelist and writer (of over one hundred books) whose work extended from realism to naturalism and social reformism. Sinclair's work was well known and popular in the first half of the twentieth century, and he won the Pulitzer Prize for Fiction in 1943. In 1906, Sinclair acquired fame for his muck-raking novel *The Jungle*, which exposed the miserable labor and sanitary conditions in the U.S. meatpacking industry, causing a public uproar that contributed in part to the passage a few months later of the 1906 Pure Food and Drug Act. His focus was largely on a group of Lithuanian immigrants being worked to death. Sinclair was what may be termed a progressive, the slightly later successor of London's working-class, syndicalist socialism, but he and London formed the Intercollegiate Socialist Society, under whose auspices London lectured on socialism at northeastern and midwestern universities. Sinclair's exposé *Oil!* (1927), which describes the working conditions of the burgeoning oil industry in California at the time, was made into the naturalist film *There Will Be Blood* by Paul Thomas Anderson in 2007.

## Special Dispatch to the Chronicle

Los Angeles, November 23.—Upton Sinclair, who is wintering in Pasadena, today paid the following tribute to the achievements and personality of Jack London:

"In the death of Jack London, American literature suffers the greatest loss it could possibly suffer today. He was one of America's most popular writers, but American critics have yet to realize what a supremely great writer he was. To foresee the judgment of posterity we have to go to foreign countries.

## His Greatest Works

"His greatest works, 'The Sea Wolf,' 'The Call of the Wild,' 'The People of the Abyss,' 'Martin Eden,' 'John Barleycorn,' are imperishable classics of literature.

"I should not be surprised if his greatest work were found unfinished among his papers. He had the sense of life and its beauty and wonder. He had begun at the bottom and he worked his way to the top, so he knew the whole of life and could portray it as it is.

"He is and will remain one of the great revolutionary forces in American letters. His work is a bugle call to the human soul, especially to the youth of the people seeking a way to freedom and justice. It may be that I am not an unprejudiced critic, but I have Jack London's own support for my opinion that the finest of his writings are the socialist essays which he wrote for love only. One of the best of these is the essay, 'What Life Means to Me.'

"My tribute to Jack London would not be complete without mention of his personal traits. He was a genial man, a delightful companion, a loyal friend and a generous herald of new talent.

"Eleven or twelve years ago when he was famous and I was entirely un-known, he wrote for the Socialist press an article about 'The Jungle' which gave that book its first impetus toward success. He was ever on the alert to do that same fine and generous thing for any writer who tried to see life as it really is.

"What we would like to say to him we have to say to the young who will read his books and thrill with the splendid vision of a world set free."

# Sinclair Lewis

## Letter to Jack London (August 1911)

> Born Harry Sinclair Lewis (1885–1951) in Sauk Center, Minnesota, he saw several generations of writers. He was the first U.S. writer to win the Nobel Prize in 1930, praised for revealing the cruelties of capitalism. He was a member of the Crowd, like London. He graduated from Yale University in 1908, having taken time to join one of Upton Sinclair's communes. His novels *Main Street* (1920) and then *Babbitt* (1922) were satires of American boosterism. *Arrowsmith* appeared in 1925 and was awarded the Pulitzer Prize, which he declined because *Main Street* had not won. His *Elmer Gantry* (1929) portrayed the hypocrisy of American life through a pastor. *It Can't Happen Here* (1935), a dystopian forecast of the election of a fascist to the United States presidency who uses the slogan "Make America Great Again," has recently become popular in the U.S. London and other writers were frequent correspondents; here Lewis seems to revel in the mention of "cut" officers in Provincetown, indicating a shared interest in the bodies of other men.

Dear Jack:

I'm finishing up my boys' book over here in the Berkshire hills. Provincetown got too rich for my blood, while writing, with about 10,000 sailors (of thin 'cut' officers especially) in the harbor—the North Atlantic squadron having its headquarters at Prtown. I shall be back in New York a week from yesterday, and back on the damned job a week from Tuesday. After this seven weeks of freedom, I want to be off the job and freelancing more than ever. Well, I shall be, I think, one of these days.

I'm glad you'd like to see some more plots. Under separate cover (that phrase shows im a damfine business man) I'm sending seventeen of them, with prices. I hope that you'll find them the thing; especially as I have made up nearly all of them, from time to time during the last few months, with you in mind, as you can see.

The poster of the Jack London cigar, of which I spoke, lived down in Washington; but I'll try to get hold of another, in New York, and send it to you. Ought to be able to, all right, for the headquarters of the United Cigar Stores are there. . . . And did you ever see the Makaroff cigarette poster quoting from you? I'll try to get hold of one of those, too. Do me demdest.

"I see by the papers" that Upton Sinclair is going to file divorce proceedings against his wife – and this after his novel "Love's Pilgrimage"!

Thanks for info. about The Abysmal Brute. I want to see that. Just kill Sam Berger while you're about it.

Hope that the rest of your trip thru the mountains will be corking. Please give my regards to Mrs. London.

For the revolution!

Sinclair Lewis

# Sinclair Lewis

## Letter to Jack London (October 1911)

London did purchase plots from Lewis. In an October 10, 1931, letter to Upton Sinclair, Charmian notes that "Jack bought three plots from [Sinclair] Lewis. Never used them. The only plots Jack ever used of George's were THE RED ONE, first story in collection under that title. And THE FIRST POET. In the latter instance, it wasn't a matter of 'plot' at all. George practically wrote the thing, and then they collaborated on it. Jack never requested plots. He picked up ideas here and there—but I've gone into all this in the biography. He bought plots to help out 'the other fellow.' Shortly before he died, Jack said: "I've got ideas here for a hundred novels. . . ."[1] Despite Charmian's statement, London did use some of Lewis's ideas for *The Assassination Bureau*.

Dear Jack:

Did you receive the plots I sent you from the Berkshires all right? I sent them about six weeks ago, and haven't heard from you yet, so I'm getting a bit anxious. Let me hear when you can.

How did you find my plots go, in general? Good investment? I sure hope they are. I've had so much fun reading the stories you have made me from them – for instance the capital "Abysmal Brute." Do they prove a good business investment? Some time I'll have to get real tactful and try to find a way to get you to make me a wedding present or some modest percent of your profits of 'em. Please tell your pleasant lady, Mme. Charmian, to tell me how to get you to ante up in this cheerful fashion to this youthful and timid partner (or is it local manager?) of yours.

Say, Jack, I wish you could make a play out of Abysmal Brute. It is so essentially fine and dramatic.

I've been trying to get hold of one of those Jack London Cigar posters, but haven't succeeded yet. A man in a cigar store promised to get me one, but I guess he's fallen down on me. I'll try elsewhere.

## Sinclair Lewis, Letter to Jack London (October 1911)

I hear that the new Hampton-Columbian magazine is very shaky financially. If they owe you anything, better collect P.D.Q., via lawyer or otherwise.

Afmo., su servidor, senior,
Sinclair Lewis

### NOTE

1. Charmian London to Upton Sinclair, October 10, 1931, Jack and Charmian London Collection, Merrill-Cazier Library, Utah State University.

# Arnold Genthe

## From *As I Remember* (1936)

Arnold Genthe (1869–1942), born in Germany, earned a PhD in philology at the University of Jena. After leaving Germany in 1895, he became a celebrated San Francisco photographer, teaching himself the craft. Genthe is best known for his portraits of San Francisco's Chinatown and the aftermath of the great earthquake and fire of 1906. He also photographed celebrities such as Sarah Bernhardt. He was an early member of the San Francisco Bay Area "Crowd" and then frequented Carmel at the Sterlings' home. He produced a series of fine studio portraits of London over the years with deep contrast but a soft touch. He later moved to New York City, making portraits of such figures as Theodore Roosevelt, Woodrow Wilson, Isadora Duncan, Greta Garbo, and Pearl Buck.

My particular cronies were George Sterling and Jack London. The latter had no home there—he lived on his ranch in Glendale [Genthe must have meant Glen Ellen] but put in many weeks as the guest of Sterling.

London did considerable writing at Carmel, for he liked to be near Sterling who was his best critic. They would write all day in adjoining rooms and in the evening would go over each other's work. Jack London in those days rarely gave a manuscript its final typing until he had submitted the drafts to Sterling, who had an eagle eye for careless writing or the misuse of words.

It was an odd circumstance that this mutual assistance sprang from the same root—a preoccupation with the dictionary. Jack London, when he was just a youngster earning a living by picking up odd jobs about the wharves of San Francisco, would spend his free hours poring over the grimy pages of a tattered dictionary which he had found in the back room of a saloon. Sterling, as he naively told me, had spent a whole year going through the Standard dictionary, making a list of words that would give color to his poetry. He had an enormous vocabulary of polysyllables derived from the Greek or Latin. London was ruthless with his blue pencil. If there were an image or expression that he thought confusing, he would persuade Sterling to change it.

[112]

Some of Sterling's poems—the simpler ones—have a beauty that has hardly been surpassed by any other American poet. That was Ambrose Bierce's verdict.

Jack London had a poignantly sensitive face. His eyes were those of a dreamer, and there was almost a feminine wistfulness about him. Yet at the same time he gave the feeling of a terrific and unconquerable physical force. When he built his boat, *The Snark*, which he had designed himself for his trip to the South Seas, some of the naval officers at the Bohemian Club insisted that it was not seaworthy. "He won't get as far as Hawaii," said a commander. "If he strikes the tail end of a typhoon, that boat will go down to the bottom like a flash."

"The boat may go down," said I, "but Jack London never will." That was the impression he gave one.

# Joan London

## Letter to Jack London (October 1911)

Joan London Miller (1901–1971) was the older of London's two daughters with his first wife, Bess Maddern London. London adored the curly-haired little girl and made some of his first photographs of her, under Bess's tutelage, to be placed in an album labeled "Joan's Book," now at the Huntington Library. Bess photographed the two of them, equally tousled and intently studying "Joan's Book." Sensitive, precocious, serious, and hard-working, Joan graduated from the University of California with a BA in history. At the time of her death she was still working to be the socialist her father inspired her to be, including speaking to rallies of farmworkers led by Cesar Chavez.[1] Her precocious, serious, and committed idealist self propelled her to prominence. She ran for office as a socialist, wrote for newspapers, lectured on socialism, worked for the Works Progress Administration, and corresponded with Leon Trotsky, traveling in Russia and lecturing on her findings back home. She advised a Hollywood production of *The Call of the Wild* for William Wellman, starring Clark Gable. In 1938 she published her biography of her father, *Jack London and His Times*.

Joan and her mother were very close, but she had difficult relations with several husbands, as well as with Flora, Eliza, Charmian, Becky, and most especially her father. He praised her for her intellect and writing ability as she grew older, but also wrote her some cruel letters when she took up for her mother; he once called her a "ruined colt." Yet after much needless pain, they reconciled. They were so very much alike. His last letter was to his girls, planning a picnic at Lake Merritt in Oakland. London loved being involved with his children, but Bess, abandoned by her husband and betrayed by a friend (Charmian), never allowed the girls to visit their father on the ranch if "the Beauty," as she called Charmian, was there, severely limiting the time he could see them, especially in view of his many travels. Joan and Charmian reconciled after London's death. In truth, the marriage of Jack and Bess was a terrible idea, Jack on the rebound from Anna Strunsky and telling Bess that he did not love her and was marrying to raise children and settle down. As a result of her parents' foolishness, Joan had a hard life.

October 22, 1911

Dear Daddy;

What has happened to you? You said that you would be down in about two weeks. Now it is over two weeks and Idora Park [an amusement park] has closed for the season.

Daddy, did you overlook those bills that I sent you for the gym, when I sent those for dancing school? A new month started Saturday for both and I will send you the receipt for them next Saturday as Miss Buttlar forgot to bring her receipt book yesterday.

I am very sorry, Daddy, that I had to stop my music lessons but mother says that you must have a reason for it and that you will let me start again at the end of six months. I am going to keep up my practicing just as though I were still taking.

Mother got me some shoes last night and just think! I wear the same width a shoe only mine in two sizes smaller than hers. I am exactly five feet tall and weight eighty-one pounds. What do you think of that? Bess weighs sixty-three pounds and is four feet, four inches tall.

If you don't come down pretty soon Bess and I will be six feet tall and weigh one hundred and fifty pounds.

Lots of love,
Joan

## NOTE

1. Joan sent Cesar Chavez four of London's books; he was especially interested in the short story "The Mexican." He wrote to her of London: "[T]hose of us who are in the struggle know your father through his books, but more importantly, we know him through what he stood for, and we know that if he were alive today, he would be here, in Delano [California], marching with us side by side." Letter. October 6, 1967. United Farm Workers Organizing Committee AFL-CIO, Joan Miller London Collection, Huntington Library.

# Joan London

## Letter to Jack London (1912)

Joan worked hard as a labor activist and author, but her life was full of difficulty. She married five times, she was alcoholic, and she suffered from throat
cancer, which eventually killed her. Her pain at her parents' divorce as well as
her fervor for being a voice for socialism leap from her letters. But her father's
treatment of her in certain letters offended her sense of personal honor, something Jack in his teens would have felt with just the same fierce intensity, and
undoubtedly her broken relationship with her father caused her to struggle
with the idea of love throughout her life. Despite Bess's nickname for him,
"Daddy-Boy," London could not be described as an attentive father to his girls.

January 21, 1912

Dear Daddy,

I am enclosing a little story that I wrote and if you think it is good I will
send it to some children's magazine. Please, criticize it severely and tell me
where I can improve it.

I will tell you where I write my stories. Up in the attic I have a sewing table
for a desk and on one side is one of the little chests you brought from Korea
for Bess and I. In it I keep my "manuscripts" as I call them.

I have a little inkstand about three inches high, whose cover is broken off
but does well enough, pens and paper, and a blotter. Sometime when I save
up my money, I'll buy a really [*undecipherable*] desk and an unbroken ink
stand but what I have now suits me perfectly. If I had one of the good desks
I wouldn't have any place to keep it except up in the attic and that wouldn't
be a very nice place.

Lots of Love,
Joan

# Joan London

## Letter to Jack London (September 1913)

The most toxic feature of divorce has to be the massive damage done to a child or children caught between the unending, begrudging pettiness of the divorcing couple. Many young people do not ever recover from the awfulness of being caught up in this, and they never really respect their parents again. What are children who thought they had a happy family, little children, to do or feel, observing the couple arguing about splitting up or witnessing a father and husband abandon his family? There was no lack of ugly feelings and mutual anger between Jack and Bess, but it really comes into focus with the pain that Joan feels. One can easily hear how close she and her father are, but Joan has matured, and like him and her mother, she has privileged the call of duty—to her mother. She is no longer willing to be dominated by her famous father.

September 13, 1913

Dear Dad,

Ever since Bess and I were small, Mother has taught us to tell the truth. No matter how bad the thing was and we told the truth about it, we were not to be punished. But, if we lied about it, we were punished, even if it was a small thing of little importance. I was not lying about my feelings when I said they were confused, because they were confused and still are. But here is what my feelings are, as well as I can make them out.

When we were little girls, from Mother's talks to us, we got the impression you were only away on a long journey. When you came to see us, it was like coming home from the journey. We continued thinking that way, until about two years ago. We always associated you with our home life. It was with this way, "Wouldn't Daddy be proud if he knew this," or, "We must tell Daddy all about it," or, "Shall we ask Daddy? He will want to know." Then slowly the truth began to dawn on us, and we learned that you had another home. Then, came the question to our minds, "If Daddy has another home, why does not Mother and Bess and I live there too?" We would ask Mother, but she would say "Wait until you are older; then Daddy will tell you himself."

Then we learned that another woman was where our Mother should be, and we wondered why. But always Mother said, "Wait until you are older." So Daddy, you see, that Bess and I, like other children, came to abhor any visit that would bring us in contact with the intruder that held our Mother's place. (You told me not to mind being harsh, so I'm telling you my feelings, as far as I can see them.)

Bess and I feel that we have one of the best Mothers in the whole wide world. So, Daddy, I'm sure you understand now, why I do not wish to visit you, when I would meet any woman that is in Mother's place.

Maybe I've not stated this clearly or maybe I've written it roughly, but I've done my best. Please, Daddy, try to understand. Here is an example of what it means to have no Daddy living with you.

At school, we had to bring home a card to be signed by our parents. Mother signed mine, and I brought it back to school. The next day, I was questioned thus, before the class. Ques. "Joan, is your father living?" Ans. "Yes m'am." Ques. "Then why didn't he sign the card?" Ans. "My father and Mother are not living together." "Oh." That is one of many. I still do not understand why you and Mother are not living together, and I hope, that until then no more reference will be made to this matter which I cannot and do not understand as yet. If I ever change my mind in the matter I'll come straight to you and tell you. So, can't we drop the subject now. I'm only a little girl and not expected to know *everything*. Adieu, mon cher pere.

Votre grand enfant,
Jeanne
Beaucop amour.

# Joan London

## Letter to Jack London (October 1913)

> Joan, an intelligent and growing teen who loved and supported her mother, eventually had to draw the line with her father's attacks on Bess. It is hard to guess how she felt, but London should have been proud of her brave defense of her mother and her honest and forthright arguments against her father.

Dear Dad:

Well, Dad, I've read over your letter, read it twice and carefully, and I understand from it that silence on my part means that I am satisfied with my present surroundings. I tried to keep silence, for I am satisfied, but you have demanded an answer. So, this I say, I am perfectly satisfied with my present surroundings and do *not* wish to change them.

I resent your opinions of my mother. She is considered as one of the finest coaches in Oakland, by the principles [*sic*] of the different schools, and Mr. Barker, Supt. of Schools. Her pupils can always be marked by their good work in both grammar and high schools. And above all this, she is a good mother, and what is greater, in this world, than a good mother! This is not only my opinion but also, of many others.

And now, Daddy, since we have thrashed this question out together, may we not leave it. I have nothing more to say in the matter, for I have given my final decree. I shall stay with my mother, and I shall keep my promise to do so, until I'm old enough to support myself.

Please, Daddy, please let me feel that this is the last of these awful letters you force me to write you; it hurts me so to write them, and yet, you demand these kind of answers and I can only write them.

Now, I'm getting so sleepy that I close one eye and then the other to keep awake and I'm yawning continuously, so Good night mon cher père, et "sweet dreams."

# Joan London

## From *Jack London and His Times* (1939)

Clarice Stasz, along with Jacqueline Tavernier-Courbin a prominent biographer of the women in Jack London's life, points out that Joan was not only the biographer of her family but also the author of numerous publications.[1] A bit overly focused on London's adherence to socialism, as she interpreted it, in his writings, Joan's book is still a key resource. But as a result of her eliding his later Hawaiian and South Seas short stories, where she did not recognize the socialist principles laid out in such stories as "Koolau the Leper" or "Mauki," she influenced other early biographers and critics such as Richard McClintock and Philip Foner to overlook the later work and more or less end with *The Iron Heel* (1908) and *Martin Eden* (1909). The cultural range of London's short fiction in particular escapes Joan; though a story like "The House of Pride," his first Hawaiian tale, may not contain the word "socialism," but it is about the failures of brotherhood and community in the face of capitalism.[2] Joan also signaled to later biographers that studying his work should be basically autobiographical. The year before Joan's biography appeared, however, Irving Stone published *Sailor on Horseback: The Biography of Jack London*, one of his fictionalized "biographies," which sold well and had a much greater effect in repopularizing London two decades after his death than did Joan or Foner. *Sailor on Horseback* gave the budding field of London scholarship a boost because it demonstrated how faulty London's biographies were and rerouted attention first to finding out the real facts, as the work of Russ Kingman began, then to London's *writings* and not just his adventurous life.[3] American political socialism, so feared by the ruling class in London's day, did not survive World War I. London increasingly became seen as a model of individualistic, not socialistic, ideals, so much so that in the portrayal of the Nazis burning books in the famous Frank Capra documentary series "Why We Fight" (1942–1945), London's and Ernest Hemingway's books are shown on the top of the burning pile. Below are excerpts from various episodes of London's life Joan relates in her account and analysis of his personal development and what his life and work have meant. In this book Joan shows herself to be a gifted writer.

For a short time Jack found this life satisfying enough. It had its share of excitement. The fishermen, ignorant and resentful of the fish laws, did their best to outwit the patrolmen; the offenders had to be caught in the act with the fish and the illegal hooks and nets, which was not always easy; and throughout his life defying the elements in a small sailing boat was to be ever a source of pleasure. He was earning a living doing what he liked; he was still his own master. Nevertheless, a deep, inner dissatisfaction was growing.

He was drinking more heavily when ashore, and his drunken decision to commit suicide one night when he stumbled into deep water is significant of the extent of his disorientation. He was drunk, but he was young and healthy and strong, his curiosity about the world still fresh and ungratified, and he could look back on his boyish exploits and achievements with nothing but pride. Nevertheless, swimming easily close to shore, he determined to go out with the tide. The events of the last years, his horror of factory work, his abrupt acquaintance with the brutally realistic water front, and the swift disillusionment of whatever ideals he had absorbed from his school years and library reading—all this was unassimilated. He knew neither what to do nor what he wanted to do, and weariness, born of alcohol, bewilderment and frustration, turned his face toward death. When it was almost too late cold water and sobriety made him change his mind, and he fought desperately for life until he was rescued by a chance fisherman.

[Even joining] the fish patrol could not hold him. . . . At Sacramento . . . [he] fell in with a number of boys who were swimming in the river. Jack listened to them in amazement. They were "road kids," and as they talked, a new world, larger than that of the bay and the pirates and the fish patrol, opened up to him. . . . Jack stayed with his new acquaintances, . . . boys who were victims of poverty-stricken and disorganized homes. In order to survive they ran in gangs and combined begging with petty thievery. During the several weeks Jack spent with them he considerably enlarged his vocabulary and knowledge of the world, exchanged his title of Prince of the Oyster Pirates for the moniker, Sailor Kid, and earned his right to be a full-fledged road kid by "going over the hill"—beating his way over the Sierras into Nevada and back.

*

With his usual thoroughness he explored New York from end to end. Its undeniable beauty, its towering skyscrapers, the bridges flung across the rivers, the pulse of traffic-laden streets, all its potentialities for progress and civilization, as well as all its evils and corruption—these struck him forcibly. But his deepest and most abiding impression was of the distress of the poor. When he saw fire escapes, parks, the Battery, filled all night long with men, women and children and hungry-eyed men and women, it needed but little imagination to picture their suffering during the bitter winter months. Neither time nor improved circumstances altered this reaction. He hated and feared New York. . . .

Jack was beginning to think, and to think hard. He had gone a long way toward identification of himself with his class, but thus far his experiences had permitted him to retain the belief that he was an exception, luckier or perhaps better equipped by "nature" to meet exigencies than most people. Disillusionment on this score was to come soon.

He left New York to see Niagara Falls. Returning in the early morning from a second view, he was arrested in Buffalo, charged with vagrancy and, after witnessing the complete disregard of the legal rights he had assumed were his, was sentenced to thirty days in the Erie County jail. He was always able to remember the approximate date of his arrest—toward the end of June— because a few days later the great American Railway Union strike broke out.

Prison bit deeply. He described it in *The Road*, as in other books he described his brief experiences with the oyster pirates and fish patrol, and the gold hunters in the Klondike, as if he had spent years there instead of a few weeks. As far as the thirty days in prison was concerned, his faculty for absorbing the experiences of others and living them in imagination succeeded in scaring him, to use his own word, into thinking through to a conclusion the problem that had been more and more clearly set before him. He grasped the spirit of the law, based on class difference and property rights, and saw how it operated. The working class lived under a system which rendered it helpless. Mere superiority in numbers did not matter. Unemployed, the workers had organized themselves into armies whose marches had accomplished nothing. Arrested, they were denied their rights and sent to prison. Awareness that he was a member of this class became knowledge, and everything that he learned stimulated him to learn more. . . .

He knew now that he was a member of the working class. He knew further that, without training, he could at best be sure of employment only as long as his muscles remained strong. But from what he had observed of . . . unskilled workers whose muscles were still good, and skilled workers whose knowledge of their crafts had not saved them from unemployment—he realized what little reliance was to be placed on selling either muscle power or skill to earn a living. He was young and strong, but so were many others whose youth and strength found no buyers. And one thing was sure: he was not going to be one of the thousands of helpless and unfit he had seen everywhere in the land. His proximity to the fate of these members of his class terrified him. Carelessly, unthinkingly, he had walked straight into the trap, but before it was too late he would get out. His decision was made: in the market where muscle and skill were dirt cheap he would display and sell, and for fancy prices, the products of his brain.

*

In the 'nineties the world of book knowledge and higher education was essentially the world of the middle class, and although he did not know it then Jack crossed its threshold when he entered high school. From the first day he found most of his school mates hostile, critical, unwilling to accept him as one of them. He was so obviously different. His manner was rough and uncouth, his clothes shabby, his general appearance careless. He was not much older than they, and yet he was a man while they were juvenile and inexperienced. And he had become a man unlike any they knew personally, but like some they had heard about, seen from a distance, and been warned against.

One of his schoolmates, a young lady who grew up to become the wife of one of his friends, always remembered her first sight of him as the French teacher, Mme Grand-Pré, attempted to call her class to order at the beginning of the term. Jack, slouched in his seat, was smiling contemptuously at the childish uproar. Georgia Loring noted his tousled hair, his wrinkled, ill-fitting blue suit, the flannel shirt open at the neck, and later, when he stood up, the long, baggy trousers with "spring bottoms," a style affected by toughs and hoodlums and in striking contrast to the neat short pants of the other boys. . . .

They thought that he was unsociable and never guessed that, although he would have died before he admitted it, their own unfriendliness had cut him to the quick. Sometimes he would stand on the outskirts of a small group, listening to their talk, his eagerness to be included visible even to them. But when, as casually friendly for the moment as they were casually cruel at other times, they addressed him, he would stiffen, answer them rudely and stride away, swinging his shoulder irritably.

It was not pleasant at first. At the time he did not know that he minded it. He was too busy. School, work, extra reading, odd jobs after school and on Saturdays, and later janitor work in the school itself, hours spent trying to apply to his writing what he was learning—these filled every available moment. But the impact stimulated him to assert himself. In conduct and activity he accentuated the differences between him and his classmates, his poverty and working-class origin, his wider experience and mature, more capable mind.

He submitted stories and articles to the school paper, the *Aegis*, and they were published week after week, a notable series to be found in such a periodical, for they were drawn largely from his hobo and sailing experiences. The little middle-class boys and girls had never seen anything like them— hunks of raw life hammered into words, inexpertly, but with undeniable effectiveness. They did not like him, he was not one of them, but they came to respect him. By his very difference he had impressed them.

*

Jack brooded over it [learning William Chaney was his father] for months, and until the end of his life the scar it left was sensitive. In old files of the San Francisco papers he read the story of his mother's attempted suicide, then set about to get in touch with Chaney. This task did not prove difficult. Chaney's reputation as an astrologer still lingered in the West, and after a brief search Jack learned a Chicago address for a reply so that Flora would not be further upset; he wrote to Chaney, asking the truth.

Chaney's reply, disclaiming any relationship, was an even more staggering blow than the first inkling of the situation had been. Several letters passed between the two before Jack, sick at heart, abandoned the correspondence. Just why Chaney chose to deny his fatherhood is not easy to say. He stubbornly stuck to his story, but every phase of his denial was suspicious, its vehemence, its slanderous attack upon Flora, even the time-worn excuse of temporary impotence dragged in for proof. Flora's few friends of the time have given ample testimony of her loyalty to Chaney during their short marriage. Chaney, on the other hand, had erred many times, for reasons best known to himself no doubt, in recording facts in his writings. One finally gives up the enigma.

What is significant is that Jack was deeply hurt by the affair at a time when his self-confidence needed bolstering, not shattering. He lived at a time when illegitimacy was regarded with horror except by the enlightened few. It also seems probable that this knowledge determined his attitude toward his mother for the rest of his life. He was gentler to her thereafter, but he never quite forgave her. At the same time his affection for John deepened.

\*

The saga of Jack London's trip over the Chilkoot to the Yukon in the fall of '97 is the saga of the thousands who came then and later on the same errand. The steamers dumped their passengers and freight at low tide on a long sand spit opposite the Indian village of Dyea and departed as quickly as possible. Long before all the boxes and bundles could be separated by their owners and lugged ashore through the shallow water the tide rose. Thousands of helpless Argonauts and tons of baggage cluttered the beach. Behind them reared the snowy Coast Range Mountains which must be crossed, and immediately, if they hoped to reach Dawson that year. The small number of Indians and horses that were available could pack but a fraction of the stuff. They went to the highest bidder, and for the average man the price was soon out of sight. Many gave up without even trying, sold their equipment and took the next steamer home. Others started out manfully only to turn back, defeated.

In later years Jack was fond of saying, "It was in the Klondike that I found myself. There nobody talks. Everybody thinks. You get your perspective. I got mine." The Klondike gave much to Jack London, but it was the speech and not the silence of his companions that enriched that gift. Night after night during the long winter months of enforced idleness men gathered together in the small warm cabins and talked. And Jack listened.

At the time he did not know what he was hearing, combined with what he saw with his own eyes during visits to Dawson and in camp on Upper Island, was story material. Only toward the end of his stay did it occur to him that he might be able to sell a few articles to the travel and outdoor magazines. He listened and egged on the old-timers to further yarns because he was as interested in the new land as any of the great audience at home. And while he satisfied his curiosity the characters, scenes and incidents of scores of short stories and several novels were being stored away.

\*

He was a simple, direct man, and his need for simplicity was urgent. Things were good or bad, black or white, and thus he chose. But when he was confronted with a third choice his indecision was painful. He had aligned himself on the side of socialism rather than accept capitalism and had been content. Now in the Klondike he found a third possibility which seemed to offer an escape from the evils of civilization by a return to nature.

What he feared and hated under capitalism did not obtain on the frontier. Its simplicity attracted him enormously. Furthermore, it already existed . . . , did not . . . have to be attained by bloody struggle through many years. It had its drawbacks, but could they not be remedied by judicious borrowing of efficiency and comforts from civilization? And could not one fight for socialism even more effectively when his strength was not dissipated by close contact with capitalism's festering cities? Certainly, he would rationalize enthusiastically, the virtues of the frontier, doomed to perish under capitalism, should be preserved, and how better to accomplish this than by celebrating them out of one's own intimate knowledge?

\*

[Back home he] had three possessions: a bicycle, a decent suit of dark clothes and John London's mackintosh, and a fourth on which he paid rent, a typewriter. All were important, even necessary to him. The bicycle saved time and carfare, for he hated to walk. The suit of clothes meant that he could call on his friends. When it rained the mackintosh protected his clothes on his daily trips to the public library. And the typewriter translated his sprawling longhand into clear type that the "silent, sullen peoples who run the magazines" could read. "If typewriters hadn't been invented by the time I began to write," he would chuckle, "I doubt if the world would ever have heard of Jack London. No one would have had the patience to read more than a page of my longhand!"

When all went well he worked, secure with his possessions around him and the rent paid on the typewriter. But when things began to go badly first the mackintosh, then the suit of clothes, and then, reluctantly, the bicycle went to the pawnshop. Last of all, the typewriter was returned to the shop, and he would sit at home, mackintoshless, suitless, bicycleless and type-writerless, the pile of scribbled sheets growing higher and higher while he waited prayerfully for the postman to bring him a slim envelope that would contain a check. Then he would redeem everything and start in again. "Am out of paper," he wrote to Ted Applegarth during one of these crises, "so have not typed it yet. Sent off 10 mss. and have 9 more ready to go as soon as I get stamps. Revised 3 more yesterday and today and expect to revise another 5000 word one tonight" [*Letters*, 54–55].

"That's the way it is," he would sum up, fifteen years later. "You look back and see how hard you worked, and how poor you were, and how desperately anxious you were to succeed, and all you can remember is how happy you were. You were young, and you were working at something you believed in with all your heart, and you knew you were going to succeed."

*

It was in the midst of his head-first success as writer and Socialist that he met Anna Strunsky, whose friendship was to be the most profoundly disturbing factor in his life for the next three years. This was not because she was a woman whose personal charm and magnetism has become legendary; not because of her intellectual brilliance, but because, instinctively loyal to certain principles and ideals, she saw the danger in much of Jack's philosophy and opposed with all her strength his socialism for the benefit of "certain kindred races," his belief that woman was inferior to man, that war was justifiable, that might made right, and his determination to use his talents for the sole purpose of making money. . . .

He had grown up in an environment which had not only discouraged sentimentality but taught him to regard any of its manifestations with contempt. The period of his submission to the agonies and ecstasies of adolescent love had been very brief. Except for this and his adoration of Mabel Applegarth, he had had a sex life, not a love life, and his sex life had been the unmawkish, spontaneous activity of a healthy young proletarian unburdened by the inhibitions of his more favored brothers in the middle class. Now, as growing success led him deeper into that class, he came into contact not only with its ugly sex moralities, but with its saccharine-sentimental and soul-probing ideas of love which had come into full flower during the mauve decade.

Listening, Jack was first incredulous, then embarrassed, and finally indignant that intelligent, cultured adults should prattle like irresponsible, love-

[127]

sick youths about subjects as significant as love and marriage. He spat his disgust in endless arguments with Anna Strunsky, a proponent of romantic love, and out of their fundamental disagreement grew eventually *The Kempton-Wace Letters*, which embodied in full the theories he tested for himself. . . .

Love, as understood by the romanticists, he defined as "a disorder of mind and body . . . produced by passion under the stimulus of imagination," in order that the human type might be perpetuated and developed. For himself, he defined love more precisely as prenuptial, romantic or sexual love, and postnuptial, by which he meant conjugal affection and sex comradeship. The former was nature's trick to assure procreation, the latter was romantic love, if the marriage endured, evolved into once the "impelling madness" of sexual love had spent itself.

He had no use for madness of any sort. He had a brain and he intended to use it. Nature might have to trick the average man into procreation, but not him. He was eager for children. Therefore, avoiding prenuptial romantic lovesickness in which his reason could not function, he would take a short cut, choosing for a partner in marriage a young woman for whom he already felt affection, and who would be strong, healthy and capable of producing strong, healthy children. "No, I am not in love," says his protagonist in *The Kempton-Wace Letters*, who is about to marry. "I am very thankful that I am not . . . I am arranging my life so that I may get the most out of it, while the one thing to disorder it, worse than flood and fire and the public enemy, is love" [*Kempton-Wace Letters*, 36].

Tracing the evolution of his attitude, he placed women in two categories. There was the wanton, "wonderful and unmoral and filled with life to the brim," and there was the "perfect mother, made pre-eminently to know the lip clasp of a child." The first he called the Mate Woman, and with her might be achieved, from the "strictly emotional and naturalistic viewpoint," the perfect love. The second was the Mother Woman, "the last and highest and holiest in the hierarchy of life." And it was this type which he married in his twenty-fourth year, "choosing a mate, not in the lust of my eyes, but in the desire in my fatherhood."

## NOTES

1. "Joan London also wrote editorials and brief articles on labor issues for *The Voice of the Federation* (Maritime Federation of the Pacific), *The International Teamster*, and *Rank and File* during the 1930s and 1960s." Stasz, "Joan London: Publications." See also Stasz, *Ameri-*

*can Dreamers* and *Jack London's Women.* For a listing of Joan's publications, see Sisson, "Chronological Bibliography."

2. McClintock, *White Logic.* Philip S. Foner's *Jack London: An American Rebel* is a combination of biography and socialist selections from London's work.

3. *Sailor on Horseback* is full of errors and fantasies, and plagiarizes directly from *Martin Eden, John Barleycorn,* and London's unpublished notes for an autobiography, "Jack Liverpool." Stone's most influential decision, to have Jack commit suicide with morphine, based on no clear evidence, stuck around for several decades in anthology headnotes and biographies. The real cause of death now agreed upon by scientists and biographers was London's heavy use of corrosive sublimate of mercury to treat the serious skin infection "yaws" that he acquired while aboard the *Snark* in the western South Pacific in 1908, ruining his kidneys. See also Labor, "An Open Letter to Irving Stone." Stone also gives a warped picture of Charmian. À la *The Aspern Papers,* Stone betrayed Charmian's trust when she caught him accessing her private papers, including her love letters from Jack, which she had declared off-limits. Stone had to be physically threatened by Irving Shepard to leave the ranch.

# Joan London, with Bart Abbott

## From *Jack London and His Daughters* (1990)

> Joan's first marriage was to Park Abbott; their son, Bart Abbott, was Joan's
> only child. London and his second wife, Charmian, had two miscarriages and
> one infant girl, Joy, who died shortly after birth. At London's death his estate
> went to Charmian, and after her death to Eliza Shepard's family. Joan and
> Becky were provided for, but the sense of loss and resentment ran deep for
> Joan. When she was older she embarked on another book, which recalls more
> personal details. Much of it is heartrending to read, especially her school ex-
> periences in the shadow of her famous father. Joan writes descriptively of her
> childhood as well as her father could have, especially the passage describing
> the Piedmont Bungalow, a magical place her parents once inhabited where she
> saw herself only as a small child. Joan died before she completed the manu-
> script; Bart Abbott finished it and published it in 1990. The book's claim that
> London threw Becky through a plate glass window caused controversy, as Joan
> insisted upon it and Becky denied it.

*Joan, Her Book* was stamped boldly in gold on the black leather cover. Inside
was page after page of pictures, taken, developed and printed by Daddy, of
myself and of everyone I had always known—Daddy and Mother and, later,
Bess, Aunt Jennie and both my grandmothers—and of a few others whom,
by the time I was four or five, I could no longer recognize. Underneath most
of the pictures were captions, written and typed by Daddy.

A magic book! One of the pictures could only have been made by a
sorcerer, while the captions, composed in a curious, archaic style and full of
incomprehensible allusions, pleasantly baffled me for years.

"Here Beginneth the Story of Joan," he wrote on the first page, and the
pictures which followed were taken at short intervals for two and a half years,
from the time I was twelve hours old until the fatal summer of 1903 when our
life together came to a sudden end. . . .

Shortly after my first birthday, we moved into the last house we were to share, the Bungalow, always capitalized thus when written, and pronounced by Mother and Daddy so that the large B was almost visible.

The Bungalow was large, rambling, many-leveled and many-roomed, with redwood-paneled walls and ceilings, and redwood shingles outside, bronzed by summer suns and winter rains. The living room in the Bayo Vista house had been large, but the Bungalow's living room was huge. Daddy used to say that the floor space of four cottages such as he had lived in as a boy would have fitted into that one room alone. The fireplace was big and welcoming, and every window framed a view of hill or bay. From spring to autumn, a broad, long, vine-covered porch was a second living room, for the Bungalow and its five acres of orchards, gardens and fields was sheltered by the eucalyptus-forested hills that rose steeply behind it and by a grove of tall, old pines on its northern side.

Over and over again when we were children we heard about the Bungalow from Mother and Daddy. There was a small, steep-roofed cottage where Grandma London lived, a barn large enough to hold a dozen horses, chicken houses and yards, a big pigeon loft, a separate laundry, even a creamery — and all for the even then unbelievably low rent of thirty-five dollars a month. They spoke of it always with love and regret, recalling the pink and white mist of blossoms in the springtime orchards and the fruit-laden trees in the summer and early fall, the riotous blooms in the garden, the little reservoir — "What a fine swimming pool it would have made," Daddy always said. And they spoke, too, of the famous view from the Bungalow: Oakland was spread out in a great half-circle, with marsh-edged Lake Merritt in the foreground, and a little further west, the silver line of the estuary fringed with the masts of sailing ships; across the bay, San Francisco climbed its many hills; straight ahead was the Golden Gate with ships almost always moving in or out; beyond lay the Pacific where, low on the horizon on clear days, loomed the Farallones; and to the north was the long, lovely slope of Tamalpais, purple against the sky.

But surpassing even these marvels was the unguessed and improbable, the never-to-be-forgotten poppy field. When they first came to live in the Bungalow the field had been like almost any California wintry hillside, with the new growth evoked by the autumn rains barely visible under the bleached, bent ghosts of last summer's grasses. But as the spring advanced and the wild barley grew lush and tall, the lacy, silver-green sprays of California poppies appeared, and seeking their multitude, Mother and Daddy realized that this would be no ordinary grassy slope, but a field of poppies.

"Every day," Mother used to tell us, "we would walk down the path to see how much taller the poppies had grown since the day before and to look for the first buds.

At last the slender bud-cones began to shed their silver caps and the first blossoms gleamed like little heaps of gold amid the swaying barley. "It's a good omen!" Mother and Daddy told each other joyfully. And when the blooms reached their peak and the golden flood lapped at the Bungalow porch and spread across the field and down the hill, their happiness and confidence were boundless.

How well it began, the year and a half we were to live in the Bungalow; how rich in fulfillment, creativeness and promise it continued to be for all of us almost to the very end.

Suddenly, magically, Daddy was famous. Critics and reviewers were saying, "A new star has risen in the West." Book sales leaped (there were three); editor and author exchanged roles: now they were begging Daddy for stories. The first summer in Piedmont a press association asked him, a struggling unknown only a few years before, to go to South Africa and do a series of articles on the Boer War. Hostilities being practically at an end by the time he reached England, he stayed in London to gather the material for and write *The People of the Abyss*, then traveled for several weeks on the continent. Six of his books were published during the Piedmont period, and many magazine stories and articles. *The Call of the Wild* was written in the Bungalow and *The Sea-Wolf* begun.

At certain especially grim moments when he was still striving to be an author, Daddy used to announce defiantly, "If cash comes with fame, come fame; if cash comes without fame, come cash!" Now both were his, and although he began at once to live beyond his income, so secure was his fame that his credit was always good. From this time on he earned a great deal of money from writing; I was still a little girl when I read in a newspaper that he had become the highest paid author in America. Surely, though, no other literary man, with the possible exception of Balzac, was to mismanage his financial affairs more completely.

But now the hard times were over at last. Mother's faith in Daddy and Daddy's faith in himself had been brilliantly justified. They were very proud and happy, and a little incredulous, I think, that success had come so quickly, for both were prepared for a longer pull. Daddy continued to work steadily and well—the quantity and quality of his output attests to that—but he began to spend more time than formerly enjoying himself and relaxing. He fashioned great, brightly colored box kites and flew them in the poppy field, fenced and boxed, went on picnics in the hills beyond Piedmont, pursued his early love, photography, with even greater zeal, bought a small sloop for bay sailing.

\*

Always when Daddy came to see us in the afternoon, he romped with us. As soon as we saw him coming up the walk, we would scamper to the front door, shouting our delight, hopping up and down, and raising our arms for him to lift us up as soon as he was inside. We scarcely gave him time to greet Mother, for the moment he put us down we would swarm over him and the romp was on.

Noisy, spontaneous, hurly-burly, the romps nevertheless had strict rules, the penalty for infraction being an immediate end to the game: no scratching, kicking, biting or hair-pulling, "be careful of the eyes," and more important than anything else, no tears, for Daddy would not play with cry-babies. For us, the aim was to make Daddy cry out, "I give up!" On his part, he was to fight us off and postpone the moment of yielding as long as possible.

I was four and Bess was two when the romps began and they were relatively mild and brief then, but as we grew older they lengthened and became more boisterous. From the start the rules were so rigidly enforced that I cannot remember, except as one remembers a tradition, any of the romps that were penalized for rule infractions. Fingers or toes accidently stepped on, heads bumped, elbows skinned on the rough Axminster carpet, no matter; we would not cry.

Singly or simultaneously, we would rush him, growling fiercely, and the next instant be tumbled back with one sweep of his arms. Sitting on the floor, he would parry our lunges with lightning-swift jabs, knock our heads together, tease us and taunt us with high good humor until we launched a fresh attack. In the end, the fortress was stormed, four small legs clambered over him and four small fists reduced him first to shouts of laughter, then to prolonged fits of giggles, and finally the three of us sprawled on the floor, breathless and content. For that little while, he was wholly ours and we were wholly his and the knowledge was good.

[133]

\*

It was during this period, also, that I became sharply aware that some-where beyond the bungalow, Daddy had a whole other life that did not in-clude us at all. This knowledge was incredible at first, and I fought against accepting it in every way I could, but it pushed past all my defenses, my furi-ous resentment, my futile efforts to ignore it. Eventually, I came out of the long struggle with little else but pride and a fierce determination not to betray my deep and bitter wound to anyone, least of all to the one who had inflicted it. How inexorably I was ruled by Daddy's maxim, "Don't cry when you're hurt," and what singularly tearless children Beth and I were!

From the start I reasoned that my place must have been taken by some per-son. Then, from a quickly hushed word here, a hint there, slowly there began to appear the shadowy figure of a competitor who lived and had her place in Daddy's other life.

Against this threat, when suspicion later became certainty, I was to mar-shal all my resources and resolution. By the time I was seven, my yearning for the father I was somehow losing had shaped my confident plans. How well I remember them! I would grow up as quickly as I could and make Daddy proud of me; I would be beautiful and accomplished; I would read and study and learn everything important; I would sing and play the piano and speak languages. And never, for one instant did I doubt that I would succeed.

\*

With my first step across the threshold of Miss Merriman's school, this shadow of a world-famous name fell upon me, and simultaneously, I, who had so lately discovered myself, lost my separate identity. I had been Joan; henceforth, for year after year, I would be Jack London's daughter. For a brief moment only, at the beginning, the public recognition of this relationship was pure joy. I was astonished and immensely pleased that my schoolmates and teachers, who had never seen Daddy, knew who he was, had read his stories and even knew he was sailing around the world in a little boat. It was a heady experience to realize for the first time that I was the daughter of such a famous man, and in all innocence, I basked in my new importance, but not for long. What had been given with one hand was ruthlessly torn away with the other.

I did not receive the full course of instruction all at once, but it was begun on the very first day, and continued for months with endless variations on the single, fundamental theme. From my schoolmates I learned that being the daughter of a famous man, in my case, meant nothing at all. My parents were divorced, and I did not live with my famous father, but with my mother. Apparently, divorce was a disgrace under any circumstances. The circumstances of the London divorce, however, were notorious because everyone had read about them in the newspapers, and that was very bad. Rewarded by the effect this produced on me, they joyously pursued their quarry. In time it became a sort of liturgy of persecution, perfected from day to day as new conclusions, implications and comparisons rose with impeccable logic out of the original premises.

My father had left us and gone away and married someone else. That showed, plain as plain, that he did not love us, for no one went away from people he loved. We probably did not even interest him very much, who was a great writer and very smart, or would he now be sailing further and further away from us on his long journey around the world? *Their* fathers would never do such a thing. *Their* fathers loved them. *Their* fathers were home every night, and bought them pretty clothes and lovely toys, and on Sundays they all went visiting together, riding in their horses-and-carriages or in their new automobiles.

What did I say? What could I say? Outraged, I tried to fight back at first, hotly denying the incredible assertions, fiercely defending myself and Mother and Bess, and even Daddy, against the insidious, slippery arguments, and got nowhere. My mother and father *were* divorced, weren't they? Well? He *did* have another wife, didn't he? He *did* expect to be gone on his trip for many years, didn't he? Did I have lots of pretty clothes? Did we have an automobile or a horse-and-carriage? Well?

And so, helpless, frustrated, I learned to be silent, no matter what they said. I would have learned not to cry when their thrusts went deep, even if I had not long before mastered that discipline. After many errors, I learned to evade my tormentors at recess times and lunch hours, but not pointedly, for that would have triggered a fresh assault. And seeking to rebuild my shattered ego, I comforted myself, thinking: wait until the report cards come out and they'll see how much smarter I am than they are! My scholastic triumph was very real, as I had known it would be, but very brief. Adroitly, they made of it a two-edged sword and turned it against me. "Your father can't sign your report card, can he?" they said. "Why, he won't even see it!" And when, throwing caution to the winds, I pointed out my uniformly excellent marks and bragged a little, they delivered the *coup de grace*: "Why shouldn't you get good marks? Look who your father is!"

\*

I was miserable that day with the onset of a heavy cold, but when Daddy telephoned that he would come to see us that afternoon, I persuaded Mother to let me move from my bed to the couch in the sitting room, once our bedroom, at the front of the house. Daddy was glad to see us, but almost at once he turned his attention to Mother. They had scarcely sat down when what I recognized as an argument began. I have no memory of what they said to each other. Drowsy with fever and baffled by their evident intention to talk over our heads, I remember only my surprise that they were quarreling, for this had never happened before.

Nine-year-old Bess, eyes sparkling and round face wreathed in smiles, was too excited by seeing Daddy for the first time in many weeks to notice the set face and anger-roughened voices. Daddy's visits always meant romps and she was eager to start, especially that day when, because I was ill, she could monopolize him. For what must have seemed to her a very long time she restrained her impatience, then, unable to endure it longer, she touched his hand: "Please, Daddy, romp with me?" Ignoring her, he brushed her hand away and continued his argument. Again, a little later, she sought to gain his attention again, bending over and looking up into his face beguilingly, and again he ignored her.

The third time she touched his hand he stopped in mid-sentence. "If you put your hand on mine again, Baby B," he told her, "I'll put you through that window!"

This was a new game, the most thrilling yet! I sat up, the better to watch. I shall never forget Bess's face as, tense with anticipation, she slowly put her hand on his: for the first, and probably the last time in her life, it mirrored the ultimate in trust.

The next moment, springing to his feet and grasping both her hands, he swung her up and thrust her, feet first as far as her knees, though the big front window, then quickly pulled her back.

Blocked off forever is any coherent memory of what happened next. The crash of breaking glass, Bess's scream of pain and terror, Mother leaping from her chair to take Bess from Daddy, the glimpse of bright blood spurting from Bess's leg—these I remember. And I also remember a special shock in the midst of the larger ones—Daddy's incredible violation of three basic laws of childhood: Bess had not done anything to merit such terrible punishment; Daddy was bigger than she; he did not say he was sorry. . . . I used to ask myself: did I really remember that he had not said he was sorry? And if that was true, then what *did* he say or do when he saw that Bess had been hurt?

*

No, I cannot question my mother's sincerity, nor will I assail as false the strongly held principles that Charmian had violated years before. That Mother had consistently chosen, at no matter the cost, what she honestly believed to be best for her daughters is impossible to doubt. She was a good mother, gentle, loyal and devoted; a generous, open-hearted woman whose special gifts and skills I admired and respected. But, deeply and painfully, I feel that her decision, like those of many mothers in similar situations, to deny to Daddy [visitation of his girls at the ranch if Charmian was there] and Bess and me the one way we might have achieved a genuine father-daughter relationship, was a tragic error. And, in my opinion, she was mistaken in her judgment of Charmian as a potential dagger to Bess and me. Years later I came to know Charmian. She was not a particularly admirable person, to be sure; she was egocentric, pretentious, had an inordinate love of material possessions; she was superficial, even a little silly; nevertheless, I am certain that she would have been a conscientious and not unfriendly stepmother, who would have welcomed us properly on arrival and watched us depart without regret.

And Daddy? His longing for his daughters was deep and true, his need for them was desperate. But did anyone ever bungle more badly in striving to realize his desire? Surely, patience, gentleness and understanding might, in time, have won some concessions, made a beginning. Instead, he lost his temper. He was not prepared, apparently, to negotiate. If his first proposal—for Bess and me to live with him on the ranch during part of each year, preferably not just during vacations—was rejected, he would, and did bring forth an alternate plan that I am sure he believed would answer Mother's objections. This plan—to build a permanent home for the three of us on the ranch—far from meeting Mother's objections, profoundly shocked her. She had been

[137]

nurtured, after all, on Victorian proprieties; even Charmian, for different reasons, perhaps, would have strenuously objected. Unwilling or unable to see any point of view but his own, Daddy met the rejection of both of his cherished plans by declaring war on Mother, a fatal, self-defeating course that would later involve me and lead irrevocably to failure and alienation.

# George Brett

## Letter to Jack London (1901)

English-born George Platt Brett (1859–1936) was London's closest reader, a close friend, a literary and business man who understood the role of a great publisher and editor in relation to a literary star in a way that is barely recognizable today: Howells with Twain, Chesnutt, and Dunbar; Cowley with Faulkner; Perkins with Hemingway and Fitzgerald. Brett was the president of Macmillan Company, London's longtime publisher. In December 1901 he wrote to London to ask him about his work, launching a very successful partnership. They worked brilliantly together, as their many letters over the years reflect. Brett was patient and obliged London with advance after advance to pay for the *Snark* and Wolf House as well as the ranch in general. In turn, London sent him bestsellers. It may be that Brett's international perspective and London's international appeal aligned so well, and perhaps also that they were both agrarian and outdoor enthusiasts. Their faith in each other and in the quality of London's artistic work paid off, not only financially but as an important friendship.

Jack London, Esq.,
Oakland, Calif.

Dear Sir:

We have had a great deal of pleasure in reading the stories that you have recently published: they seem to us to represent very much the best work of the kind that has been done on this side of the water.

We have wondered as to whether you have happened to write at any time, a longer story, which perhaps while not so suitable for serial publication would be likely to be more successful in book form. If so, may we not have the pleasure of making you an offer for its publication?

It would give us great personal pleasure to publish for you both in this country and in England, all our arrangements with authors being for production of their books on both sides of the water. If, for any reason, you have not made arrangements for the publication of your next work in book form, we should be much pleased if you would permit us to consider it.

Trusting that you may find our letter timely and that we may, in due course, have a favourable reply to it,

We are,

Yours very truly,

George Brett, President

The Macmillan Company

# George Brett

## Letter to Jack London (1902)

The Macmillan Company, Publishers
66 Fifth Avenue,
New York

My dear Sir:

I was very much obliged to you for your prompt reply, which has just reached me, to my recent letter. I am most sorry to hear that the arrangements for the novel are already made as I should very much have liked to have been able to make you an offer for its publication both here and abroad.

Your northern stories have always appealed to me, as I think I told you in my last letter, as being by far the best work of that kind that has been offered in America, and I shall, accordingly, be more than glad to be able to arrange with you for the publication, both here and abroad, for the book entitled "The Children of the Frost." I will then gladly avail myself of your kind offer to place the stories comprising the book in my hands with a view to their book publication, and shall expect to be able to make you an offer for their issue which will be entirely satisfactory to you. If you can in the meantime very kindly tell me as to when this book "The Children of the Frost" will be likely to appear I should like to make such memoranda in regard to the date of its appearance as will enable me to keep a satisfactory place for it on our list.

Yours very truly,
George Brett.

# George Brett

## Letter to Jack London (June 1906)

June 10, 1906

Dear Mr. London:

I read "Before Adam" last night, and it really is a wonderful re-creation of the times of which it treats and shows, I think, more strongly than anything else the truth of my belief in the greatness of your imagination and power to delineate things of which other people can only make vague surmises.

If you are going to revise the story in any way again before publication, it might perhaps add an appeal to a certain class of readers if you would refer by incident in it to the common hate and fear of rats and mice by women, a fear which is almost never shared by members of the male sex.

Of course, I may be wrong entirely in the matter, but I should judge that this fear by women of the rodent came out at about the time of which you are writing, and arose out of the occasional or constant overrunning of the caves by rats and mice or similar animals, which made it impossible for the women to leave their offspring a moment either day or night or to venture out of sight of them, the male of the times caring little or nothing as to what happened in the matter.

As far as the sale of "Before Adam" is concerned and its appeal to the large reading public at the present day, I miss a certain human connection between the story and the present day readers, which may result in its not having so wide a sale as some of your books, so that if you are to revise it at all before publication this aspect of the matter, if I am right, might perhaps be taken into account, i.e. the fact that the story seems to need an everyday appeal to present day readers not especially interested in the science or psychology of the situation which you are considering.

The story will, however, find, if it does not achieve great popularity, success, add to your reputation, and I think obtain the sale that your books always do on publication. Its illustration, however, is a very important matter and before taking up the question of its illustration I should like to know whether the story is to be serialized or not, as we should enter into the matter of its illustration together. . . .

I am sending the manuscript on to the printer and will print in advance copies of the book for copyright purposes here and abroad at once, and I will also put the map in the hands of an engraver and send you a proof, so as to be sure that it is what you want.

In arranging for the serial publication of these books which we copyright in advance of publication, if you insist, all installments of the story will be published in the magazines so that copyright notice shall be included, which will in this instance read "Copyright 1906 by Jack London."

I am so sorry to hear of the accident to your riding horse. I spoiled a pair of colts once with barbed wire and have wished ever since that the stuff had never been invented.

Yours very truly,
George P. Brett.

# George Brett

## Letter to Jack London (September 1906)

The Macmillan Company, Publishers
66 Fifth Avenue,
New York

Dear Mr. London:

Before we finally pass the matter of the paper edition of "People of the Abyss", would you mind telling me, if you have time, as to any special direction where you conceive there would be a demand for a cheap paper edition of this book. We could readily manage the book at fifty cents (50¢) provided we could sell five thousand copies and it ought not to be difficult to dispose of that number provided any special section of the public would take to an interest in helping circulate the book, one of the difficulties being that a book is hard to advertise at a cheap price like this, with profit: hence the advertising of a cheap edition of this book would have to be done by its friends if it were to be successful.

. . . I shall be keen to see the manuscript of "The Iron Heel", and shall make arrangements for copyrighting it here and abroad in your name upon receipt.

Of course I cannot tell you what the story is from your letter, but it sounds very much as if it might be the story for which we have all been waiting. I won't tell you what I think this is, but your letter has raised great hopes that this story tells of some of our modern life and institutions the exact truth in fiction for the first time.

I wrote you a short time ago asking you kindly to let me know what we were to do in regard to the renewal of the contract between us for next year, and what was to become of the monthly payments during your absence. Pray give me specific directions in regard to the matter when you have time to write, Yours very truly, sig. George Brett

P.S. By the bye, someone told me the other day that you had been obliged to put off the date of your sailing to November 1. I should be glad to have any account of your itinerary that you can give me, as friends in Australia and elsewhere have asked me about when you might be expected in various parts of the world.

# George Brett

## Letter to Jack London (October 1906)

Dear Mr. London:

Many thanks for your letter of the 16th, which arrived this morning and brought me the contract for next year's work.

I am enclosing to you herewith the cheque for five thousand dollars ($5000.00) for which you ask, this to be a payment on account of general royalties on your books to be published.

"White Fang" comes out on the 25th and advance copies have already been sent to you. I trust you like the book's appearance. I have been re-reading it and like the contents of it more and more. It seems to me to be a much better knitted piece of work than any other long story that you have written, and to show a clear advance in your art, especially in being much stronger throughout than "The Sea Wolf," a book which seemed to me to have enormous interest through two-thirds and then in some way to let a little of the interest escape in the conclusion.

I am hoping to find "The Iron Heel" a still further advance in this direction and there should then be no limit to what you will be able to do and the public that you will be able to command.

There is, by the bye, no reason that I know of why you should not serialize "The Iron Heel" if you would like to do so, as the book, although finished in December as I understand the matter (I am to receive it by January — am I not?) could not very well be published until next fall; so that there would be nine or ten months or even eleven for its serialization if you wanted to arrange it, and in these days of multiplicity of magazines there should be no trouble whatever in getting a very good price for it indeed.

I shall be very glad to attend to the delivery of copy or any other matters of detail in connection with this, if you like to entrust it to me, and I will also try to arrange for its serialization if you care to give me this commission and tell me what you want to get for the serial rights.

I am telling them to publish the play as early in November as possible. The printer reports all the second proofs not back yet.

One thing I envy you most tremendously and that is the thing you are congratulating yourself about—the ranch. A place such as yours must be I have always had in mind as a place to retire to as a home for remaining and declining years. The most beautiful valley is the most beautiful country in the world! I certainly hope some day to see it and when you allow me to come you will have only one difficulty and that will be getting rid of me again.

I do not think there will be the slightest difficulty in arranging to use the design from "Everybody's" for the cover of "Before Adam." I will see what can be done and if possible have a dummy of that book ready to show you in the course of the next few weeks.

I shall, of course, want your itinerary, as there will, I hope, be many things to write you about and letters and other matters to forward.

You have not told me where I am to send the monthly cheque from the time you start on December 1. Pray give me detailed instructions about this before you leave.

Yours very truly,
George Brett

# Becky London Fleming

## "Memories of My Father, Jack London" (1974)

> Bess "Becky" London Fleming (1902–1992) was London's second daughter,
> born when he was on the Continent after his time in the East End of London,
> England, writing *The People of the Abyss* (1903). The Londons' marriage broke
> up when Becky was an infant. She graduated from the University of California
> with a degree in history and a teaching certificate. She became a secretary but
> discovered she was pregnant out of wedlock. She claimed she was raising an
> adoptee, naming the baby Jean. She married Percy Fleming, and they had a
> son, Guy. As she grew older, her older sister Joan tended to take her mother's
> side in the divorce and all the arguments it led to over the years. Becky, how-
> ever, seemed more sympathetic to her father and, like Joan, wrote from her
> own perspective on him, though she was never the professional writer Joan
> was. Joan and her father carried on an intense correspondence and were often
> furious with one another, yet Joan went on to be his biographer and a socialist
> activist. Most of Becky's reminiscences come in interviews and letters. After
> Joan's death in 1971, Becky's public profile grew. She lived out her last years
> cared for by Russ and Winnie Kingman in Glen Ellen, owners of what was then
> the Jack London Bookstore and Research Center. Becky lived long enough to
> see her father's reputation revive and expand post–Cold War, and she pro-
> moted scholars and scholarship on him.

My young memories of my father were of a big, friendly playmate, one who
would romp and roughhouse with me, or who would listen, as though he
were really interested, to what I had to say about friends or school or the
books I had read or the theatres and vaudeville shows I had seen. When we
went to amusement places such as Idora Park in Oakland, or the chutes in
San Francisco near the Cliff House, he seemed to have as much fun as Joan
and I did. Looking back, I am sure he couldn't have enjoyed the merry-go-
round or the scenic railway as much as I did, but he made me think he did.

I will never forget the last night the three of us, Joan, Daddy and I, spent
together. First we went to San Francisco to a big restaurant for dinner. I had

never been in such a place before. About half the men and women dining there were in formal evening clothes. (Remember, please, this was 1916, and people "dressed" for dinner, especially if they went to a "fine" restaurant.) I kept staring, I had never seen such fine dresses. Behind some palms at one end of the dining room, some musicians played softly all the time. It was a wonderland to me.

When the meal was served I turned my attention to our own table. Doubtless we had soup and salad, bread and butter, but I don't remember. However, I'll never forget the steaks we had. They were the thickest I had ever seen, crisp and dark brown on the outside, and pink—no, red—and very juicy when cut. I remember feeling so grownup when neither Daddy nor the waiter offered to cut my meat for me.

Daddy said the steak was the best he had ever eaten, and added that he wanted to thank the chef. Right then, for the first time, I realized Daddy was "somebody." No ordinary person could ask for the chef to leave his kitchen and come into the dining room. I was almost bursting with pride. As he turned to leave, the chef asked Joan and me what we would like for dessert: we could have anything we wanted, he said. I remember Joan asked for bananas and cream. But I felt that here was an opportunity to get something I had asked mother for any number of times and been refused. So I spoke up and said, "Half a cantaloupe filled with whipped cream, not ice cream." It was delicious. (Incidentally, it is an excellent dessert because the whipped cream doesn't melt as ice cream does!)

When we left the restaurant we took a taxi to the theater though it was only a few blocks. You see, Daddy had small feet for a man, and hated to walk on city pavements.[1] He would have preferred a horsedrawn cab because he didn't like autos or machines of any kind. But horses "wouldn't do" in San Francisco: there was too much traffic, too many hills, and there were still some cobblestone streets.

I can't remember when I didn't go to the theater. Mother had several cousins who were well-known actresses—the most illustrious of these was Minnie Maddern Fiske—and whenever one of them came on tour and played in San Francisco and Oakland, we went to each of her different plays. Sometimes we sat out front, sometimes we were behind the scenes watching everything. Besides these relatives we saw all the well-known theatrical men and women of the day because they all played in both San Francisco and Oakland.

Also, there were the Orpheum and Pantages theaters which showed vaude-ville, and Joan and I were taken by our mother, Bessie Maddern London, practically every time the theaters changed their programs. The young people of today who know nothing about the "life" of the theater of that time and who have never seen a vaudeville show have missed some great entertain-ment.

At the theater that last night with Daddy we went to see a very famous actor of that period, Henry Miller, in "The Great Divide." This was some-thing Joan and I had been looking forward to for some time, and now we were to see it *with Daddy!* It was a wonderful climax to a wonderful evening. But it was something that was never to happen again!

This might seem to be a mere handful of memories, but I treasure them all. The greatest regret of my life is that I was not older when Daddy passed away: it would have meant so much to me to have known him more intimately as a man and my father as well as a playmate. . . .

When I was a little girl there were not many books for children as there are today; but I do remember four very well. All were about animals, and of these, three were about dogs. They were *A Dog of Flanders*, *Gallopoff the Talking Pony*, *Gypsy the Talking Dog*, and John Muir's *Stickeen*, another Alas-kan dog story like *White Fang* and *The Call of the Wild*.

Daddy gave Joan and me a puppy called Glen—after Daddy's ranch in Glen Ellen, California. He told us the puppy was the son of White Fang. This meant nothing to me until one day when I was dusting our books I noticed that one was titled *White Fang*. It was on a shelf with a lot of other books which I had been told were "Daddy's books." I had thought this meant they belonged to him. Then I noticed that under the title of each book there was the name "Jack London." That was when I first realized that my Daddy had written all those books! It was a thrilling moment for me—a revelation! And it still seems thrilling to me now, more than six and a half decades later,—one of the most memorable moments of my life.

### NOTE

1. Following his broken ankles from a fall on the steamer to Yokohama in 1904, London was troubled with rheumatism and joint pain for much of the rest of his life, and by 1916 he also had some gout.

# Becky London Fleming

## "Becky Remembers . . . Aunt Jennie (Daphna Virginia Prentiss)" (1982)

> Mrs. Virginia Prentiss (1832?–1922) was born a slave on a Virginia plantation and sold to a plantation owner near Nashville, Tennessee, from which she escaped during the Civil War. She married Alonzo Prentiss and moved to Oakland, where she became a pillar of the burgeoning African American community, especially the church. She became London's wet nurse the night he was born, when her own baby died in the same hospital as Flora was in. Alonzo and John London worked together, and the Prentisses were neighbors of the Londons. Mrs. Prentiss seems to have given London the maternal love he missed from his own mother, whom he found cold. She lived to be 91 years old, caring for Flora, Bess, Charmian, and the girls. She died at Napa State Hospital on November 22, 1922, only six years after London himself.[1]

I saw more of Aunt Jennie when I was young than I did of Grandma London. I don't think Grandma ever liked any other child but Johnny Miller,[2] maybe she just didn't like children because we were very good friends when I was 15 and older. But I started to tell about Aunt Jennie. . . . I figured out that she was 12 or 14 when the Civil War was started and that would have made her nearly 60 when she used to come to the 31st Street house.

Aunt Jennie . . . always insisted on preparing all our birthday dinners and all holiday dinners, except Christmas. She would arrive early, put on a big, stiffly starched white apron and head for the kitchen and it seemed no time at all until everything was ready. Somehow she always found a moment or two to show me how I could help. But I doubt if I ever did more than cause her trouble, at first, but just about all I know today about cooking I learned from Aunt Jennie.

Much as I liked "to help" her, what was far better and made me happier came after work was finished and she would sit in the big rocking chair, hold me in her lap and tell me stories about plantation life when she was a little girl. You see Aunt Jennie was born a slave, but she never mentioned that. She

[151]

was always happy and cheerful, a hard worker, independent and the most loving and affectionate person I have ever known in my life.

There were only a few colored people (that is what I was taught to call them) in Oakland when I was little and the other children in the neighborhood stared at her at first, but soon they became used to her and wished they could hear her tell stories which I tried to repeat to them, but I could never make them as interesting or exciting as she did when she told how she and her mistress "refuged" to St. Louis from the plantation during the Civil War.

Aunt Jennie never learned to read or write. She did learn to write her name and was clever enough to learn about money, but that was all the education, perhaps learning is a better word, that she had. She never knew where in the South the plantation was, nor the family name of her master and mistress. She didn't know when she was born, nor how long it took to journey from the plantation to St. Louis.

In 1876 Aunt Jennie was living with her husband and children in San Francisco. When Daddy was born, January 12, 1876, Grandma wasn't able to nurse him and had to find a "wet nurse." (In case the expression is no longer used, a wet nurse was a woman who had just had a baby and was willing and able to nurse another child.) Grandma found Aunt Jennie and so began the loving relationship between Daddy and Aunt Jennie which lasted as long as he lived. No—longer, because Daddy left Aunt Jennie enough to take care of her as long as she lived.

Daddy always said that the only love and affection he knew as a child came from Aunt Jennie. He never remembered his mother kissing him. Well, I don't either. Grandma was not demonstrative. Aunt Jennie not only loved Daddy she helped him in many ways, loaned him money, backed him in everything he did. She was a wonderful woman and a friend to everyone. Not only to Grandma but to Daddy and me—a loving friend.

Never called, by me, Mammy, always Aunt Jennie Prentiss. She was the person who meant the most to me as a little girl, (aside from Daddy.) She loved me, and I loved her. I knew that, never doubted it. It made a great difference to me when I felt I was an outsider, not part of the family with mother and Joan. I'll never forget her. She has a place, a big place, in my memory and in my heart.

Joan and I never lost contact with Aunt Jennie. We saw her often after she "retired," [which] meant she was waited on instead of working. It was sad when her memory began to fail near the end of her life and she had to be watched closely because she would wander away. But Joan and I took charge of her funeral and saw she had a good one. I don't remember exactly, but I think she died in 1923 or 1924.

**NOTES**

1. See Lasartemay and Rudge, *For Love of Jack London*; and Reesman, *Jack London's Racial Lives*, 24–29 et passim.

2. Johnny Miller was Flora's stepson.

# Charmian London

## From *The Book of Jack London*, Vol. 1 (1921)

Charmian Kittredge London (1871–1955) was London's second wife. With his marriage to Bess Maddern London falling apart, in 1903 he fell in love with Charmian, the niece of Ninetta Wiley Eames, who wrote for the *Overland Monthly* and interviewed London in 1900. Charmian, daughter of a U.S. Army captain, Willard Kittredge, and a poet, Dayelle Wiley, was a child of westward migration. She became his dream "Mate-Woman," someone who could share love and adventure, and who was also devoted to writing, music (playing her grand piano and singing), and the arts. He had longed for an androgynous woman or a "man-comrade"; Bess was interested in her home and children and not in his friends, his love of fun and travel, or his unpredictability. Where Bess was taciturn, reserved, and conventional, Charmian was outgoing, sexually uninhibited and experienced, and used to supporting herself as a stenographer, a valuable skill for a woman in those days. She was athletic, a lifelong believer in exercise and vegetarianism, a nimble horsewoman and swimmer. She also knew her way around sailboats. After their marriage in Chicago in 1905, she spent much of her energy helping support Jack's career and his adventures, trying to get him to lead a healthier life, and remaining by his side through many a storm in their lives. She had great pluck and pertinacity (as London named a short story), but she was also unreservedly feminine; she dressed beautifully. Charmian had miscarriages and bore their daughter, Joy, in 1910, but the baby died as a result of the doctor's using forceps. Like Jack, she had a tendency to depression and was a lifelong insomniac, but her good health helped her rally each time, and she lived into the 1950s. London's love letters to Charmian throughout their relationship brim with devotion: "My thoughts are upon you always, lingering over you in a myriad ways. . . . Ah Love, it looms large. It fills my whole horizon. Wherever I look I feel you, see you, touch you, and know my need for you. . . . I love you, you only & wholly. . . . [E]ach moment I am robbed of you, each night & all nights I am turned away from you, turned out by you, give me pangs the exquisiteness of which must be measured by the knowledge that they are moments and nights lost, lost, lost forever" (*Letters*, 391). After Jack's death Charmian worked side by side with Eliza to save the copyrights, publishing contracts, movie contracts, and the ranch, which was in danger of being foreclosed. London left the two women nearly penniless.

It is impossible to overestimate the critical importance of Charmian to London's writing career. She was his muse and his typist, to be sure, and his companion on adventures, but she was also highly disciplined and trained for the modern business world. Before he met her Jack threw his manuscripts away, not thinking they were of any value. Charmian saved every one, every note on Big Chief tablets, every dictation, every pocket notebook, every scrawl Jack London ever made from then on, down to matchbooks. It was she who made carbons, organized his contracts, filed, edited, and remembered, who at her deepest core really cared about the writing of Jack London. Without Charmian, biographers and literary scholars might have little to go on today.

Charmian published four books: her biography, *The Book of Jack London* (2 vols., 1921); *The Log of the* Snark (1915); *Our Hawaii* (1917); and *The New Hawaii* (1923). Her unpublished diary of the *Dirigo* voyage is held at the Huntington Library. In it appears some of her best descriptive writing about herself and her sailor husband: "[O]ur machinery of life, shot with love, resumes." For her this voyage was about them: they confronted Jack's drinking, planned for a new pregnancy, and made plans for their beloved ranch.[1] In another entry, she writes:

> I went on the main deck later and found it bright moonlight. So I had to rouse my man. Together we trudged to the fore, to look back upon the swaying sprays of tight white pearls gleaming in the dazzling radiance. One simply is cowed by the impossibility of wondering what one sees and feels in the bows of a wind-propelled vessel. The first means made by man, by man the sailor—himself the original adventurer in the civilizing of the world through discovery of other peoples. I looked at Jack London, there beside me. His short-Greek face was upturned, and his deep-sea eyes were wide upon the unspeakable glory from deck to maintruck, of those snowy flowering petals of pearl. Presently he came back and looked at me. Jack said: 'Is it Possible, Mate Woman, that we are seeing this together, and have been together on this full-rigged ship, have made our Westing around Cape Horn—our dream since childhood?"[2]

She also noted in her diary of the *Dirigo* voyage that she felt *The Valley of the Moon*, which London completed on the *Dirigo*, would "bind together all readers of all nations, for its health, its thought, its lovingness and a charm all its own."[3] Such passages echo *The Log of the* Snark: "'We have lived a little, you and I, Mate-Woman,' Jack said this morning, as we took our book under an awning out of the glare. We had been talking over our travel experiences and the people we had met; from Cuba to Molokai, from Paris to the Marquesas. A vivid life it is, and we hold it and cherish it, every minute, every hour of to-day, and yesterday, and the fair thought of days that are coming."[4]

The most remarkable thing Charmian did, however, is not listed above. She kept a diary, every single day. There Jack London scholars can find an enormous trove of information, from such famous pages as the ones marked in red "Earthquake!" to the intimate details of their marriage, all written in her tiny, loopy handwriting, accurate and detailed. Her *Book of Jack London* used these diaries as a primary source, and later Russ Kingman used them to put together his *Jack London: A Definitive Chronology* (1992). Her diaries and her *Book of Jack London* grow increasingly grim toward the end of London's life, as his illnesses and bad habits started to take their final toll.

Turning to *The Book of Jack London*, we find her wondering if London's promise was being "unfulfilled" as his "will to live" weakened but recognizing how he fought for egos other than his own, "causing two blades of grass to grow where one grew before" (2:323–324, 327). She also wondered if he were "doomed to remain unsatisfied because of 'the white logic,'" his struggle with "his perception of futility" (2:376). She records his plans for a trip to Japan, his discovery of Carl Jung, and his final illness. He became easily enraged and bitter, and was receiving heavy doses of narcotic for kidney pain. He was still drinking. He lost all interest in guests and declared himself "tired to death" (2:385). After dictating his last letter to his girls for an outing at Lake Merritt in Oakland, that next morning she records his purple, swollen features, his doubling up with pain, and his stertorous respiration. Just two days before, on November 20, she wrote, "Mate rides to top of ranch and further, looking at new land he wants to buy—good land, watered. Full of enthusiasm over quality of soil, etc. Wants me to ride up with him but I don't feel fit" (2:395). Yet despite the painful last chapters, most of Charmian's lengthy book focuses upon the happy times they enjoyed together.

Jack London's inscriptions to Charmian in her copies of his books are all different, but they all describe what she meant to him:

"Dearest My Woman—
Whose efficient hands I love—the hands
that have worked for me long hours and
many, swiftly and deftly, and beautifully in the
making of music; the hands that have steered the
Snark through wild passages and rough seas, that do
not tremble on a trigger, that are sure and strong on
the reins of a thoroughbred or an untamed Marquesan
stallion; the hands that are sweet with love as
they pass through my hair, firm with comradeship as
they grip mine and that soothe as only they of all
hands in the world can soothe.
Your Man and Lover—
Jack London
The Road, Macmillan, 1907[5]

By land and variant water-ways I have traveled with Jack London: by
steamer—tramp and liner; windjammer, sampan, pleasure craft of all sorts;
in railroad trains of many countries; by automobile, bicycle, saddle, and
horse-drawn vehicle from cart to tally-ho; even on foot, which was least
to our mutual liking; and we but awaited opportunity to take to the blue
together—this chance coming to me alone after he had gone beyond that
blue. But it was upon the liquid two-thirds of earth's surface that I saw him
the most blissfully content. Dawn or twilight, he loved the way of boat upon
the sea. His bright inquisitive spirit might have sailed to its human birthing,
so native was he to the world's watery spaces. The sea nurtured a gallant and
adventurous spirit that made us all watch his banner. His influence was felt
like a great vitalizing breath from the West—wide land of red-veined men
in which he lived and died. "Seamen have at all times been a people apart,"
curiously so, from the rest of their kind; and the sailor Jack London was a
man apart from the rest of himself. Imagination, nerves, work, pleasure, all
ran in smoother grooves when his feet stood between the moving surface and
the blowing sky, his own intelligence the equalizing force amidst unstable elements. Seldom in waking hours without book or spoken argument exerting
upon his wheeling brain, yet at the helm of his boat, braced for a day-long

hours he would stand rapt in healthful ecstasy of sheer being, lord of life and the harnessed powers of nature, unheedful of physical strain, his own hand directing fate.

\*

School finished, what play-time remained after "hustling" newspapers and performing odd jobs was spent in a fourteen-foot, decked-over skiff equipped with centre-board and flimsy sail [the *Spray*]. Questing a new world beyond the tide-ripped mouth of the Estuary, out upon the treacherous water of the Bay proper he ventured to Goat Island, more formally Yerba Buena, now conspicuous in all the array of a naval training station. The fish he bore home gave him economic sanction for his favourite recreation. Very important he felt with those still dimpled fists closed about the rickety little tiller — captain of the ship, and soul, salt spray upon his parted lips, and the free west wind sweeping through his young lungs, that came, unlike other blessings, without price. Sitting high on the wind'ard rail, sheet in hand feeling out the strength of the breeze, with wistful eyes he watched great vessels tow Golden Gate-ward, breaking out their gleaming canvas, and longed to run away to sea. Or, slipping along with slack sheet before a light zephyr, one eye on the sail, one hand at the helm, he devoured countless tales of voyageurs, the covers of which he first protected with newspaper against injury by dampness or salt spray.

In this wise he applied himself to master the manners of a little craft until their management should become automatic to hand and brain. Here he laid foundation for the consummate small-boat sailor to whom I, yachtswoman long in advance of our meeting, entrusted my life seventeen years later in ocean voyaging on a forty-five foot ketch. "The small-boat sailor is the real sailor," was his opinion, although he courteously prefaces the remark with "barring captains and mates of big ships." And he goes on: "He knows — he must know — how to make the wind carry his craft from one given point to another given point. He must know about tides and rips and eddies, bar and channel markings, and day and night signals; he must be wise in weather-lore; and he must be sympathetically familiar with the peculiar qualities of his boat which differentiate it from every other boat that was ever built and rigged. He must know how to gentle her about, as one instance of a myriad, and to fill her on the other track without deadening her way or allowing her to fall off too far." As for the captains of liners as well as officers and able seamen, I have heard them frankly admit: "No, I can't swim; and I don't know the first thing about handling small sailing vessels." It is an art by itself, Jack London became a past master of it during his early teens.

Never did he forget his astonishment upon encountering his first modern deep-water sailor—runaway from an English merchantman. He sat in breathless wonder-worship of this sea-god who discoursed lightly of hair-raising hurricanes and violent deeds in strange lands and oceans. One day the superior being consented to sail with him. "With all the trepidation of the veriest little amateur I hoisted sail and got under way. Here was a man, looking on critically, I was sure, who knew more in one second about boats and the water than I could ever know. After an interval in which I exceeded myself he took the tiller and the sheet. I sat on the little thwart amidships open-mouthed, prepared to learn what real sailing was. My mouth remained open, for I learned what a real sailor was in a small boat."

*

He had deliberated earnestly about a pursuit for which he should qualify, and it seemed that he must definitively abandon music, and poetry, and other alluring ways of what he had thought of as "the wide joy-fields of art." The more he pondered, the more convinced he became that fiction writing would pay the best, bringing to him the means of good living for himself and others. In writing he would still be creating art, which seemed necessary to a full realization of himself. It would not take him long to get where he could incorporate art and beauty into form that would sell for several dollars a column, if rumors were dependable. . . . I cannot refrain from wondering if he had not set up for his motto Washington Irving's "Great minds have purposes; others have wishes."

"And no brother of mine is going to take any chewing tobacco into High School," Eliza announced her disapproval of an unsavoury habit he had brought home from his tramp society. Whereupon Jack submitted the excuse that he had to keep chewing incessantly, when he was not smoking incessantly, to prevent his teeth from aching. Suiting action to his defense, he opened his square jaws and exhibited a pitiable array of cavities in every tooth that the Kelly's army dentist had spared from his forceps.

"You ought to be ashamed of yourself—you needn't have had a mouth like that if you'd take half-decent care of it," Eliza scolded full righteously. He owned she was justified, and then proffered the bargain that if she would get him some new upper-fronts, and have the cavities filled, he would quit the abhorred "chewing." Which he did, except on one of two surreptitious occasions when, sailing and fishing up-river for a rest, alone or with some unregenerate compatriot, he renewed acquaintance with "plug cut!"

"Well," he remarked when the plate had been adjusted, "here I am with my first store teeth and my first tooth-brush I ever bought—I got them both at the same time, at nineteen years of age."

"Well, it's nothing to be proud of," his sister flashed back with rising colour. "It's your own fault, because you knew better. I didn't bring you up that way! And I wouldn't brag about it before anybody. It's no credit to you."

... Jack's first mishap while he and the new plate were becoming accustomed, was upon a day when he rode the spic and span "safety" to call upon a girl schoolmate. Coasting downhill, a violent sneeze ejected the teeth, and in his lightning effort to catch them midfall, they and he and wheel went down together. Although his sensitiveness was acute, he would hide it under a bold brusquerie at such times. Once, I remember, at Piedmont Swimming Baths in Oakland, he lost his plate in the tank, and failing to recover it by crawling along the bottom in eight feet of water, he finally gave up secret methods and offered a dollar to the boy who would find it for him. Great hilarity ensued, in which he as noisily shared, and there followed a mighty splashing and engulfment of small divers. When one strangling brat had emerged successful, the owner concealed his blushes under water while he slipped the teeth into place. "Be a good sport, no matter how it hurts," was the word.

*

If Jack London's roving feet had failed to be drawn into the Klondike stampede of 1897, his future audience would have ceased not from asking why. But, of course, he could not fail of response to the lure of this golden adventure—accent on adventure. With all the naiveté of previous self-justifications when yielding to his passion for boating, the material treasure-trove in itself formed but an adjunct that made all at ease with his conscience.

It was Klondike or bust. But how, how, How?—he beat at the obstacle of poverty. The steamer *Umatilla*, of recent memory, carrying the great jam of mad gold-seekers, was to sail in four days on the irresistible tide of the enterprise. Klondike or bust—oh, he would somehow get to go; but there was not a cent in sight for grub and gear, and his automatic practical sense warned of meager welcome for the unprepared in the bleak Northland.

Two days moved swiftly by, while he hustled about Oakland to find some one reckless enough to grubstake him into the Arctic. He even called upon Joaquin Miller;—blockhead, why hadn't it occurred to him sooner! There was a man, a true sport who would understand. Would he! He had understood so well that when Jack reached the door, the Sweet Singer of the Sierras had already pulled out on his own hook—"The son of a gun!" Jack ruefully appreciated.

As the hours lessened, he grew reckless; he would depend upon strength and luck, and chance the thing, outfit or no outfit. Unavoidably he had thought of his sister; but this being so expensive an undertaking, and she having done much for him of late without his having proved he could make good, for once he could not bring himself further to burden her.

Yet it was from her household that help emanated, although from an unanticipated member. Jack stricken dumb when his brother-in-law fell as sudden and hopeless—or hopeful—victim to the gold-fever as any youngster in his unlicked teens, boldly announcing his own intention of the Klondike or bust. He furthermore declared that if Jack would trade the benefit of his youth and experience and see him through, he should be grubstaked in partnership. Jack, with shrewd judgment born of bedding with hardship by land and sea, was markedly unenthusiastic in view of the slender and ailing veteran's age and other disqualifications. Still, he was up against a disappointment he could not brook; it was Klondike or bust, and he could ill balk at such last-moment opportunity. Upon the instant he decided, as was his habit in crises.

The elder man's generosity of a grubstake consisted in sinking his own earnings of the firm of Shepard & Company, along with his wife-partner's, in addition to the hundreds she promptly realized by mortgaging the home, which was her own. Then, having bowed her sensible head to the impregnable fusion of their juvenile insanity—"both as crazy as loons one no worse than the other!"—she abetted with might and main. Since they were minded to make idiots of themselves, they should have the best outfit that could be purchased; moreover, she would shop with them to see that it was complete in every detail. And the following year her brother was able to happily to assure her that nothing to beat it went over Chilcoot that fall of 1897.

## NOTES

1. "Diary of *Dirigo* Voyage around Cape Horn," March 13, 1912, Jack London Collection, Huntington Library, JL 208, 4.

2. "Diary of *Dirigo* Voyage," June 1, 1912, 43–44.

3. "Diary of *Dirigo* Voyage," March 17, 1912, 35.

4. Charmian London, *Log of the* Snark, 171.

5. See Jack London, *With a Heart Full of Love*.

# Charmian London

## From *The Book of Jack London*, Vol. 2 (1921)

In Tremont Temple, and in historic Faneuil Hall, under the noted Gilbert Stuart of the Father of His Country, to packed audiences Jack London sent forth his voice for the Cause. In the latter auditorium, the sweet and unvanquished fighter, "Mother Jones," marched up the central aisle to the huge rostrum and greeted the young protagonist of her holy mission with a sounding kiss on either cheek. He spoke also at socialist headquarters. The Intercollegiate Socialist Society had been organized for a month or two, and the Harvard members got together and saw to it that the first President, Jack London should be heard in Harvard Union.

Aside from Mrs. Sheldon, myself, and one or two others, there were no women present in Harvard Union that night. We sat with Frank Sheldon and Gelett Burgess in a tiny gallery hung upon the rear wall of the high hall. A thrilling sight it was, that throng of collegians, not only those crowded both seated and standing on the floor below, but the scores hanging by their eyebrows to window casements, welcoming Jack with round upon round of ringing shouts and cheers — an ovation, the papers did not hesitate to call it.

He gave them, unsparingly, all and more than they had bargained for, straight from the shoulder, jolting "revolution" into them. Once, when a statement of starvation facts, concerning the Chicago slums, was so awful as to strike a number of the chesty young bloods as a bit melodramatic, a laugh started. Jack's face set like a vice, and he hung over the edge of the platform, a challenge to their better part flaming from black-blue eyes and ready, merciless tongue. Be it said that the response was instantaneous and wholehearted, the house rising as one man and echoing to the applause until I, for one onlooker, choked and filled with emotion at the human fellowship of it. At the close of the lecture, Jack and Mr. Sheldon were carried off to the fraternity houses and royally entertained the rest of the night.

*

That year of 1906, sketchy as was our domestic ménage, many visitors came to Lodge Annex, and auntie let us now spill into the main house. Among the names in my journal was custodian of the welfare of Jack London's troublesome teeth to the end of the patient's life; Mr. Bamford; I. M. Griffin, the artist, a number of canvases, painted in the neighborhood, Jack purchased; Professor Henry Meade Bland, of San Jose, at all times one of Jack's most tireless biographers; Felix Peano, sculptor, in whose house, La Capriccioso, Jack had once lived; young Roy Nash, of whom "The People of the Abyss" had made a socialist; Ernest Untermann, author and translator of Karl Marx; the George Sterlings; different members of the talented family of Partingtons; George Wharton James, who charmed with his social qualities and music, and later published most readable articles upon his visit; Elwyn Hoffman, poet; Herman Whitaker; Xavier Martinez, artist and prince of bohemians — "Sometimes I think," Jack once remarked, "that George Sterling and 'Marty' are the realest bohemians I have ever known!"; Maud Younger, settlement worker and philanthropist; and a long list beside.

Our amusement consisted in exploring alone or with our guests, the infinite variety of the one hundred and twenty-nine acres of Jack's "Beauty Ranch"; driving or riding to points in the valley — say Cooper's Grove, a noble group of redwoods; or to Hooker's Falls across in the eastern range; or to Santa Rosa, as when we drove Professor Edgar Larkin, of Mt. Lowe Observatory, to call upon Luther Burbank, or to the valley resorts to swim, for a change from Sonoma Creek, in the warm mineral tanks.

*

On April 18, 1906, there came, in a sense, the "shock of our lives." One need hardly mention that it was the great earthquake, which, most notable of consequences, destroyed the "modern imperial city" of San Francisco as no other modern imperial city has been destroyed. If it had not been for this stunning disaster to the larger place, the pitiable ruin of our county seat, Santa Rosa, in which many lives were crushed out, would have commanded the attention and sympathy of the world. As it was, refugees from the Bay metropolis began presently to straggle up-country, only to find the pretty town prone in a scarcely laid dust of brick and mortar and ashes.

Jack's nocturnal habits of reading, writing, smoking, and coughing, or sudden shifts of posture (he could not move his smallest finger without springing alive from head to foot), not being exactly a remedy for my insomnia, we ordinarily occupied beds as far apart as possible. A few minutes before five, on the morning of the 18th upstairs at Wake Robin, my eyes flew open inexplicably, and I wondered what had stirred me so early. I curled down for a morning nap, when suddenly the earth began to heave, with a sickening onrush of motion for an eternity of seconds. An abrupt pause, and then it seemed as if some great force laid hold on the globe and shook it like a Gargantuan rat. It was the longest half-minute of our lives. . . .

When Jack and I ran over to the barn still rented at the Fish Ranch, we found our saddle animals had broken their halters and were still quivering and skittish. Willie, the chore-boy, said the huge madroño tree near by had lain down on the ground and got up again—which was less lurid than many impressions to which we listened that weird day.

In half an hour after the shock, we were in our saddles, riding to the Reach, from which height could be distinguished a mighty column of smoke in the direction of San Francisco, and another northward where lies Santa Rosa. In the immediate foreground at our feet a prodigious dust obscured the buildings of the State Home for the Feeble-minded.

"Why, Mate Woman," Jack cried, his eyes big with surmise, "I shouldn't wonder if San Francisco had sunk. That was some earthquake. We don't know but the Atlantic may be washing up at the feet of the Rocky Mountains!" . . .

With no luggage except our smallest handbag, which we left with the restaurant cashier of the last ferry-boat permitted to land passengers that night, we started up old Broadway, and all night roamed the city of hills, prey to feelings that cannot be described. That night was the closest we ever came to realizing a dream that came now and again to Jack in sleep, that he and I were in at the finish of all things—standing or moving hand in hand through chaos to its brink, looking upon the rest of mankind in the process of dissolution.

Having located relatives I knew had been overtaken, and found them unharmed, Jack and I were free to follow our own will.

"And I'll never write about this for anybody," he declared, as we looked upon one or another familiar haunt, soon to be obliterated by the ravaging flames that drove us ever westward to safer points, on and on, in our ears the muffled detonations of dynamite, as one proud commercial attempt of the city fathers to stay the wholesale conflagration. And no water.

"No," Jack reiterated. "I'll never write a word about it. What use trying? One could only string big words together, and rage at the futility of them."[1]

One impinging picture of that fearful night was where two mounted officers, alone of all the population, sat their high-crested horses at Kearney and Market Streets, equestrian statues facing the oncoming flames along Kearney. Hours earlier, we had walked here, two of many; but now the district was abandoned to destruction that could not be retarded.

In my eyes there abides the face of a stricken man, perhaps a fireman, whom we saw carried into a lofty doorway in Union Square. His back had been broken, and as the stretcher bore him past, out of a handsome, ashen young face, the dreadful, darkening eyes looked right into mine. All the world was crashing about him, and he, a broken thing, with death awaiting him inside the granite portals, gazed upon the last woman of his race that he was ever to see. Jack, with tender hand, drew me away.

Oh, the supreme truth of desolation and pain, that night of fire and devastation! Yet the miracle persists, that one saw nothing but cheerful courtesy of one human to another. And I was to learn more of my husband's cool judgment in crises. Now and again it seemed as if we would surely be trapped in some square, where the fourth side had started to burn. But he had always, and accurately, sensed and chosen the moment and the way out, when we should have seen all we could risk.

Toward morning, finding ourselves on the doorsteps of a corner house on "Nob Hill," very near the partially erected and already burning Hotel Fairmont, Jack fell into a sleep; but I was unable to still the tingling of heart and nerves long enough to drop off even from exhaustion. Presently a man mounted the steps and inserted a key in the lock. Noting Jack and myself on the top tread—he had had to pick his way through a cluster of Italians and Chinamen on the lower ones—something impelled him to invite us in. It was a luxurious interior, containing the treasures of years. His name was Perine, the man said, and he did not learn ours. Suddenly, midway of showing us about, he asked me to try the piano, and laid bare the keys. I hesitated—it seemed almost a cruel thing to do, with annihilation so very near. But Jack whispered, "Do it for him—it's the last time he'll ever hear it," sent me to the instrument. The first few touches were enough and too much for Mr. Perine, however, and he made a restraining gesture. If he ever reads this book, I want him to know that none in poor, racked San Francisco that week was more sorry for him than we. We must have tramped forty miles that night. Jack's feet blistered, my ankles were become almost useless.

*

All a piece of wonder it was, on and round the small precipitous deck of the Snark, herself a mere scudding fleck of matter advancing upon the vast un-dulating plane of the Pacific. How could a true sailor be bored, the longest day under the arching blue sky — the excellent trades hunting his ship to its purple havens? For Jack found me sailor, too, albeit a lamentably untechnical mariner — ever he stood aghast at the hopelessness of getting me to present, "so that the Man from Mars could understand," certain ordinary, primary principles of seamanship. But my love and true feel for the very shape of the boat, and for her performance, and for the whole world of water, easily he saw were not to be questioned; while always, in the entering and leaving the most dangerous passages, he sent me to the wheel to co-operate with his piloting. "It's this way," he had it: "There are man boats, but only one woman; boats will come and go, and captains will come and go, but Charmian will be with me always, at the helm."

Here I am tempted to digress, in order to word a still but not small worry that was mine throughout our married life. Jack's correlations between brain and body were exceptionally balanced. But there was in him one inexacti-tude that led me to nurse a dread that my own hand, under his command, might some most inopportune time wreck a boat. I do not know when I first began to notice that at intervals he would say "right" for "left," but some-times I would promptly call his attention to the mistake while his voice was still in the air. My principal fear was that, some irretrievable consequence having occurred, the responsibility might not be easy to place; and I prided myself upon unquestioning obedience aboard the ship. Jack liked that, and only once did we, personally, come to grief. It was upon a midnight in the Solomon Islands, dark as a hat, and Jack, ill and apprehensive, was trying to make out a certain plantation anchorage on Guadalcanal. Suddenly, . . . I started to put the wheel hard down at Jack's swift, tense command. "Hard down! Hard down! Quick!" he repeated. And I, like an idiot, "Oh, I am! I am!" It was too much for the disciplined sailorman. Not of babbling cour-tesies nor babies nor women was he thinking, but of saving the vessel that insured the safety of all the souls on board. And I let me own silly, mawk-

ish, fever-worked nerves go up against this intellectually-cool, efficient ma-
nipulating of a real issue. Since Jack never apologized for his sharp reproof:
"Obey orders and don't talk back!" I believe that no realization of his harsh-
ness entered the mind so bent upon a life-and-death issue.

\*

No, we did not know the meaning of boredom. And "Aren't you glad I'm
your husband?" Jack would laugh over my enthusiasms. Or, tenderly, "You
would marry a sailor!" when I floundered into the head-splitting fever attacks. But dearest of all was his assurance, reiterated in illness and its brief
discouragement: "You do not know what you mean to me. It is like being lost
in the Dangerous Archipelago and coming into safe harbour at last."

It is all a piece of wonder, the sea, to such as we: still magic of calms, where
one's boat lies with motionless grace upon magic of calms, where one's boat
lies with motionless grace upon a shadow-flecked expanse of mirror; or when
one laughs in the pelt of warm sea-rain from a ragged gray sky of clouds; or
peers for night-blue squalls darkling upon the silver, moonlit waves; or lifts
prideful, fond eyes to the small ship's goodly spars standing fast in a white
gale; or gazes in marvel at those same spars lighted to flame by the red-gilt
morning sunrays from over some green and purple savage isle feared of God
and man; or braces to the Pacific rollers bowling upon the surface of the eternal unagitated depths; or scans the configuration of coasts from inadequate
charts; or steers, tense breathless, through the gateways of but half-known
reefs, into enchanted coral-rings below "the lap of the Line"; or looks with
misleading candor into the eyes of man-eating human beings; or being received ashore on scented Polynesian "fragments of Paradise" aplume with
waving palms, with brown embraces, into the "high seat of abundance." It
is all wonder and deep delight, this "smoke of life"; and often and often we
surprised ourselves thinking or voicing our pity for the "vain people of lands-
man" who have no care for such joys as ours. Jack, embodiment of fearless-
ness, so vivid in thought, and action, and physique, was a ringing challenge
to any who were not half-dead.

\*

Our main meal was at 12:30. This hour better suited our work and Ranch
plans generally. At twelve the mail-sack — a substantial leather one bought before we sailed on the Snark — arrived at the back porch, and Nakata brought

it to me to sort the contents. In the half-hour before dinner, Jack had glanced over the daily paper, read his letters, indicated replies on some of them for my guidance, and laid the more important ones in their wire tray; one of many such nested on a small table beside the Oregon myrtle roll-top desk, where he transacted business. I always endeavored to have his ten pages of hand-written manuscript transcribed—an average of two-and-a-half type-written letter-size sheets—before the second gong belled the fifteen-minute call to the table. That gong was an ancient concave disk of brass and bronze, brought from Korea by Jack. He implored me to be on time to the minute's tick, and attend to seating the guests, so that he might work to the last moment.

In many minds, I am sure still lives the vision of the hale, big-hearted man of God's out-of-doors, the beardless patriarch, his curls rumpled, like as not the green visor unremoved, pattering with that quick, light step along the narrow vine-shaded porch, through the screened doorway and the length of the tapa-brown room to his seat in the great koa chair at the head of the table. . . . How he doted upon that board with its long double-row of friendly faces turned in greeting, ever ready with another plate and portion! It was his ideal—carried from old days with the Strunskys. "In Jack's house," one writes me, "I met the most interesting people of my life and of the world." And perhaps, while we fell to our portions, before his own was tasted he would read aloud newspaper items or newly received letters; or he might launch out in a fine rage of his eternal enthusiasm, upon some theme that has claimed him, or strike into argument, whipped hot out of his seething brain and heart.

\*

How shall I say? Jack could not traffic in small things any more than he could deftly handle trifling object with his fingers. All he did was in a large way. His boyish memories were of moving from one small, inadequate wooden domicile to another. Being what he could not help being, and remaining true to himself, lover of large and enduring things, he must invite spaciousness and solidity—room to breathe in. . . . The ancient frame cottage in which on the ranch he lived and worked and received all men at his table was wholly disproportionate to his needs. Being so indefatigable and systematic a worker and thinker he required everything to his hand. A smoothly running domestic ménage made for efficiency in other matters. Here where he had to live during the three years while the Wolf House building went on intermittently, the rooms were crammed and jammed and spilling over with the very implements of his many branches of endeavor. Only the combined efforts of the two of us, and later a third, a secretary, made it anything less than distracting for Jack to function in the cramped quarters. Three-fourths of his library was packed away moulding in the big stone barn half a mile away, and many the time he could not lay his hand upon some volume especially needed.

Wanderer, yet deeply fond of his own home, a place for the permanence of his treasures — curios, blankets, books, "gear" — he sighed content knowing that in the big house there would be a story in one wing devoted to the library; above that, his roomy work-den; on the first floor, dining-room and kitchen. The middle story of the opposing wing was to be mine — a place where I might retreat to rest and call my soul my own when the outside world was too much within our walls. Above, Jack's sleeping tower reared. Beneath mine were the guest chambers, and, still below, servants' quarters and the like. The connecting link of these two wings formed a two-story living-room, partially flanked by a gallery; and underneath this high hall lay what Jack termed the "stag room," where no female might venture except by especial ukase from the lords of creation, who might lounge and play billiards and otherwise amuse themselves therein. The house foundation measured roughly 80 feet from corner to corner.

It should be thought of, that house, in connection with Jack, not as a mansion, but as a big cabin, a lofty lodge, a hospitable teepee, where Jack, simple and generous, despite all his baffling intricacy, could stretch himself and beam upon you and me and all the world that gathered by his log-fires. I know a friend who appreciated this largeness of the man, and who with man's tenderness call him the Big Chief. . . . Why, the very form of the rough rock hacienda was an invitation, with its embracing wings, its sunny pool between the wide, arched corridors and grape-gnarled pergola! The reason that seekers after the truth about Jack London find more reminder of him in the aching ruins of his great house is because they do not know the all of Jack London. He was a man before all else — big, and solid, and spacious, and unvaryingly true to himself.

So with his ranching. There, too, he wrought largely. "No picayune methods for me," he would vow. "When I go into the Silence, I want to know that I have left behind me a plot of land which, after the pitiful failures of others, I have made productive. Can't you see? Oh, try to see! In the solution of the great economic problems of the present age, I see a return to the soil. I go into farming because my philosophy and research have taught me to recognize the fact that a return to the soil is the basis of economics. I see my farm in terms of the world, and the world in terms of my farm. Do you realize that I devote two hours a day to writing and ten to farming? — my thought-work, my preparation, at night, and when I am out-of-doors."

Similar revelation of himself he gave on the witness stand only a few days before his death, when suit had been brought to restrain him from using his share of the waters of a creek in the whole sad affair, which contributed its weight toward his break-down, not one iota of understanding was accorded him by the prosecutors, among whom were some near and dear to him.

From time to time I would ask: "When, in the years to come, do you think you will ever pull even, financially, with your ranch project?" And it was always with a laugh that he would return: "Never, my dear—at least, I want and expect to have the place eventually sustain itself. That would be the natural object. But it will never make money for me, because there is so much developing I want to keep on doing, endless experiments I want to make."

A noted socialist lecturer, with misapprehensions and prejudice in his eye, spent a day or two on the ranch. "At last I see," said he. "I was wrong. In your work here as you unfold it to me, I see a social creation!"

Once more, let me impress: temperamentally Jack London was a builder— of books, of houses, of roads, of soil, of things that would outlast merely temporary uses. . . . Little call to point out that he did not build for himself alone.

### NOTE

1. London changed his mind and published "The Story of an Eye-Witness" in *Collier's Weekly* on May 5, 1906.

# Charmian London

## From *The Log of the* Snark (1925)

> Charmian's *Log of the* Snark was published in the United States and Great Britain. This book is one of three by members of the *Snark* crew: Charmian's *Log*, London's *The Cruise of the* Snark (1911), and Martin Johnson's *Through the South Seas with Jack London* (1913). Whereas London's book is a medical memoir from a disease-infested "paradise," Martin's is sensationalistic, as befits a 19-year-old from Kansas out to see the world. But Martin is excellent on the details of the yacht, how the crew felt, and local customs. Charmian's *Log* is part travelogue, part personal reverie.

## The Beginning

It was all due to Captain Joshua Slocum[1] and his *Spray*, plus our own wayward tendencies. We read him aloud to the 1905 camp children at Wake Robin Lodge, in the Valley of the Moon, as we sat in the hot sun resting between water fights and games of tag in the deep swimming pool. *Sailing Alone around the World* was the name of the book, and when Jack closed the cover on the last chapter, there was a new idea looking out of his eyes. Joshua Slocum did it all alone, in a thirty-seven-foot sloop. Why could not we do it, in a somewhat larger boat, with a little voyage was our dream. He and Roscoe fell at once to discussing the scheme, the rest of us listening fascinated.

This was a few months before we were married. "Say we start five years from now," Jack, who always seems to be making plans for a tangible eternity. "We'll build our house on the ranch and get the place started with orchard and vines and livestock, at the same time going ahead with boat drawings and building a yacht to suit. Five years will not be too much time."

Then, privily, he asked what I thought of it. Too good to be true, was what I thought; but why wait so long? We'd never be younger than we were, and besides, what was the good of putting up a home and leaving it for seven years? — seven years being the time roughly calculated to carry out our far-reaching plan. I won the day.

And the boat. She should be ketch-rigged, like the English fishing boats on the Dogger Bank.[2] We had never seen a ketch but knew that for our purpose it combined the virtues of both schooner and yawl. There should be six feet of head-room, under flush decks unbroken save by companionway, skylights, and hatches. The roomy cockpit should be sunk deep beneath the deck, high-railed and self-bailing. There should be no hold, all space being occupied by accouterment, and engines—one a seventy horse-power auxiliary, and one five horse-power to spin out electric lights and fans. Forty-five feet should be her water-line, with a length over all of fifty-seven feet. She should draw six feet, with no inside ballast, but with fifty tons of iron on the keel. There should be used only the strongest and best materials of every kind—a solid, serviceable deep-sea craft, the strongest of her size ever constructed.

But we counted without the Great Earthquake of April 18, 1906. The vessel was already begun, and the iron keel was actually to have been cast the night of April 18. Following that date, what we did not suffer from damage to other property, was inflicted by post-earthquake conditions which made our ship-building triply expensive and incomprehensibly protracted. Everybody and everything went mad; and it was nearly a year after the delayed laying of her doughty keel that the yacht, unfinished, unclean, her seventy horse-power engine a heap of scrap-iron from the ignorant tinkering that had been done to it, sailed from California for Hawaii, manned, or unmanned, by a more or less discouraged crew, whose original adventurous spirits and efficiency had been sorely dampened by the weary postponement of departure dates. The final one was set behind an extra week-end by a ship chandler who libeled the yacht because he was afraid he would not get his last bill paid, the while Jack was settling accounts right and left aboard the boat, one pocket full of gold and silver, the other containing check-book and fountain pen.

*

At Sea, Saturday, April 27, 1907.

Toward night the weather looked very nasty (I knew I'd have a chance to report some weather), the waves seemed enormous to me, the *Snark* rolled and pitched, water running deep across her deck, water sloshing around below and squirting up through the floors, water squeezing in through the buried side and into the galley stores and all over the dishes and stove. But the boat acted well in the heavy seas, until it came to putting her through the paces of heaving to. *Heaving to* means bringing a vessel's head up into the wind, the sails being trimmed to hold her that way any length of time. This means safety so long as a sail stays on a boat.

Now, listen well; the *Snark* refused to heave to. Not all the efforts of three men for hours and hours could make her heave to. She simply wallowed—and most creditably wallowed, it must be confessed—in the trough of the sea, but would come no farther into the wind. Fortunately the gale did not increase, nor was it cold. But oh, the hills and valleys of the ocean! There may be real storms for the *Snark* somewhere on the wide ocean of our adventure; but the waves this day loomed quite large enough on my new horizon. If they had been really big waves, we, rolling there in the trough, might have been turned over and over, with only a stray life-preserver left floating upon the boundless briny to tell that the *Snark* had been lost with all on board. And, of course, the wind *might* have blown harder, and the worst *might* have happened, with the yacht acting as she did. The final thing to be done, in a case like this, or in any extreme case, is to put out a sea anchor, a contrivance of canvas and half-hoops that I warranted to hold to the wind the head of 'most anything that floats. So our sea-anchor was rigged up. And it failed. Then Jack and Roscoe stood by the mizzen and talked it over with serious faces. They had tried everything, every possible combination of sails that they could think of, and failed to bring the yacht up nearer than eight points into the wind, which means that we were rolling in the trough, as I have said. The men talked it over, wondered at the incredible fact of the failure, and could solve nothing of the wonder. I wish I had a picture of the three, in the pale grey moonlight that drifted through the flying clouds, leaning over the forward weather rail watching the sea-anchor. It will be with me always, that grey scene, the three darker grey forms in oilskins, the heads on sou'westers, leaning at the same angle, hanging upon the success of that sea-anchor.

There is no explaining these things that happened this day. I can only tell the facts and leave folk to wonder as we wonder.

All these hours I stood in the cockpit hovering over the compass, wheel hard down, watching vainly, oh! how vainly, for the yacht to round up into the wind, and at the same time marveling that some of the grey seas which brimmed to the very lip of the rail did not come aboard and whelm us. I remember, some years ago, figuring out that I was too old to die young; but this grey night, especially after I went to bed in my rubber boots, I caught myself dwelling on the conclusion that I was too young to die!

At sea, April 28, 1907, Sunday

The Sea is not a loveable monster. And monster it is. I thought a great many thoughts about it last night, those hours I studied the binnacle or watched the men make their fight. It is beautiful, the sea, always beautiful in one way or another; but it is cruel, and unmindful of the life that is in it and upon it. It was cruel last evening, in the lurid low sunset that made it glow dully, to the cold, mocking, ragged moonrise that made it look like death. The waves positively beckoned when they rose and pitched toward our boat laboring in the trough. And all the long night it seemed to me that I heard voices thought the planking, talking, talking, endlessly, monotonously, querulously; and I couldn't make out whether it was the ocean calling from the outside or the ship herself muttering gropingly, finding herself. If the voices are the voices of the ship, they will soon cease, for she must find herself. But if they are the voices of the sea, they must be sad sirens that cry, restless, questioning, unsatisfied—quaint homeless little sirens.

Saturday, May 4, 1907.

We are bowling fast into the Torrid Zone, into Hawaiian weather. I am sitting on the rudder-box, steering with my feet while I write. Oh, this water, and this brave trade wind. The big sapphire hills of water, and this brave trade wind. The big sapphire hills of water, transparent and sun-shot, are topped with dazzling white that blows from crest to crest in the compelling wind. Just now a huge swell picked us up and swung us high, and the merest little fling of salt spray was in our faces. The *Snark* is what sailors call a "dry" boat. And she sails easily, without jerks or bumps. Along comes a blue mountain that looks like disaster; and we slip over it and down into the blue abyss on the other side, without a jar—just a huge, rolling slide. And ever the strong sweet wind blows from behind to send us forward to the isles of our desire.

The steering-compass has become a part of my consciousness, sleeping and waking; and I often go amidships and hover over the big Standard Compass. I think in terms of "south by west," and "south half west," and other expressions that were Greek to me a month ago. I can "luff her up," too, when the men are aloft fixing something. And I can box the compass. Jack calls me various jolly names, such as "The skipper's sweetheart," "The Crackerjack," "Jack's wife," and I swell with pride and feel very salty indeed. And I am reminded to mention that when we call each other "Mate," this has no connection with boats, but is an interchangeable nickname.

## NOTES

1. Joshua Slocum was the author of *Sailing Alone around the World* (New York: Century, 1899).

2. The *Snark* was actually modeled after East Coast boats, which made it stand out in California.

# Charmian London

## Letter to Upton Sinclair (1951)

Charmian spent more of her time actually writing—in letters using her long, looping cursive or a typewriter, her shorthand, her tiny diaries with her tiny script, her articles, typing London's works and her own—and continuing a lifetime of correspondence. She was a newsy, faithful, and welcoming friend, though she could flash with anger when she felt slighted or when she felt her husband had been slighted, as in her letters involving a competing biography of Jack London from an acquaintance, Rose Wilder Lane, or when she chastises Joan for rudeness. Her letters to Joan are important—they illustrate the way that Charmian and Jack London approached things, to stand one's ground but never neglect to embrace one's family, one's true trailmates. Her great two-story stone house she called the House of Happy Walls is now a museum at the Jack London State Historical Park. The walls were "Happy" because on their interiors she hung hundreds of mementos from their *Snark* journey.

Dear Upton:

Yes, Viereck's article in LIBERTY is rather nicely done. I furnished the material—the Sinclair Lewis stuff (with his permission, but did not know that Viereck's was to do the article). I have a note from him today (I met him long ago at the luncheon in New York of which he writes). He hopes that I will like the article and that there is nothing in it that displeases me or that would have displeased Jack.

Jack bought three plots from Lewis. Never used them. The only plots Jack ever used of George's were THE RED ONE first story in collection under that title. And THE FIRST POET. In the latter instance, it wasn't a matter of "plot" at all. George practically wrote the thing, and then they collaborated on it. Jack never requested plots. He picked up ideas here and there—but I've gone into all this in the biography. He bought plots to help out "the other fellow." Shortly before he died, Jack said: "I've got ideas here for a hundred novels"—and he was not referring to the plots bought from friends, but to the grist he had collected. One favorite way of his was to drift when listening to music—and many a story came to him then. But all this is in the biography.

THE RED ONE, aside from the suggestion of the great round possibly meteorite, (except for some of the description of the quality of the red orb—I did it) is entirely Jack's own work—and one of his biggest short-stories in my opinion. It is magnificent from its various viewpoints. Outside of the above about THE FIRST POET, there is nothing whatsoever in Jack's work collected in book-form (and nothing else I know of) that was written by any one but himself. He bought plots—and didn't use them, except in these instances. I would not at all object to revealing it if the facts were otherwise. I don't remember any title like OG, THE SON of OG, or anything like it. They probably looked over a lot of things. At the time of Jack's death, there was some manuscript by neither of them, that they were discussing for moving-picture. Nothing came of it. I returned the material at George's request. I shall go into this subject a little more fully when I come to it in the revision I am at work on of the two-volume biography. I recall no cave-man material that Jack used that had connection with George. I can generally speak with authority because Jack and I worked right together for sixteen years, and I typed everything he wrote, and he was the sort who shared everything almost moment by moment.

Sincerely always,
Charmian London

# Charmian London

## Letter to Joan London (1917)

Dear Joan:

Do not ever forget, Joan, you and your sister, that when your Mother is willing, nothing would please me more — and your Aunt Eliza — than to have you girls come up to the ranch. It is so great an achievement of your father's, that it will be a pity if you should not see what he did here. Also, it is really the most beautiful place in the world. Just now there are young colts and calves and kids and things, and everything is very beautiful and green. I am far too busy to do much personal entertaining; but you and your sister would find no boredom roaming over the trails and the mountain meadows.

It all lies with your Mother and you girls. I am always ready and glad to welcome you and turn you loose upon your Daddy's mountainside.

Sincerely yours,
Charmian London.

# Charmian London

## Letter to Joan London (April 1919)

My Dear Joan:

Your letter is just at hand, and I hasten to assure you that your trip to the Ranch next Saturday, May 3, will be perfectly convenient. When you get to Glen Ellen, inquire the road, and follow along until you come to the stone barns, and you will see Aunt Eliza's shingled cottage on a smooth knoll, with the mountains behind. She will direct you to the Little Hill of Graves, and anywhere else you wish to go.

Long ago, Joan, I wrote to you how welcome you would be at any and all times on the Ranch. And now that you are really going to set foot upon it, I shall hope that you may look at the occasion in the way, and not deny yourselves the pleasure, sad pleasure though it be, of seeing your daddy's "workroom," and everything else about the place. Try, won't you? The older I grow, the more I think the most valuable thing in the world is to get down to the simplicities of life, to eliminate the complex unworthwhile emotions as much as possible. To be concrete: Here is your daddy's beloved mountainside. . . . You would love it; knowing it would do you good; you are free as the sunshine, as far as I am concerned, to roam it. For me to know that you and your sister were enjoying it, would be the best joy in the world to me.

Think it over—and with open mind. Hard feelings, stern convictions, bring nobody anything but sour unhappiness. And life is so short.

In conclusion—when you motor to the Ranch next Saturday, I hope you will come to my house and let me show you everything that will bring you nearer your lost daddy. It will do us all good.

If you wish, why not bring your luncheon, and enjoy it up at the lake. And if you bring your swimming-suits,—"the water is fine," they tell me, although a bad attack of neuritis has kept me out of it so far.

I want you to feel that I am entirely consistent in my old desire to share the beauty of the Ranch with you. I haven't expressed myself well, perhaps; but you can read between the lines. You should know, by this time, what my intentions are toward you all.

And again, I shall hope that thinking it over will bring you all to my welcoming door. If you cannot see it my way this time—why, I shall keep on hoping that you will some other day. In ANY event, Joan, Aunt Eliza will see that you find your way about to what you do wish to see.

# Charmian London

## Letter to Joan London (May 1919)

My dear Joan:

This, unless I greatly mistake, will be my last letter to you. And you can, with all the wisdom of your eighteen years (to refer to your latest letter to me), be able to guess the reason.

It seems so strange, with all the wisdom of your eighteen years, plus the half of a college education wherein you certainly must meet a percentage of persons of good breeding, that you should be guilty of so absolutely indecent a faux pas as upon last Sunday. Indecent seems to be the best word, since there are certain decencies of social conduct.

I do not need, seeing you are so shameless, to call your attention to the fact that you have in every respect had considerate treatment from myself. The "letter of the law" has been supplemented, as you may be able to recall, by various things of the spirit which materialized in benefits to you—sometimes proffered by me, sometimes solicited by you, and at times not paid for out of money due to you father's work, but out of my own earnings. These things were yours for the asking and sometimes for no asking, and with my full heart of well-meaning towards your father's children. I never expected actual gratitude—I only expected the courtesy of acknowledgement.

Now, since you been sheerly mercenary (not a pretty word) in keeping upon terms of merest courtesy—though grudging—with the goose with the golden egg, why has not all the wisdom of your eighteen years kept you from killing the goose! As I said above, certainly you must meet and observe persons of good breeding who do not accept hospitality in the home of one to whom they turn their backs. Do you not know, really, Joan, do you incredibly not realize that the sort of thing you did last Sunday was in the nature of the behavior of children and peasants?

I took a Southern gentleman out for a horseback ride over the Ranch. I was not anxious to run into you, this not on my account so much as yours, because of your youth and any embarrassment you might feel. I suspected you were picnicking on the Ranch, because one of my men, coming up in the machine, said a party had acted so peculiarly as to attract notice—jumping up and turning their backs upon him as if scared. So, when I saw through the trees ahead your party (curiously enough on a place where your father particularly did not like to have people picnic or even ride across), I purposely avoided the direct road and cut off to the left to pass you. The Southern gentleman, accustomed to courteous women and good breeding generally, said to me:

"Did you see how funnily those people acted?—they jumped up off the ground and all turned their backs in a row! Who could they be?"

I admitted to him that out of the corner of my eye I, too, had witnessed the phenomenon, which, let me say here, was positively the most laughable thing I ever saw—a line of adult human beings' backs that had been so comfortable picnicking a moment before. Why, do you always turn your back on your life? Your father loathed a coward—surely you're not one? Have you no character for emergency—even the accidental meeting of your hostess on her own land! It's beyond me. But to my Southern guest I replied:

"I am ashamed to tell you that two of those very rude persons are Jack London's own flesh and blood—his daughters."

And I WAS ashamed, Joan. Don't you really know any better to lose entirely the manners of civilization when you are out in the world? Or, and I hate to think it, but I seem forced to do so, are you so hardened, with all the wisdom of your eighteen years, that you can take favors from a person, even ask favors, and turn your back upon that person in her own house? Think it over. I can only interpret you to mean that you wish no further favors of any sort from me, and walk accordingly. My gate is closed. . . .

Your father had no commerce with smallness, with any spirit that could not face the music; with mercinariness [*sic*]; with pridelessness. Your actions last Sunday were inexcusable, prideless, and very, very short-sighted. You can hardly gain anything in the mercenary way, because I, like your father, have huge disgusts, and get through things—quite, absolutely, positively through. You will, with all the wisdom of your eighteen years, understand what I mean. Your father gave you up in the end, as hopeless. I thought him prejudiced; I see now, that he was right. Any girl of Jack London's with the accumulated wisdom of her eighteen years, and the benefit of his advice concerning the big things of life, who would demean herself to the abysmal point reached by you last Sunday, is hopeless.

This letter is not for your sister. She hasn't all the wisdom of her eighteen years, as yet. I only wish you could both have seen that row of backs last Sunday! It was so funny, Joan, so very funny. And very expensive. You have regarded me as rather a fool — an easy mark; but you have shown your hand, and I now show you mine.

And, please believe, there is no hurt in all this — there was no hurt last Sunday, except in one particular. And this particular was: that it was a shame and a sorrow under high heaven, that any person possessed of such a spirit as you manifested, should have stood beside the grave of so great a man as Jack London. It was a desecration to the symbol of simplicity that reigns on the Little Hill of Graves.

This letter you will destroy, in anger of course. The wisdom of your eighteen years is not of the kind, I sadly fear, that will help you to a logic in the matter. But I am keeping a copy for myself, and I shall file it with the copies of your father's letters to you, which so wonderfully prove that your actions of last Sunday, with all your wisdom of eighteen years, are far, far from what your "daddy would like."

Good bye.

# Charmian London

## Letter to Joan London (March 1925)

Joan, I am the luckiest woman that ever lived. The luckiest thing about it, too, is that I know it. In view of the admirable restraint in your quite-perfect letter to me, I dread seeming garrulous. You cannot quite understand, because there is so very much you do not know, have no possible way of knowing until I can tell you. But not now, in a letter. I am about as mushy as a freckle-faced hoodlum; yet I was near to tears when I read into your letter, and turned to the end to learn the writer. Oh, shame and pity that your writing was strange to me!

Oh, Joan, I was wrong, these seven years—since your visit to my Ranch that awful day, awful to me, I mean. Then I said: "It is no use trying any longer. The material is not there; there is nothing to work on." And now to find myself all wrong—let me be quick, quick to shout it at you. I am giving you the honor, and making myself the happiness, of being frank. Because, you see, unless you were the very essence of deceit, you could not have written so frank a letter deceitfully. I rush to believe you; and I have a grief to think of your life's experiences that have brought you to my door. Then joyfulness.

Another thing let me be quick to say: you *do* speak for yourself alone when you refer to bitterness. I have never been bitter; why should I be? Besides,— please do not accuse me of triteness—I do not allow bitterness in me about anything, because, first, I am too selfish; it makes me unhappy. I must maintain a happy-free heart or I should die. Bitterness is a palpable poison. I know you will understand. And that brings me to your phrase, "that things are as they are." But they're not, if you will allow the paradox. They've never been—everything was all right between us if you had only known it. All that was needed was for you, in full time, to say the word, wave your torch. I vainly tried to wave mine after your father died; there was no response. The time wasn't full. And I was so afraid—only afraid of misunderstanding. Well,

[185]

I got that, and it was inevitable under all circumstances. That I was not made bitter, I hope this letter of mine will prove.

Now Jack's daughter has waved her torch, mine has taken light again, or flared up anew. For we shall not meet as strangers, if you will have it so, Joan. It has been said, in many lands, if I may say it, that I am not a stranger to any one who meets me in the right spirit. Again, that is because I deliberately want things right—a result perhaps of living for over a decade with one so illuminatingly wide of vision as Jack London. . . . I think, myself, that you are passing courageously through a sort of mild Purgatory in your life, a transition from earth-earthy things to a good, clean, interesting—therefore happy—existence. It's up to you, that.

At the moment, I cannot make an appointment. My impulse is to send you a ticket to come here immediately and talk with me beside the lake, long hours; for I have much to say. Much more than you, because I know more. But I am not well, and am crowding a terrific lot of work into small space of time. (As if seeing you were not paramount! It is, Joan; but then one is sometimes restrained from things one most wants, by circumstance.)

If I should be in San Francisco soon, how could I get hold of you at short notice? And, being reticent of my personal affairs . . . , I wish to meet you quite alone, where nothing, nothing, Joan, can distract us from each other. Remember, as a preparation, that to me you are Jack's daughter and, insofar as I was a vital part of your father, so, in my consciousness, you are somehow joined to me. It has always been so. I tell you this simply, quite as a matter of course. Remember, do please, as a further preparation, that I want this meeting to be on the basis of a sort of frankness we can both be proud of as two intelligent women (thank you for that word—it is a favorite of my own); thrusting aside prejudices as much as possible—I want to state mine, and I think I know yours. Let us wipe the big slate clean, Joan London, and talk over things that must be said, without bitterness—say as if we were discussing a proposition removed from personal equation. If you cannot do it, you are not the girl who wrote your letter to me day before yesterday. . . .

If his daughter and I, after all that has gone between, can build a house of friendship upon a rock as steady,—well, it would seem too good to be true; yet nothing is too good to be true—I know that—if wrought out of pure material. The English use simple, straightforward, controlled words to express big fundamental things. "Decent" is one of them, and it means essential sportsmanship in life and living. Let us be "decent," friendly and, who knows, we may find, "out of all that remains," together, something finer and more potent for true happiness than anything that has yet come into our lives.

If you can open your mind to what is in mine — I could hardly say this to you if I were not fairly sure from your letter — free of any latent desire for misunderstanding, why can this not be?

It is my dearest wish. I shall compose myself for our meeting, when we first look really into each other's eyes, with a feeling of sacredness. It is something that belongs to you and me and no one else. Yet I wish Jack could know — trusting us both to shed our skins and stand out plain in sight of each other. Joan, Joan — how ridiculous otherwise!

I have so many things to ask you.

Please write me immediately, here. I may be gone on Sunday, for a few days.

This morning, having my slight breakfast on a sunny porch of this ramshackle old cottage, it seemed to me that the meadowlarks and mountain quail, instead of singing, were yelling, out of all bounds of harmony, as if they had something too good for restraint of rule of thumb! I wonder if they knew!

Charmian London.

# Charmian London

## Letter to Joan London (May 1925)

Joan, I'm glad you liked me. I liked you. And, best of all, I liked and like the way we came together: frankly, with perhaps some sentiment but no sentimentality. It was a big experience in its way, and I do feel that we have struck a note that may loom large to us both. Yes, we must be better acquainted. We haven't even started. In some ways it was and is easier for me than for you, because I am older, more experienced in the matters of history that concern us both. It was splendid, the way you let me talk to you; and I truly feel that you understand that I spoke without personal grudge or criticism, only in order to make clear to you what my attitude had been toward you, in one way or the other, as the years and circumstances fled by. For our mutual understanding now, I do not know any young woman, I am sure, who could have met it more fairly and squarely than you did. It is remarkable, and a great glory, if you can really "value, place, and keep that equilibrium" that is so necessary for you—and all of us. I think, as time goes by, we can be of help to each other—each in our separate sphere, bridged across with comprehension.

Always,
Charmian.

# Charmian London

## Letter to Ernest Untermann (1921)

My dear Ernest:[1]

There is nothing "dutiful" about my living up to Jack's memory. There is a deep and lasting making good for what I have had from him, if you want to put it that way. Jack was an unceasing wonder to me, and he shared with me every breath he drew. It would take me many a lifetime to express what I learned from him; he made me, in fact. I mean he made it possible for me to develop what I am now—such as I am.

My biggest compensation for the loss of him, is my utter independence. I know, you know, that just as soon as one even hints at letting down the barriers with the opposite sex, the possessive element begins to creep in. I know I couldn't stand it. I do not want a restraining finger on me. I may carry this too far; I may make mistakes. But they will be my mistakes. I know wonderful men; the men who would be my lovers now, are, in several instances, old friends of Jack's and mine, who are kind enough to think I'm a pretty good scout. But I have not yet seen any one for whom I could sacrifice one jot of my glorious freedom. If Jack hove in sight, bless him, I'd undoubtedly fall a slave to my great love for him. I am a REAL man's woman, Ernest; when I care for a man, I WANT to be a slave. But it's got to be "some" man, by gum! I couldn't stand the wear and tear of daily life with any man, howsoever splendid—and I know some who are—who has yet come into my vision. I do not think I could give again a real big love. And without that, I do not care to sacrifice too much of the comfort I find in my delightful aloneness, in wedlock or out of it. . . .

My marriage was a series of honeymoons; right up till the last. The woman who says that her husband "never spoke an unkind word to her in her life," or "Never did we know a moment's unhappiness," or "Never did we quarrel," is a fool and a liar, whether she knows it or not. Every married pair has its up and downs; most them DOWNS. But Jack and I, with our level spaces, always came together in recurrent madness. He could not believe it of himself. He

[189]

marveled at it. There was no hopelessness nor emptiness in our lives. Don't, for God's sake, Ernest, confuse George and Carrie with Jack and me. The cases are not analygous [*sic*].

I haven't time to write a book to you. Wait for the biography, Ernest. You'll have an eye opener. It's terribly frank; you'll be astounded at the latter part. I'm telling a lot of things, and indicating many more that the general public will not "get." I'm inclosing herewith my Preface. RETURN IT IMMEDIATELY. You'll get from it a sense of what it all meant to Jack and me. And the "little irks" of a long journey are not what counts. And there were so few.

On August 6, 1916, three months before Jack died, he gave me two books — one, *The Acorn Planter*, and the other *The Little Lady of the Big House*. In the former was written:

"Darlingest:

"You remember when I wrote this, you typed it; and we joy-sailed together on the good, old, dear, and forever dear, 'Roamer'?

"Husband-Mate,

Alias

"Jack London."

In the latter:

"Dearest Mate:

"The years pass. You and I pass. But yet our love abides — more firmly, more deeply, more surely, for we have built our love for each other, not upon the sand, but upon the rock.

"Your Lover-Husband,

"Jack London."

*The Turtles of Tasman* was the last book of his Jack ever saw. In it, a month before he died, he wrote:

"Dearest Mate:

"After it all, and it all, and it all, here we are, all in all, all in all.

"Sometimes I just want to get up on top of Sonoma Mountain and shout to the world about you and me.

"Arms ever around and around,

"Mate-Man."

Listen: At the present time, I have a lover who is very famous indeed.[2] If he keeps on, he will be nearly as famous as Jack, because, besides being an artist, he is a thinker, a live-wire. He is NOT an old friend; he is a comparatively new one. So, you see, I CAN command the worldly aspect of the situation, Ernest. But if I fell in love with a quite obscure person, who was all man, attractive to me, congenial to me, my famous name would mean absolutely nothing to me. I am NOT going to marry the famous man. I am not going to marry anybody, because I don't want to.

As for Jack's name, and being Jack's widow, my only interest in the worldly aspect of that is TO MAKE GOOD. A big name won't buy anything, unless one can back it up. I write under my own name. I am known under my own name. I make use of "Mrs. Jack London" just as Jack and I made use of his name together, to get us things. It is useful. But underneath that, it is only a name.

You don't know me at all, Ernest. Don't think I am egotistic when I say it would take a-many years to get to know me. I'm so various, and so much more various in this new, individual development of myself, that I don't know myself. I'm an awful proposition for myself to handle!

I haven't said half what I could; but I've written a terribly long letter. Read it "good and plenty," and THEN DESTROY IT. Or, better, RETURN IT TO ME. I often like to see what I have written on a given subject, long afterward.

Some day I may write a novel. It will be made up of what DIDN'T go into the Biography! Along with a lot of other things I know. Meantime, don't ever make any mistake that the love of Charmian and Jack London was at base one of the biggest things that ever happened.

Charmian.

**NOTES**

1. Ernest Untermann (1864–1956) was a German-born painter, seaman, journalist, and one of the founders of the Socialist Party of America. He was an old friend of the Londons and visited them frequently.

2. One of Charmian's lovers after Jack's death was Harry Houdini, whom she had met with Jack when he performed; Jack got to take the stage with him. After hosting Houdini and his wife at dinner at Saddle Rock, she wrote in her diary, "Charming Houdini. Shall never forget him." Labor, *Jack London*, 36–63.

# Charmian London

## Letter to Lorrin Thurston (1925)

This letter to Lorrin Thurston, editor of *The Honolulu Advertiser* and a close friend of the Londons in Honolulu, demonstrates that despite Thurston's outraged editorials against Jack when he published the Hawaiian stories of *The House of Pride* (1908), attacking the *haole kamaʻaina* elite in Honolulu over labor conditions and mentioning his trip to Molokai and the leper colony, they made up, and he remained a good friend when they visited in 1915 and 1916, as well as a friend to Charmian after her husband's death. Ironically, it was he who made arrangements for the Londons' trip to the Ewa side of Oahu together with Alexander Hume Ford and some dignitaries. That was where the indentured plantation workers were; it gave direct rise to the title story of *The House of Pride*.

Now that I am writing you, I'm going to mention something I want you to know: A new novel (Harper's) has lately appeared under the title HE WAS A MAN, by Rose Wilder Lane. It is a fictionalized biography of Jack. The biography was written by Mrs. Lane shortly after Jack's death, and we had a world of trouble about it—even to lawyers, though it did not come to trial. VERY briefly, the lady came to me, quite apparently, as it turned, on false pretenses to obtain material for an ARTICLE on Jack, for SUNSET MAGAZINE. A few days after she had been generously entertained and given all help to that end, she wrote me that she had misunderstood—it was a full biography she was expected to write. Like a fool (having listened to hard-luck story of this woman who had to earn her way, and being loath to stand in her way), I did NOT stop the writing of the biography right there. Imagine ME, with my already formulated, even started, life of my husband under way! So, being an idiot, I let it go ahead. The first issue of the SUNSET's serial brought Jack's sister to me with the seriousness of what I had allowed. Anyway, when later on she asked if I would allow her to publish the biography, I restrained and refrained and everything! The American publishers were afraid to touch it. I forgot England! First thing I knew while my London was feeling about for serial publication of *My Jack London*, Mrs. L's started to run in JOHN O'LONDON'S WEEKLY. Cables, inquiries, and so forth, from my publisher and agent!!! I then, to my distress, had to make known to them the whole painful story! Result, that her "life" came to an abrupt end in John O'London's, and that no publisher in the Empire dared to touch the book. I LOST MY SERIAL PUBLICATION IN ENGLAND ON ACCOUNT OF MRS. LANE. She lost her book publication, so, if one wants to look at it that way, we are even! But, LISTEN: She now takes her "life" and makes a novel of it which has stirred up much controversy. Some of our best reviewers and writers pronounce it "great," and all that. Personally, and quite without prejudice, I do not think it is great or anything like it. The lady is cold-blooded, you see, and that always tells. Other big critics are violently antagonistic to it, both as fiction and as a picture of Jack London—no matter what their individual opinion of Jack London! THAT is interesting, isn't it?

Harper's wanted me, evidently, to express myself about it, and sent the book to me—saying it was to appear shortly. It was already in the hands of all reviewers, and, I believe ALREADY ON THE BOOK STALLS. After consultation with Mrs. Shephard, one Assd. Press correspondent, and one famous writer who knows Mrs. Lane to his own sorrow (she claims co-authorship with him in a famous book, and a lawsuit is eating up the funds of both without coming to trial—dangerous lady, she!)—after consultation, I say, Mrs. Shephard (Jack's sister) and I decided to remain ABSOLUTELY MUM, as anything, especially anything antagonistic, would only boom the book—a consummation devoutly, etc., etc.

I do not know if your paper has already reviewed HE WAS A MAN. If not, I am wondering if your reviewer, whosoever he or she be, could be influenced in one particular—that as a PICTURE OF JACK LONDON, "He Was a Man" falls hard at the end in having him marry a woman of excessively alien blood—in view of Jack's almost rabid propaganda for pure human breeding. You see, Mrs. Lane has taken, say Anna Strunsky (Jack's old collaborator in KEMPTON-WACE LETTERS), who is a Russian Jewess, and myself as Jack's "love-woman," and rolled us two into one, and called it a Turk, or a Syrian, or both! It is to laugh. Anyway, it is a blatant weak spot in a life of Jack.

Always the same.

# Lloyd C. Griscom

### From *Diplomatically Speaking* (1940)

> Lloyd Carpenter Griscom (1872–1959) was an American diplomat and news-
> paper publisher; he was appointed Envoy Extraordinary and Minister Pleni-
> potentiary to Persia (Iran) and Japan, and was then appointed ambassador
> to Brazil and then Italy by Theodore Roosevelt. While serving as minister in
> Toyko, he was summoned to defend Jack London against arrest by the Japa-
> nese military and confiscation of his camera. Although other evidence sug-
> gests that London's fine for accidentally photographing a military site in Moji,
> Japan, was paid and that his camera was returned courtesy of the Japanese
> press who saw him as a fellow newspaperman, Griscom's version is more
> widely repeated.

By the end of February Japanese soldiers by the thousand were being trans-
ported to Korea, and there under General Kuoki were being assembled along
the Yalu River ready to invade Manchuria. . . .

Although the world was clamoring for news, a censorship of unparalleled
strictness blacked out all reports from the mainland. Hardly a day went by
without some veteran American newspaperman turning up at the Legation
and protesting, "Here, what is all this? I've been to the War Department and
they won't give me a pass to the front. It's preposterous. How's anybody
going to know about this war?"

I explained to Baron Komura that these fellow countrymen of mine represented the leading American papers, that upon their reports depended
American public opinion, and that nobody had ever tried to keep war correspondents away from the front before.

Baron Komura hemmed and hawed, mentioned military exigencies, said
Japanese success hinged on surprise, arrangements would be made as soon
as possible.

The correspondents were somewhat put out, but at first were satisfied to
wander all over Tokio with copies of Murray, collecting atmosphere, writing laudatory accounts of Japanese character, and describing Japanese gar-

dens, street scenes, personalities. Some took advantage of the delay to travel through the country, but again promptly encountered restrictions.

One day I had a frantic appeal from Jack London. He was in jail; I must have him released immediately. Investigation showed he, with his camera, had strayed by mistake into one of the fortified areas along the Inland Sea; and on my assurance that he intended no harm, the Japanese released him. However, he turned to Tokio sputtering with wrath because his valuable camera had been confiscated; he could not replace it; it was essential to his livelihood; a war correspondent without his camera was like a plumber without his tools.

On my next visit to Baron Komura, after I had gone through my other business, I brought up the matter of the London camera. He was in a rather irritated mood and said that he did not see how he could grant this request, but to make certain he would summon the legal counsel of the Foreign Office. I knew very well that when a Foreign Minister rang the bell for his legal adviser, it meant he needed support, and I would not get what I wanted.

The counsel arrived, an extremely clever lawyer, who, according to the quaint Japanese custom, had sat on the bench for many years to gain experience before being allowed to practice and have clients. As soon as the case was put to him he answered, "What you ask, Your Excellency, is absolutely forbidden. The statute declares that the weapon with which a crime has been committed becomes the property of the court."

"There you are," Baron Koumra said to me.

"Does that apply to every crime?" I asked the lawyer.

"Yes, to every crime of every description."

I turned to the Foreign Minister. "If I can name crime to which this does not apply, will you release the camera?"

Regarding me doubtfully for a few seconds, Baron Komura replied, "Yes, I will."

"What about rape?"

Baron Komura's Oriental stolidity dissolved in a shout of laughter. "That's a good one. Wait until Count Katsura hears it."

Later the Foreign Minister called me on the telephone. "Mr. Griscom, your story broke up the Cabinet meeting. Mr. London gets his camera back."

# Martin Johnson

## From *Through the South Seas with Jack London* (1913)

Martin Elmer Johnson (1884–1937) was a teenager fixing watches in his father's jewelry store in Independence, Kansas, when he read of Jack London's planned around-the-world cruise. In his initial letter he described himself as a "rolling stone" like the famous author, in search of adventure. Martin is the only crew member besides the Londons who stayed with the *Snark* for the entire two-year cruise. His skills with cameras and photography became useful to London, though his cooking remained a subject of jokes for many years. He stayed in touch with the Londons as he and his new wife, Osa, whom they saw several times, began their careers as travelers and filmmakers to exotic and often dangerous places, such as North Borneo, New Hebrides, the Solomon Islands, and Central Africa. They made numerous films and were the celebrity couple of their day, as Jack and Charmian had been in theirs. They were among the first wildlife cinematographers, producing numerous films. Martin's need to get close to wildlife in Africa helped with the invention of the telescopic lens. He toured a slide show about the *Snark* around the Midwest, wherein he sensationalized aspects of the voyage such as head-hunting and cannibalism. A large number of Martin's letters to Jack involve either begging for a loan or apologizing for not repaying one. After Jack's death, Martin often wrote to and visited Charmian; indeed, he was killed in a plane crash while flying with Osa to visit Charmian at the ranch. His wife, who was injured but survived the crash, wrote a memoir of their times together, *I Married Adventure* (1940).

## "On the Trail of Adventure"

In my native Independence, Kansas, I sat long hours in my father's jewelry store, and dreamed as I worked. I ranged in vision over all the broad spaces of a world-chart. In this dream-realm, there were no impediments to my journeying. Through long ice-reaches, across frozen rivers, over snow-piled mountains, I forced my way to the Poles. I skimmed over boundless tracts of ocean. Giant continents beckoned me from coast to coast. Here was an island, rearing its grassy back out of the great Pacific. My fancy invaded it. Or here was a lofty mountain-chain, over whose snow-capped summits I roamed at pleasure, communing with the sky. Then there were the valley-deeps; dropping down the steep descents on my mount, I explored their sheltered wonders with unceasing delight. Nothing was inaccessible. I walked in lands where queer people, in costumes unfamiliar, lived out their lives in ways which puzzled me, yet fascinated; my way led often amid strange trees and grasses and shrubs—their names unguessable. To the farthest limits of East and West I sallied, and North and South, knew no barriers but the Poles. I breathed strange airs; I engaged in remarkable pursuits; by night, unfamiliar stars and constellations glittered in the sky. It is so easy, traveling—on the map. There are no rigid limitations. Probabilities do not bother. Latitude and longitude are things unnoticed. . . .

I did my best to convince Mr. London that I was the man he needed. I told him all I could do, and some things I couldn't do, laying special stress on the fact that I had at one time made a trip from Chicago to Liverpool, London and Brussels, returning by way of New York with twenty-five cents of the original five dollars and a half with which I had started.

\*

The letter was long and detailed. It spoke of the ship, of the crew, of the plans—to use Mr. London's own words, it let me know just what I was in for.

There were to be six aboard, all-told. There were Jack and Mrs. London; Captain Roscoe Eames, who is Mrs. London's uncle; Paul H. Tochigi, a Jap cabin-boy; Herbert Stolz, an all-around athlete, fresh from Stanford University; and lastly, there was to be myself, the cook. We were to sail southern seas and northern seas, bays and inland rivers, lakes and creeks—anything navigable. And we were not to stop until we had circled the planet. We were to visit the principal countries of the world, spending from three to six months in every port. It was planned that we should not be home for at least seven years.

"It is the strongest boat ever built in San Francisco," ran the letter. "We could go through a typhoon that would wreck a 15,000-ton steamer. . . . Practically, for every week that we are on the ocean, we will be a month in port. For instance, we expect that it will take us three weeks to sail from here to Hawaii, where we expect to remain three months—of course, in various portions of the Islands.

"Now as to the crew: All of us will be the crew. There is my wife, and myself. We will stand our watches and do our trick at the wheel. . . . When it comes to doing the trick at the wheel, I want to explain that this will not be arduous as it may appear at first. It is our intention, by sail-trimming, to make the boat largely sail herself, without steering. Next, in bad weather, there will be no steering, for then we will be hove-to. But watches, or rather lookouts, must be kept at night, when we are sailing. Suppose we divide day and night into twelve hours each. There are six of us all-told on the boat. Each will take a two-hour turn on deck.

"Of course, when it comes to moments of danger, or to doing something ticklish, or to making port, etc. the whole six of us will then become the crew. I will not be a writer, but a sailor. The same with my wife. The cabin-boy will be a sailor, and so also, the cook. In fact, when it's a case for all hands, all hands it will be.

". . . Incidentally, if you like boxing, I may tell you all of us box, and we'll have the gloves along. You'll have the advantage of us on reach. Also, I may say that we should all of us have lots of good times together, swimming, fishing, adventuring, doing a thousand-and-one things."

\*

My thoughts kept constantly turning upon the man whom I was journeying to meet. What sort of being was he, that had compelled the attention of the world by the magic of his pen, and by the daring of his exploits? One thing I knew. The places I had roamed in fancy, his foot had trod in reality. And he had sailed over the seas. In '97, he was a gold-seeker in the far North. He had been a sailor and a tramp, an oyster-pirate, a Socialist agitator, and a member of the San Francisco Bay fish-patrol. His voyages up to this time had carried him far over the earth, and his experiences would overlap the experiences of an ordinary man a score of times and more. Above all, he was a student, and a writer of world-wide celebrity. Wherever civilized men congregated, wherever books were read, the name of Jack London was familiar. . . .

When I rapped at the door, a neat little woman opened it, and grabbing my hand, almost wrung it off.

"Come right in," cried Mrs. London. "Jack's waiting for you."

At that moment a striking young man of thirty, with very broad shoulders, a mass of wavy auburn hair, and a general atmosphere of boyishness, appeared at the doorway, and shot a quick, inquisitive look at me from his wide grey eyes. Inside, I could see all manner of oars, odd assortments of clothing, books, papers, charts, guns, cameras, and folding canoes, piled in great stacks upon the floor.

"Hello, Martin," he said, stretching out his hand.

"Hello, Jack," I answered. We gripped.

And that is how I met Jack London, traveller, novelist, and a social reformer; and that is how, for the first time, I really ran shoulder to shoulder with Adventure, which I had been pursuing all my days.

\*

## "The Building of the 'Snark'"

There was much protest from the Londons' friends. Many freely expressed the sentiment that they could not see how sensible people would even think of such a trip. And they all knew, with profound certitude, that we were to be drowned. But we paid very little attention to their ominous head-shakings and pessimistic predictions. We who were setting out in search of Adventure were not to be balked by mere words. Also, a number of Jack's Socialist friends wrote letters, urging him to abandon what they evidently considered folly. On every side of us, the conviction was openly aired that we were on our way to the bottom of the sea.

\*

During my long stay in Oakland, I had ample opportunity to get intimately acquainted with both Jack and Mrs. London; indeed, we were all like one big happy family. Fame and popularity have not spoiled them. Jack is just like a big schoolboy, good-natured, frank, generous, and Mrs. London is just a grown-up schoolgirl. They are good comrades, always helping each other in their work. Mrs. London I found to be as full of grit as any of us — as we were later to discover, there was hardly a thing on board that any of the men could do that she couldn't do; and she was a practised swimmer, and could ride on horseback with grace — a gift not vouchsafed all women. And they were both amiable Bohemians.

\*

Daylight broke at last. That 23rd of April, 1907, I shall never forget. Thousands came to the wharf to bid us good-bye and to wish us a pleasant and successful voyage. Photographers from a popular western magazine took what they announced would be the last views of the *Snark* and her crew. Among the dozens of telegrams I received was one from an Independence friend, which read: "Good-bye, Hope I may see you again." Surrounded by hundreds of people who were prophesying that we would never reach Honolulu, this telegram was a rather gruesome sound to me. Strangely enough, I never did see this friend again. I did not meet my death in the water, but he did. He drowned in one of the rivers near Independence.

Among those who came down to say the farewells were many members of the Bohemian Club of San Francisco, to which Jack belonged. There were writers and artists and newspaper men. George Sterling and James Hopper were on hand, as was also Martinez, the artist. Mrs. London's friends came in a body. Then there were Oakland Elks, and San Francisco Elks, and friends of Tochigi, and Bert's friends, and all the friends of the Eameses, and other who came merely out of curiosity to see the world famous author and his crew sail off in one of the most unique little boats that ever rode the waves.

It was a beautiful, bright, sunshiny day when we passed out of the Golden Gate, with hundreds of whistles tooting us a farewell salute, passed the seal Rocks, and turned her bow to the westward. My duties on the smallest boat, with only one or two exceptions, that ever crossed the Pacific Ocean, had begun; but instead of getting busy cooking meals, I sat in the stern looking gloomily toward the land, which was the last I would see of good old American soil for nearly three years. I was thinking of the friends and the home I was leaving, and wondering if we were really bound for the bottom of the sea as so many had foretold; and I could not altogether down a feeling that I would just a little rather be on the full-rigged ship that passed us on her way into the harbor. But on the *Snark* I was and on the *Snark* I must remain. Gloomy dreams soon ended, and we settled down to life on the high seas. So it was that we put forth into the wide Pacific, in a mere cork of a boat, without a navigator, with no engineer, no sailors, and, for that matter, no cook. This lack of a cook did not bother much just then, however, for soon we were all too seasick to care to eat.

When night came, land was out of sight, darkness wrapped us about on every side, and the *Snark* rose and fell rhythmically, the sport of every wave.

### "On the High Seas"

The galley or kitchen of the *Snark* was tucked away to one side, and was not large enough for two small men to enter, close the door, and then turn around. As a matter of fact, if I was handling a dish of any size, I had to back out of the door to turn around, myself. For the first meal, I decided that I would try some fried onions, a nice roast with dressing, some vegetables, and some pudding; so I got out about a half-peck of onions, and by the time I had finished peeling those onions in the little galley, I decided that onions were all that was needed for that meal. Did you ever peel onions in a kitchen cupboard? That is practically what I was doing. My eyes were watering so that I couldn't see, and my nostrils and throat were burning so that I couldn't talk. The entire crew was kind enough to say that they liked onions, anyway.

Tochigi served the dinner, and we all ate. Then I made for my bunk, feeling, as Captain Eames put, "rather white around the gills." As soon as Tochigi had served the dinner, he got out his flute, and as the last note died away, rushed precipitately up on deck and relieved his deathly sickness at the rail. Mrs. London speedily joined him. But Jack and Bert and Captain Eames were as yet unaffected.

The boat was leaking like a sieve. Yes, the *Snark*, the famous *Snark*, that had cost thirty thousand dollars, that had been built by expert shipbuilders, and that was declared the tightest craft afloat, leaked! The sides leaked, the bottom leaked; we were flooded. Even the self-bailing cockpit quickly filled with water that could find no outlet. Our gasoline, stored in non-leakable tanks and sealed behind an air-tight bulkhead, began to filter out, so that we hardly dared to strike a match. The air was full of the smell of it. I got up from my bunk, staggering sick. Bert started the five-horse-power engine, which controlled the pumps, and by this means managed to get some of the sea out of our quarters below.

At intervals, I was obliged to spend some necessary moments at the rail. The rail was only a foot high; one was obliged to crouch down on deck, clinging tightly, and lean far out, confronted ever by the stern face of the waves. The unutterable, blank sickness of such moments it is beyond the province of words to portray.

Never had I known anything like it! My head ached, my stomach ached, every muscle in my body ached. There were times when it seemed impossible that I should live. When the sickness was at its height, I was blind, deaf, and—need I say it?—dumb. All stabilities were shattered. The universe itself was rocking and plunging through the cold depths of space. And then, for a brief instant, the sickness would subside, and sight and speech and hearing return, and I knew I was on the *Snark*, the plaything of the waves, and that I, the most desperate of living creatures, was gurgling and babbling my troubles to the uncaring sea. Later, it was laughable, but ye gods! at the time laughter was a stranger to my soul.

It did not ease matters much to discover that the water pouring into the boat had ruined the tools in the engine room, and spoiled a good part of three months' provisions in the galley. Our box of oranges had been frozen; our box of apples was mostly spoiled; the carrots tasted of kerosene; the turnips and beets were worthless; and last, but not least, our crate of cabbages was so far gone in decay that it had to be thrown overboard. As for our coal, it had been delivered in rotten potato-sacks, and in the swinging and thrashing of the ship had escaped, and was washing through the scuppers into the ocean. We found that the engine in the launch was out of order, and that our cherished life-boat leaked as badly as did the *Snark*. In one respect, however, I was especially marked out for discomfort. I had the misfortune to be somewhat taller than any of the rest; and so low was the ceiling of the galley and the staterooms downstairs that I could never stand upright, but was obliged to stoop. The only place where I could be really comfortable was on deck, and even here things were so tightly packed that there never was room for a promenade.

We didn't discover all our handicaps at once. It took about a week for us to see all there was to see, and to get acquainted with our little floating home. One of our greatest drawbacks was the fact that never for a moment could we let go of one hold unless we were assured of another. To have let go would have meant being jerked off our feet and thrown sprawling until we fetched up against something stout enough to check the fall. Circus gymnastics is as nothing compared with it. I have seen many acrobatic feats, but nothing resembling in mad abandon the double handspring Mrs. London turned one day when her hand missed its hold and she landed down the companionway in the middle of the table, on top of a dinner which I had just cooked, and which Tochigi was serving.

*

The next day found us in a fierce sea. We were all soaked with water. Indeed, it was impossible to step on deck without getting wet. Great waves, many times higher than the *Snark*, kept sweeping down as if to swamp us, but always we slid along the top of them, seeing for miles around; then would come the dive down into the slough, where everything was blotted from view but a wild swirl of waters. It was next to impossible to cook. Dishes defied all laws of gravitation, and skimmed like birds through the air; and the stove was a sight, what of the things that slopped over it. We were covered with bruises from being thrown up against the vessel. Mrs. London made another aerial descent of the companionway that night, but was only slightly bruised. Captain Eames scraped the skin off his head in the course of one tumble. I got my punishment in burns from the stove. Far above, in the tropic sky, the lightning flashed and the thunder rolled. Lightning had an awful significance to the crew of the *Snark*. We were far out at sea; the copper and other metals would tend to draw the current, and had a spark ever reached us, and ignite the eleven hundred gallons of gasoline on board, there wouldn't have been a splinter left to tell the tale.

Like all sailors, we did not love the sea. It was the eternal menace. Looking upon its placid surface in moments of calm, we could almost forget that it was forever yawning, and that into its maw had gone many a brave ship, of greater tonnage than ours. But in raging storms, with the lightning shooting in fiery lines across the sky, and the artillery of heaven rumbling and banging overhead and echoing on the storm-lashed waves, we came to appreciate the true meaning of things, and to assign to earth and sky and sea the proper values. At such moments, I repeat, we did not love the sea; but we did love the *Snark*. Its ten tons of wood and metal stood between us and destruction. It made life possible to us. It was in such reflections as these, miles and miles from any land, that the words of Jack London rang again in my ears: "Life that lives is life successful. The achievement of a difficult feat is successful adjustment to a sternly exacting environment."

\*

### "The Long Traverse"

We did not know what to do. We had been forty-five days out of the Sandwich Islands, had not sighted any land or a sail, and were in the uncertain doldrums and not half-way to the Marquesas Islands. Jack immediately ordered the remaining ten gallons of water put under lock and key, and one quart of water per day was our allowance.

One has no idea how small an amount a quart is until he is put on such an allowance. Before the middle of the afternoon, we would have our water drunk. Our thirst raged. It grew worse because we knew there was nothing to assuage it. At meals, when tins of provisions were opened, we tried to buy each other's share of the liquid from the can. . . .

How we longed for rain! None came. At last, after nearly a week, we saw a storm blowing up, and black clouds gathering. Here was promise! We rigged lines on either side, between the main and mizzen riggings, and from this spread out the large deck awning, so disposed that it would catch and pour into a barrel as much water as possible. The storm swept on toward us. We gazed at it with parted lips. Gallons of water were descending a few hundred yards away from us, and the heart of the squall was making directly for us, while we stood there and exulted. And then, to our infinite disappointment and dismay, the squall split, and the two parts drew off away from us.

Twelve hundred miles from land, and no water!

Death leered at us from the dark sea. There seemed no possible chance for us. And what did Jack London do?

Almost dead with thirst himself, he went into his cabin and wrote a sea story about a castaway sailor that died of thirst while drifting in an open boat. And when he had finished it he came out, gaunt and haggard, but with eyes burning with enthusiasm, and told us of the story and said:

"Boys, that yarn's one of the best I ever did!"

That night a heavy, soaking tropical rain came on; we spread the awning again and filled our water tanks; and as the big barrel ran over the gurgling water, Jack said:

"I'll not kill that sailor; I'll have him saved by a rain like this; that'll make the yarn better than ever!"

That water was the best we ever tasted. We couldn't deny it. After seeing that we had a good supply, we set all the sail we could crown on the boat and crossed the Equator. When the sun rose the next morning, and we awoke for the day's duties, we knew we were out of the doldrums.

\*

*Friday, December 6, 1907.* — Midnight. We are anchored in the prettiest bay I ever imagined. But let me begin at the first. My brain is so full of things to write that I know I will never do them justice, for I have not the time or paper. Early this morning captain awoke us with "Land ahoy!" and in the quickest time anyone ever got on deck we were trying to make out in the hazy atmosphere *land*. At last we succeeded. Ua-huka was straight ahead, and away in the distance could be seen the ragged crags of Nuka-hiva, the island we were heading for. How good those big green mountains looked! Only men who had been sixty days on the sea could appreciate the scene. In a few hours we were within three miles of Ua-huka, seven miles long and thirty-three hundred feet high. It looked like a big rock. Soon Nuka-hiva loomed up straight ahead. It seemed as if we were in another world as we sailed past several low cocoanut islands, sometimes going so close that with glasses we could see villages of grass houses, and we knew that at last we were in the real South Sea islands.

By five o'clock we could make out the two sentinel rocks, between which we must go to get into the bay. It was nearly midnight as we sailed up the coast of Nuka-hiva. A fine bright moon had been shining earlier in the evening; but just as we sighted the opening of the bay (called Taiohae Bay on the chart), a squall struck us and we were in the most dangerous position we had ever been caught in: rocks and reefs on every side, so we could not turn back. We did the only thing possible—drove right for the place of which we had sighted the opening, and left to luck that we would find it. Luck was with us. We sailed in the opening, just missing a large, rocky island at its mouth. We passed so close that thousands of sea-birds were sent crying and frightened off their rocky perch. After getting inside the bay, the mountains on every side shut off the storm, and the wind dropped so low that we were an hour getting from the mouth of the bay to the upper end, where the water was shallow enough for anchoring. At last we are at anchor. It seems that we must be in paradise. The air is perfume. We can hear the wild goats blatting in the mountains, and an occasional long-drawn howl from a dog ashore. It is so near morning now that the cocks are crowing; and we are so proud of ourselves for doing what the Sailing Directions said was impossible, and so happy at seeing land again! Well, now we shall get a much-needed rest.

\*

### "In the Marquesas"

Finally, we came to a clearing where the old village of Typee had once stood. But now only the foundations of the buildings of this once strong tribe remained to show where they had been. The cocoanut trees we found growing in the fantastic arrangement that Melville had spoken of, but the natives were gone. Everything was quiet except the chirping of the birds, and the rustling of palm-leaves. We rode on until we came to a frame house that had been built by a trader, but he had left, and now a family of natives lived in this old house on the edge of Faiaways Lake. How delightful this little lake looked, with the background of mountains, but how sad this one family! When we came to them and asked for a drink of water, the woman brought a large gourd full to the brim, and as she extended it, we saw upon her flesh the curse of the islands, leprosy. The man came out, dragging a big heavy foot behind him. He had elephantiasis, and the children that played in the yard showed signs of leprosy.

Perhaps we should have gone back without seeing any more of the Typee tribe, had not the girls urged us on. We shortly came to another clearing — the new village of the valley. Here we found about twenty grass houses and perhaps fifty or seventy-five people, all that remained of the once strongest tribe in the Marquesas Islands.

About thirty years ago, there were six thousand natives in this valley, with nearly as many in the opposite valley of Hapaa. But the two tribes were continually at war, until the Hapaa tribe was totally exterminated. Then came ships in search of sandalwood and copra, and came also missionaries. With them they managed to bring leprosy and elephantiasis, and a venereal disease that, in the tropics, is worse than either of the others. As a result, the native hosts are gone, and only the few remain. Still, these people we saw looked healthy enough, though here and there we could see a leper lurking in the background.

Better had it been had the natives never seen the missionaries. What happened in the Marquesas has happened in many other South Sea islands, and no doubt is happening to-day. My conscience smote me. To think, the very pennies I had given in Sunday School for foreign missions had contributed to the calamitous end of the inhabitants of this beautiful garden spot!

But the great attraction for the natives was our graphophone.[1] When evening fell, they came about us in swarms to hear the playing, and they could never get over the belief that we had a little dwarf caged in the "talk-box." At times, there would be as many as two hundred brown people squatting on the grass, and they would never leave until we stopped the graphophone. In the Hawaiian Islands, we had secured records of *hula-hula* music, which so delighted the Marquesans that sometimes we would have half a hundred dancing in front of the machine. . . .

These natives are considerably larger than the average white person. Their skin is a light brown colour; their hair is thick, straight and black. Dark eyes and eyelashes make them appear a fine, handsome race. The only unfortunate thing is their tendency to age so soon. At fifteen the girls are fully developed women, and at twenty-eight or -nine they are old women. They seem to have no vitality; though they look strong and healthy, if one were told that he was going to die, and had the idea impressed on his mind, he would be sure to lie down and die.

*

## "South Sea Cannibals"

[Malaita] *Tuesday, June 30, 1908.* — Again this morning we traded with natives until we are wondering where we will put the things. About one hundred spears alone are hard to pack away. After lunch, Jack, Mrs. London, and I went ashore in the launch. As we could not get clear up to the beach, Tehei had to carry us out of the boat. We had our guns strapped on, and carried four kodaks. We went up to the trader's house. Imagine our surprise to find a whole beachful of naked girls. Absolutely naked. Jack looked at me and then at Mrs. London, and I looked back at them. Each was anxious to see how the others would act. But these people did not appear sensual or unnatural at all. They were just like animals. We each turned our eyes shoreward and tried to look unconcerned and as if we had been used to such things all our lives. We sat on the porch and talked with the trader, while the girls got us cocoanuts. These girls, from ten to twenty years of age, had a few strings of beads around their waists, some had a single string hanging in front, and there were anklets and armlets and necklaces; but of garments to hide their nakedness there was nothing at all. Some of them were not bad looking, save for the black pointed teeth and hideously red lips. I was told the teeth were coloured by chewing the betel-nut. With Peter guiding us, we tramped around a quarter of a mile to the village, a hundred natives in the path ahead and a hundred behind. And we kept our hands on our guns all the time, for this would be a fine place for the islanders to get some *kai-kai* (food) for a cannibal banquet. And I have little doubt that our heads are vastly coveted.

At length, we came to a log bridge, over a shallow stream of water. Mrs. London was not allowed to go over—she must wade through, as this bridge is taboo to women. Jack could not resist chaffing Mrs. London, for up to this time she has been treated like a lady by the natives we have come in contact with, but here a woman is only a woman, and has none of the rights of men.

[207]

Poor Mrs. London was humiliated, but Jack enjoyed it. We came into the village. Men and women too old and feeble to walk would peep at us through their grass houses. We came upon a mammoth grass house, facing the sea. This place was as large as a good-sized store-room. From the front protruded the ends of war canoes. We wanted to see them better; but Mrs. London was again stopped, and in company with Peter, Jack and I went inside and inspected two canoes large enough to hold fifty men each, and a dozen smaller ones. These were the war canoes, used only for the fighting. At the rear of the house was a large coffin-shaped grass box. We looked in, then stepped back in horror; and holding our noses, Jack and I beat a hasty retreat, for inside the box was the body of a man, looking like a pin-cushion, so full was he with barbs. Peter told us that he was the best king that ever ruled them, that he had been dead a week, and that the points in his body were the arrow points used in their envenomed arrows. Everyone knows that a dead body contains the most virulent poison in the world. By steeping their arrow-points in a chief's body, they think that the poison will be more effective. I bought one hundred and fifty of these arrows. But I shall have to be careful how I touch them.

As we passed out, we saw several old men squatted in front of the house, making hollow wooden fishes by the use of stone axes. We were told by Peter that these men were chiefs, and that after they die their bodies will be allowed to putrify. Then, after the arrow-points have been poisoned in their decaying flesh, their bones will be put in one of the hollow fishes and set on a shelf in the canoe-house, where we saw about a hundred such fishes. The old men were making their own coffins.

We went through the village, which is closed in by a fence of small sticks woven together. The houses touch one another, so that the whole village covers only a few acres, with streets about ten feet wide. In a small square at the centre stand tall carved images. At the foot of the village, in a small enclosure about twenty feet square, they showed us the graveyard. Everybody goes into the same hole. The pit is simply opened up, the body tossed in, and then it is covered over again. Scores of naked women and children followed us about, and large men with clubs and spears. I really did not feel any too safe. They showed us another boat house in which rested a big log-fish, filled with the bones of chiefs. I made photographs of the women and men. Jack made head studies. . . .

All these cannibals are head-hunters. One may see tiny mummified heads stuck up outside the huts. The more heads a man has, the stronger he imagines himself to be. .... The bones are all drawn out, and then the head is dried until it is only the size of one's fist. To possess the head of a white man is a special honour. A village with a white man's head considers that it has a wonderful talisman. Naturally, we took great care not to become luck-bringers for any of the natives among whom we sojourned.

Some years ago, a party of German scientists landed at Malaita, one of the most inaccessible islands in the group, to explore. They very much wanted to take back some of these heads as relics, and offered fifteen sticks of plug tobacco for each. The market was brisk for a few days, but soon all the posts outside the huts had been stripped, and the supply slackened. Then suddenly trade revived again—but it was noticed that the heads brought in were fresh! It turned out that the natives had been doing a little private killing in order to keep up the supply. One native had sacrificed several relatives in his desire to please the Germans and get their tobacco.

**NOTE**

1. The graphophone was invented by Alexander Graham Bell in 1886 as an improvement on the phonograph.

# Martin Johnson

## Letter to Jack and Charmian London (1909)

Dear Mr. & Mrs. London:

Have not heard from you since I started the Snark Theatre, and have been afraid all along that you would not like my idea of running this theatre.

A prominent druggist in Independence was so taken with the idea that my experience around the world would make a drawing card in this part of the country, that he closed out his store and we have built the finest little theatre in this state. And for the boat have as near an exact duplicate of the Snark bow as it was possible to build here in the interior, where the carpenters never saw a ship.

The enclosed book will explain better than I can what my talks are and everyone I give is an advertisement for you, it never seemed possible that this trip could of taken the interest it has and every man, woman and child in this country is interested in the trip.

Some things in these travelogues my partner Mr. Kerr insisted on me giving that I did not want to but they are not what they would seem in the pamphlet—for instance in the table on Molokai I quote your article on the island and explain what leprosy is and how it is caught, Tuamotus, I tell of Stevenson's experience there and of the Pearl Fisheries that make their headquarters in Papeete.

Near Death's Door is the experience Tehei had when wrecked in the Tuamotus.

Eating human flesh I quote from Woodford's (what's his name at Tuleai) book about "A Naturalist among the Head Hunters." (I've just ordered about twenty books on the South Seas.)[1]

The slides I am having made by a photographer here who I know and who gives me the negatives and I color most of them myself with the help of a girl here, I have sent to Beattie in Tasmania for all the photographs that he has of the islands and sent to Honolulu for photos from there. After I have shown these slides I keep them listed here at home and if you ever want any of them you can have them, you see there is no possible chance of them being used by anyone else.

And you may not credit it, as I did not when my father wrote me the same thing, but your books are being read in nearly every home in the country and your articles in the *Pacific Monthly* will sell more of that magazine than anywhere else in the United Sates.

Your curiosities I have packed and will send next week. And on account of not putting any money in the show (I had more to put in) I will not get any until $700 has been put in the bank in order to make me a half partner, then I will get half the profits, we have put $200 clear profit in the bank in the last ten days so before Christmas I will send you part or all of what I owe you.

You see this is the one chance I will get to make some money and at the rate we are going I will make good money this winter.

You promised to pay me a visit as soon as you had time after you got home and if you will come and spend Xmas with me, I'll do all I can to show you one of the best times, it would be possible to show you in a state where it does not rain all the time, you can have plenty of room to work and not be disturbed. And I'll give you my room full of curios and pictures that every person in this country is surveying.

Am sending a clipping from today's paper and as soon as I get time I'll send a whole of them.

=A, NII I= [*sic*] was with me for a couple of days—says he staid with you for a several days in the summer. It's queer that neither you or I ever spoke of him while on the trip—for I have known him before I started with you.[2]

Well until next time I'll knock off—give my regards to all my friends—and write me that you are coming this way soon.

> Yours,
> Martin

I've got the promise from the Pathé Frères Moving Picture Company of the pictures made by Sutto in the Solomons and they will be good to show and explain in any part of the U.S.[3]

> M.

## NOTES

1. *A Naturalist among the Head-Hunters: Being an Account of Three Visits to the Solomon Islands in the Years 1886, 1887, and 1888* (1890) was written by Charles Morris Woodford.

2. Leon Ray Livingston (1872–1944), also known as "A No. 1," one of America's best-known tramps, wrote several books about his tramping including one (mostly fictionalized) about Jack London.

3. Martin worked with the Pathé Frères film company in the South Seas to shoot footage for a film with London in it. The film was made—*Jack London's Adventures in the South Sea Islands* (1913)—but has been lost.

# Martin Johnson

## Letter to Jack and Charmian London (1911)

Dear Mr. and Mrs. London:

I just received your autographed copy of the *Cruise of the* Snark and I can not thank you enough for it as it now furnishes me actual proof to

Snark and I can not thank you enough for it as it now furnishes me actual proof to skeptical people that I am not lying to them when I tell them of the South Sea Islands—you know many of the people we saw and many of our adventures would sound a little fishy to tell and some times people say perhaps I am lying but now comes your book and it will from now on be my bible for proof.

We have been showing up here in Canada for nearly six months now and have been doing fine—some nights I have made as high as $150.00 for myself and have never showed in a town that I did not make money—so far we have given Travelogues in 204 towns and cities, now when we quit the "Snark"... — perhaps you will censor me for this but I did not know how far we were in debt until we started winding up the affairs of the shows and as my father was safe, it naturally put him in a bad way, now I am nearly out of debt to the bank—they had the notes of a six months time and it was all we could do to get them to extend again, but at the end of the second six months as I had paid up so much of the original bill they consented to another renewal and now I have three months more to clear the rest in, but as my father is expecting a big Christmas trade I think he can attend to the remainder if I do not have it by then.

We will be in Chicago in about three weeks to get a try out on the Orpheum vaudeville circuit, if we make it we will get 90 weeks straight time at $250.00 a week—if we make good money anyway—but I know we have a show good enough for the Orpheum people to feature—the only trouble we might have is that we have no pull and the Orpheum time is mostly secured through pull.

Now we will go home to rest up for a month during Christmas and if we possibly can I want to come out to Glen Ellen right after New Years—or if you are needing a vacation why not come and spend Christmas with us in Independence—I have a dandy place to put you at home, where you could keep right on with your work with out interference.

Now I know you would like to tell me where you stand and I stand in regards to what I owe you and I would like to know exactly what I owe you, and as I don't want to discourage Osa in her work write me a letter at once without your letter head to some fictitious name as I will give below, I can then get the letter without any one knowing about it.

Any way you can rest assured that you will get all I owe you and interest too as soon as I am sure my father is clear from the clutches of the bank—while I feel mean every time I think of what I owed you you must own that my first duty is to my father. Of course another way to look at it I would never have the advantages that I have if it had not been for you.

Martin

# Martin Johnson

## Letter to Jack and Charmian London (1912)

Dear Jack and Charmian:

Now folks I will need a big enlargement of the Snark, and I want to enlarge several of the pictures that I am using in slides, these pictures are all for lobby display, then I must have something to fill out my men only show for I have not enough and it means big money to me to get it in good shape and I want something that I know you put a high value on but I want them bad, in fact if I can't get them it will seriously cripple my new show, you know I can't fake so much in New York for some one is liable to catch me and I have got to have everything strictly South Sea Island.

I want you to send me every South Sea negative we made since the Snark was built, also the album of Samoan girls (nude studies), I still have about twelve of the men only film that I got while I was in California and the head sail picture that you sent me, these pictures are in Chicago now having slides made from them, I had quite a bit of trouble getting them made up for the slides I had made in Kansas City were so poor that I would not take them, and then I sent the picture into New York and they sent them back saying that they had nothing but girls doing their work and they could not do the men only kind, then I found a man doing slide work in Chicago and he is working on them now.

Now if you dislike to send these pictures to me, just think what a big thing it means to me and I believe you will let me have them, I will take the best of care of them and I will also pay you the remainder I owe right away in the spring as soon as things are running smooth. I don't mean this as a bribe but these pictures will help me get the money a great deal quicker.

Another way you can figure it out the pictures will help you a little for every show is an advertisement to Jack.

I expect you think I am taking quite a little trouble in squaring this but I want the pictures so bad that I want you to see just how bad.

If you feel that you can send the pictures to me, have Nakata bundle them up in a little box and send to me Collect, I will have the enlargements made in Indianapolis and send the negative in to Chicago for slides and then inside of two weeks from when I receive them I will return them all to you in good condition. I will not return them in installments but all in the original packages just as you sent them to me.

Excuse this poor typewriter ribbon, this town is so small that I don't suppose I could get another and will wait until I get to Indianapolis.

If you send the pictures at once I will get them when I get into Indianapolis.

Martin

# Martin Johnson

## Letter to Charmian London (1917)

Dear Charmian:

After three days in Noumea, a day in the Loyalty Islands we arrived in Vila yesterday and the "Pacifique" dropped anchor within fifty feet of the Snark.—Our poor old Snark—she had just been raised after having been under the water for two months—in a former wreck her stern had been crushed in so it was chopped off into an ugly shape—our fine cockpit was gone—the fine diamond screw steering gear was gone and in its place a rusty chair apparatus—everything below was gutted out—the gasoline tanks—the engine room—the bathroom—the gallery—cabins, etc—nothing below except a big dirty hold—on deck everything is gone—the bows have been stove in and repaired so that the word "Snark" cannot be seen. And the stations where I labored with brass tacks in making designs are gone—But worst of all I missed the cockpit where we spent such happy days—and strange to say she lay abrupt exactly where we did nine years ago.

We lay in Vila one day—and I went around mad at everyone—I do not know just why, but I knew our old Snark had been mistreated and some one was to blame—I do not know where—Osa and myself looked for old remembrances but could find but few.

We are now going to Ayr, where we will see Donald Frazen, then to Malekula—Santo—Ambrym, then south to Erromongo and Tanna to my old friend Rev. Watt (?).

Osa sends love. Excuse haste as we are leaving the ship in an hour to go abroad a schooner.

The enclosed pictures were only placed in Hypo so it will fade, but I have made several pictures of the Snark—in a month when we make Vila again on our way south I will make more pictures of her when she is in better repair.

Martin.

# Martin Johnson

## Letter to Charmian London (1932)

Dear Charmian:

I received your letter a couple of weeks ago—and Osa's letter arrived yesterday, but have delayed writing because I thought I might have some news about our next trip to California, but so far don't know just where I stand. Am afraid we may have to remain here all summer, for the theatrical season is nearly over, and it is probable that we will have to stay here in New York for the opening of "Congorilla"[1] and then tour with it in the fall, although Osa and I are both anxious to get back home to Nairobi. However, we have put everything we have into this film and must get it back.

Your several mentions of the Snark cause me to sit back in my chair and dream over our glorious adventure—the most wonderful time of my life, but kid like, I'm afraid I could not realize it then, at least the full value of it. Of all the adventure I've had since then, and any I may have in the future, nothing will ever equal the Snark voyage. Why, I doubt if anyone ever had the good times that we had, and honestly, Charmian, I think of getting the money to pay for the trip, the worry of the crew, two years of sailing through those glorious South Seas! And I had you and Jack for companions! You never made me feel like one of the crew; and you can never realize what your influence did for me—made everything possible in later years.

Then I wrote that fool, inconsistent letter to Jack just before he died. I didn't give it much thought at the time for I didn't realize what a fool I was.

IF I had money now, I would like to buy the old Snark, even if it is a wreck. I would fix it up again just as we had it—then loaf again in the South Seas—you, Osa and I.

Gosh! When I think of the great time I had living on the Snark at Hunters Point, and at the foot of the Atlas Machine Works in the Oakland Estuary—the nights when the tide would go out and the Snark would lay over in the mud, and I slept on the side of the hull—the things I cooked for my meals—the hours with the old whalers who were then watchmen on the old whaling hulks laid up in the Estuary—the poker games with you and Jack, George Sterling and Dick Partington, and the rest of your crowd—that rainy night I arrived in Oakland in the midst of a poker game—and—oh Hell! I'm getting to be a sentimental old fool.

But Charmian, it was all wonderful; a young, healthy fellow—big adventure.

And now I must keep a stenographer to answer all the thousands of letters that come from boys (and girls) who want to go adventuring with Osa and me. I answer them all for I remember it was just such a letter as these boys write to me, that I wrote to you and Jack which made it possible for me to make the Snark voyage. Gosh! How I hate to turn down these youngsters who want the opportunity to do just what I did!

I'd better stop before I blub all over the paper—it's a beautiful spring day out and I'm feeling sorry for myself. It was never intended that I sit at a desk.

I hope Osa answers your letter soon, but don't look too hard for it. She is the world's champion rotten letter writer. One letter a year is a very good average for her. However, she did ask me to send her love when I wrote.

I'll write you all about "Congorilla" when it gets started to a good opening.

As ever,
Martin Johnson

**NOTE**

1. *Congorilla* was a film made by Osa and Martin Johnson based on some of their African experiences.

# Osa Johnson

## From *I Married Adventure* (1940)

Osa Helen Leighty Johnson (1894–1953) and her husband Martin Johnson were international celebrity travelers and photographers originally from Kansas. They were good friends of Jack and Charmian's and frequent visitors to the ranch. In 1912 the young husband, recalling his *Snark* days, told her that they were leaving for the Solomon Islands, where they returned to make several films. Though on their first visit Osa was seized by islanders as directed by their chief, they returned to the United States and showed their film *Captured by Cannibals* to astonished audiences. Their collaborations included travel, exhibits, slide lectures, and films. Flying their twin planes, one with tiger stripes and one with leopard spots, they traveled in many lands and stopped to visit where they pleased. Their books include *Jungle Adventures* (1921) and *Headhunters of the South Seas* (1922). Their films, often with sensationalistic titles, include *Simba: King of the Beasts* (1928), *Congorilla* (1932), *Wings over Africa* (1934), and *Baboona* (1935). (In January 1935, *Baboona* was shown on an Eastern Air Lines plane, becoming the first sound movie shown during flight.) The Walt Disney Company was the first organization to license a Johnson film from the Martin and Osa Johnson Safari Museum (still open in Chanute, Kansas) for the 1976 television program *Filming Nature's Mysteries*. Osa was able to lecture from a wheelchair and travel to study the lives of the Maasai people. Television's first wildlife series, *Osa Johnson's Big Game Hunt*, premiered in 1952. Adrienne Rich mentions her and Martin in her poem "In the Waiting Room."

Martin had tried with everything that was in him to adapt himself to the confining routine of his father's jewelry store. He sat on the high watchmaker's bench, a glass screwed in his eye, his movements restricted to a finger or two, his vision if not his thoughts narrowed down to an escapement pin or the hairspring of a lady's watch. He designed monograms and made, in the bowls of spoons, free-hand engravings of the city's [Independence, Kansas] more important buildings. He got the knack of handling phonograph springs and wondered at his own and his father's pride over the first one he had fixed. He sold engagement rings, wedding rings and silver baby cups, and secretly and ashamedly he was miserable.

That he was of interest to the younger set of the town for awhile, because of his vagabonding abroad, was of no consequence to him. He couldn't even be persuaded to talk about those four years. His only impression was of great masses of humanity, dependent on one another, defeating one another, and of men's struggle, often cruel, for supremacy over other men. He wouldn't care if he never saw another big city as long as he lived.[1]

Several times lately his father had felt him out about expanding the business. He broached the subject again one chilly evening in the fall. They had locked up the store for the day and were on their way home for supper.

"We could rent that vacant store next door and carry the finest supply of photographic stuff in the whole state." He paused. "What do you think, Martin?"

"Uh, yes. Sure. Sounds like a great idea." . . .

"Photography's your line. I thought we could have a fine dark room at the back too. Do developing. You take charge of the whole thing. . . . And I was thinking we could have a sign made to go clear across both stores, and it could say, 'Johnson & Son.' ". . .

Mrs. Johnson was in the kitchen getting supper ready; Martin said something sure smelled good and wandered into the living room. Freda [Martin's sister] was there poring over the fashion section of a magazine. Tall for her age, flaxen haired and graceful, she was beginning to have beaus, and Martin, as well as checking up on these, teased her unmercifully. To-night, however, he paced the room.

Johnson & Son. Johnson & Son.

His sister giggled and asked him what he was mumbling about. He denied mumbling. Then as she went into the kitchen to help with supper, he said it aloud.

"Johnson & Son."

Idly he leafed through the magazine Freda had left in her chair, when suddenly, with an impact that was almost physical, an article by Jack London met his eyes. It told of the proposed seven-year trip around the world in a forty-four foot boat.

The story was told in Jack London's own words, of how the ship, though small, was to be the finest of its kind ever built; that only the most carefully selected woods and finest metals were going into its construction, and the most skilled of craftsmen had been employed to do this work. The article went on to say that when finished this small but perfect ship was to carry Jack London, his wife, Charmian, and a crew of four on a trip without schedule or predetermined route to distant lands far removed from the sea lanes of regular travel. And then Martin read with astonishment that one of the crew of four was to be someone in the United States still unknown, who had only to write a letter to Jack London of sufficient convincingness to win him a place in the crew.

"This is it! This is it!" something in Martin shouted.

"I'm going with them! I'll steer the boat! I'll take pictures! I'll scrub decks—I'll do anything—"

The flame of excitement dimmed as quickly as it had lit. He was crazy even to think of such a thing—he, a small-town Kansas boy, without the slightest knowledge of navigation or of boats—a total stranger to the famous Jack London—how could he even hope to share so great an adventure.

Martin got up, the magazine slid to the floor, and without even a thought for his supper, he went out into the street and walked rapidly and without direction until nearly midnight.

His stomach was hollow with desire.

"Why not write Mr. London?" he heard himself arguing. "He can't do any more than say 'no.' He probably won't even answer, but at least you'll have tried."

Martin ran all the way home. The folks were in bed. His mother had put some milk and sandwiches in his room. He bolted these as he got out his meager supply of writing materials; then sat for hours chewing his pen.

He began writing. He rewrote. He tore up page after page of the most careful writing to which he had ever applied himself. Finally down to his last two sheets of paper, he cursed himself for not having paid stricter attention to composition when in school. Then, with something both of recklessness and despair, he wrote what came. Briefly he told Jack London how he had knocked and fought his way over a small part of the world, what he could do with photography, that he wasn't afraid of work, and, finally, that he was as strong as an ox. And then, so he wouldn't tear up his final effort, he shoved it in an envelope, addressed it and pounded the stamp into place with his fist. Dawn was just edging the horizon.

When the westbound train stopped at Independence a few hours later, Martin was waiting for it. He gave his letter into the hand of the mail clerk, watched the train from sight, and then sat down as suddenly as if his knees had had jelly in them instead of bones.

The mail carrier now became the most important person in Martin's life. Each day the shrill whistle up the block brought him tingling to his feet, and each day as it went back it left him sick and cold. When a week had passed, he berated himself for writing in the first place. It just didn't seem possible that he could have been such a fool. He'd simply forget the whole thing, that's all.

Late one afternoon some ten days later, a Western Union boy delivered a telegram at the store. Martin's father signed the book and was about to open it when he saw it was for Martin.

"A telegram for you, Martin," he called to the back room.

"Telegram!"

Martin came to the doorway and gaped. Then he pounced. In his clumsy fingers the envelope seemed made of some indestructible material. Next he was staring at the message. Altogether there were just five words:

"Can you cook? Jack London."

Can you cook? It sounded crazy. Can you cook? The words beat a sort of tattoo into his brain. Canyoucookcanyoucookcanyoucookcanyoucook . . .

"What's the matter, Martin?" his father asked anxiously.

"He wants to know if I can cook!" Martin shouted.

"Who wants to know?"

"Jack London!"

Martin leaped to the back room and looked at the wall calendar. It was Monday, November 12, 1906. The article had said December 15th was the sailing date.

There wasn't time! Maybe there was! There wasn't time! Maybe there was!

He ran out the back door, down the alley and into the rear of Milton Cook's White Front Quick Lunch Room.

Jess Utz, the lean, lank chef, was just sticking a fork into a pot roast.

"Listen, Jess," Martin panted. "How long would it take a man to learn to cook?"

Jess deliberated.

"Me," said Jess, finally, "Me, I bin cookin' somepin' like ten years and ain't larned yit."

"I don't mean to be a first class chef," explained Martin. "How long will it take me to learn to cook enough to keep six people from starving—including me?"

Jess eyed him suspiciously.

"Say, what are you up to?"

"Look, Jess," pleaded Martin, shoving the telegram into the cook's hand. "If I can cook I've got a chance to go with Jack London on a trip around the world. And I can't go with Jack London if I don't learn to cook. Jess, I've just got to!" Martin was almost incoherent.

"All right! Don't get so excited! Don't you understand that cooks are born, not made? Yer either a good cook or ye ain't—and I don't think ye are."

Jess looked into the oven and shut the door with a bang.

"A'course," he said, "efen ye want to come in here and work, I'll show you what I kin, and Gawd have mercy on the stomicks of them as has to eat your vittles."

Ten minutes later Martin was in the telegraph office composing his answer to London's wire. It read:

"Sure, just try me."

## NOTE

1. In 1906 the teenaged Johnson had stowed away on a ship and spent six weeks in London and Liverpool.

# Alexander Hume Ford

### From "Jack London in Hawaii:
### Rambling Reminiscences of the Editor" (1917)

> An energetic newspaperman in Chicago, Alexander Hume Ford (1868–1945) moved to Honolulu to try his hand at entrepreneurship. He met London upon his arrival there and introduced him to many people, some of whom would become lifelong friends. In April 1908, Ford arranged a trip to the Ewa, or western side of Oahu, to see the profitable sugar cane and pineapple plantations, owned by the *haole kama'aina* ruling class of descendants of missionaries and other early immigrants to Hawai'i from the Eastern Seaboard of the United States and England. Though he was trying to show London Hawai'i's agricultural productivity, Ford found that London's attention focused closely on the plight of the indentured workers from China, Japan, Chile, Portugal, and elsewhere. This experience led London to his first Hawaiian short story, "The House of Pride," an unambiguous indictment of the white ruling class. A friend he was with that day, Lorrin Thurston, editor of *The Honolulu Advertiser*, briefly became an enemy upon the publication of that story. In this and subsequent visits to Hawai'i, Ford invited London to speak to many organizations, including the Pan-Pacific Union promoting "Pacific Rim" trade, especially with Japan in its "Hands-around-the-Pacific" movement.

I first met Jack London on the lanai of the Old Royal Hawaiian Hotel. It was ten years ago, he was still young in his glory, and I having not yet abandoned writing for the English and American reviews and magazines to become a Mid-Pacific editor, was known by reputation to the young author.

"Jack London, I believe," I said to the young man huddled up beside a slim girlish woman (Charmian, his mate). "I came here first and I'm not going to leave. My name is Ford; *Aloha* (welcome). You, too, will stay—it will get you."

"Alexander Hume Ford?" were the first words spoken to me in query by

London. "I heard you were here." There was a firm clasp of the hand, and a friendship began that never wanted, but grew closer as the years flew by.

There are less than half a dozen men in all the world who so became a part of my life and entered partnership with me in my life work, as did Jack London. His last letter, written a few days before his sudden end at Glen Ellen, was to express his sincere regret that the paragraphs he had prepared on "Aloha Land" (Hawaii) for the "Cosmopolitan" Magazine, had been omitted, some of these describing the objects of the Pan-Pacific Movement. He sent the original manuscript to show his sincerity, and an assurance that the paragraphs would appear as he had written them when the work appeared in book form.

It was Jack London all over. The reply I sent to the effect that no editor's blue pencil could convince me of his lack of interest in the movement he had helped to create, never reached him in this world.

For ten years Jack London had sent me as it left the press, each new volume from his pen, and on the fly-leaf was always a warm letter of friendship. In Hawaii it was my privilege, that of an old friend, to read his manuscript ever as it left his pen. Often I would read with interest of an afternoon his penciling of the morning hours. Even on the last day of his stay in Honolulu, but a few weeks before his departure for other worlds, I was permitted to read words that will appear in his last written romance, and as I put down the MS strips, the great author and great friend took from his writing tray a fountain pen, on which his name was engraved, and said, "Ford, this is the pen that has turned out my stories written in Hawaii. I want you to have it."

"I want it, Jack," was my reply, as I slipped it into my vest pocket; and so Jack and I parted lightly, and forever. I did not see him off on the steamer, as neither of us wished it.

As I ask myself, "Why did I like Jack London from the start?" I know it was because I intuitively guessed that he loved Humanity more then he loved himself, his work, or life itself.

It was Jack London, Joe Cooke, Lorrin Thurston, Walter F. Frear (then governor of Hawaii) who first got together and talked of a Pan-Pacific Movement, and for ten years each of us has worked heart and soul toward its attainment. Jack London was one of its sponsors, and to the end one of our coworkers.

I arrived in Hawaii but a few weeks before Jack London left San Francisco in his yacht the "Snark" for a Pan-Pacific cruise. One evening, after dinner, on the lanai, or great tropic verandah of the Honolulu home of J.P. Cooke, the head of the most progressive sugar house, we discussed the possibility of securing the co-operation of all Pacific lands in a movement to bind us together to advance our combined interests. A friend present, Frank C. Atherton, who was to come into the movement years later as one of its leaders, gave assurance of his hearty support, and a few days later at a small luncheon at the University Club, the Hands-Around-the-Pacific Movement was born. In the meantime, I had met the author of the "Call of the Wild," with the result that there was planned an automobile trip around the Island of Oahu; and so Jack London was brought into the circle of the Pan-Pacific Movement, my first snapshot of "Jack" being at the Pali or precipice, six miles from Honolulu, between Joseph Cooke and Lorrin A. Thurston, two men who from that day were to become his life-long friends, and one of them, L. A. Thurston, an oft-time companion on many island excursions.

Jack London, during the two or three days of this outing aroused the boy that slumbers in every man. True to his resolve, which I have never known him to break, he put in certain hours of work before he would consent to take his enjoyment. Up at four in the morning, on the day we were to start, he had written his prescribed 1000 words before we were ready to start at 9 a.m., and the next day at Haleiwa Hotel he was up and at work before daylight without our knowledge, that he might not delay our proposed early morning start.

We had begun by calling our guest Mr. London.

"Nothing doing," was his laughing reply. "I'm out for a good time: I'm first, 'Jack'" (we had stopped for a swim), and it's "Ford" and "Thurston," and I'm going to duck you, "Joe," and under the water went the great financier of Hawaii. Then began a boyish romp. Jack wouldn't listen then and never would in later years to our playing the grown-up. After he was through with his day's work he longed to be a boy again. . . .

The boyishness never left Jack. He would come down to the Outrigger Canoe Club on Waikiki Beach, which, by the way he and I were instrumental in organizing ten years ago—but he tells of this in some of his books— and it was here on these grounds that he used to have his tent house, and in the surf in front I taught him to ride the surfboard. It was the spot we both loved best of any in Hawaii, and here, every afternoon after his work was over he would come and romp with the children before his daily swim with Charmian, his mate.

Jack had a hundred ages. He would drop the most serious conversation for a moment to show her some new trick he had learned. To the boys of the Outrigger Club he was an idol. When he would read aloud they would sit around and worship; in the surf he was one of them. . . .

It was on the Outrigger Club grounds, on that spacious lanai over the sea, that Jack and I held our weekly Pan-Pacific dinners. One week I would invite a dozen of the leading Japanese "lights" of Honolulu to meet with the man who wished to know them, and the next week the leading Koreans, and then the prominent Hawaiians, and the Portuguese, and the people of every race of the Pacific; and they in return would invite London to their homes. . . .

When the Congressional Party visited Honolulu last, we arranged for a Pan-Pacific dinner under the *hau* trees on the Outrigger Club grounds, and there three hundred men of every race of the Pacific, and sixty Senators and Representatives sat down together, and Jack London made the speech on the "Language of the Tribe," that brought us closer together and made us begin to understand. . . .

It will never seem real to us, it will never be true. It is only that he is back in Glen Ellen on a visit, and to us there will always be that "some day" when he will return to Hawaii to be our companion once more.

# Armine von Tempski

## From *Born in Paradise* (1940)

The section printed below is from the writer's autobiography about growing up on the side of Mt. Haleakala on Maui, daughter of Louis von Tempski, manager of a large cattle ranch. Armine von Tempski (1892–1943) became a friend of the Londons and visited them at the ranch after they first met her at age 16 on Maui in 1907 on the *Snark* voyage. They treasured their ranch time on the slopes of the volcano, especially the exciting riding opportunities. Though London gave her some pretty sharp criticism, she became the most popular writer in Hawai'i in her time, focusing her work on the lives of the *paniolos*, or cowboys, as they worked the cattle on Maui. Her books include a sequel to *Born in Paradise* called *Aloha* (1946), together with *Hula* (1927), *Dust* (1928), *Fire* (1929), *Hawaiian Harvest* (1933), and *Ripe Breadfruit* (1935), the latter illustrated by Don Blanding.

A while after Dad returned from the session of the Legislature in Honolulu, Lorrin Thurston, Editor of the *Advertiser*, and a lawyer of distinction in Hawaii, wrote saying that he was bringing Jack London over to the ranch for ten days.

Lorrin Thurston had been one of Dad's first friends in the Islands. As young men they had hunted wild cattle together on Mauna Kea. Kakina, as Dad called him, came from Missionary stock. He didn't smoke, swear, or drink. Dad did all three, but their affection was unshakeable. Kakina was a tall, heavy-set, noble man with burning dark eyes, who moved and gestured in the large sweeping way of Hawaiians. The fact that he was Dad's closest friend, and an Editor, made me admire him greatly. Of course his stock, where I was concerned, went to an all-time high when I found he was bringing one of the most famous writers of the day to the ranch.

I was going to see Jack London, whose books I'd read avidly. It seemed too good to be possible. Dad took me to meet them. Because they were such notables they were breakfasted and lunched en route to the ranch and a special plantation train brought them from Kahului to Paia.

I was prepared for an awe-inspiring person. Kakina jumped off the train followed by a sort of breezy, boyish-looking man with brilliant blue eyes and a mop of rather untidy hair. Intelligence, vigor, and a gusto for life emanated from him. He and Dad looked at each other, laughed, hooked their fingers in their own shirt collars and shook them with a sort of delight, signifying they were one breed. In a day when men wore stiff detachable collars, they both wore soft-collared shirts. It was an immediate bond of outlawry.

Tall Aunt Hattie, Kakina's wife, got off the train and Jack's wife, Charmian, followed. She was a small, vivid person whom I loved instantly.

It was a memorable ten days. The August round-up was going full blast. From dawn til dark the bawling of cattle being drafted, counted, and branded filled the air. Jack rode all over on his horse, like a sailor. Charmian was such a finished performer that I lent her Bedouin, who had never carried another woman on his back—and she managed him perfectly. She was out with us at daybreak; Jack joined us around noon, after he'd written the thousand words which were his daily output.

I was in heaven. All day we did the things I loved best, riding, working with the cattle. In the evenings I listened to flashing conversation. Jack had a mind like a sword and when he grew eloquent about some subject which was close to his heart the air crackled. Of course, I shyly showed him a couple of my manuscripts. He was honest and straight from the shoulder. "Writing's the hardest work in the world," he told me. "The stuff you're producing is clumsy incoherent tripe, but every so often there's a streak of fire on your pages. You're only a kid, but everything registers with you and you've a zest for life. If you're game enough to take all the lickings that will come to you, and keep on writing and writing, you'll make out."

That was enough for me. I determined I would keep on, until I was ninety, if necessary.

# Yoshimatsu Nakata

## From "A Hero to His Valet" (2000)

In 1907 a young Japanese man in Honolulu signed aboard the *Snark* as London's valet and remained in that position until 1916, when he returned to Honolulu, started a family, and became a dentist. Yoshimatsu Nakata (1889–1967) accompanied the Londons to the South Seas on the *Snark* and sailed aboard the *Dirigo* in 1912. To replace him, the Londons hired Tokinosake Sekine from Toyko, a college graduate who served London until his death. Nakata was extremely dear to the Londons, and he knew them as well as anyone could. Charmian wrote a good deal about him in her various publications, describing him as "temperamentally and mentally, a type of human being who would be at home in any land, with any race." She praises his vigor and dutifulness, especially his delicate touch with the services he rendered, as well as his "virtuosity" with language. She wonders in her notes about how he feels serving others—and what the *Dirigo* voyage means to him. She reflects that he was not asked whether he wanted to go. On the journey, Nakata, like the Londons, was crew, but to his duties he added making special foods, special furnishings, and combs of turtle shell that Charmian treasured. She writes that he is trusted "with out scruple," but she also feels for him, that he may have a good position as their valet, but he is still a "race-lonely boy."[1] On the *Dirigo* Nakata proudly joined Charmian in her typing and organizing. She felt that knowing Nakata helped London see things from a Japanese point of view, especially his stories of Asians in Hawai'i.

> Nakata is inexpressibly precious to us both. We have, we three, been through hell & high water to-gether. He has nursed us many a time in frightful set-upons of South Sea (Solomon's) fever, and other troubles have been eased by his patience and his tiny, baby-like brown hands. And Jack and I once, saved his life, when he had got poisoning from salmon left too long in a tin, at sea. More than once he started to get rigid, but we toiled, and dosed him desperately, with did [*sic*] everything that the books told—experiences of others had ever suggested to us.... [T]he thought of losing Nakata in any way, is just not tenable. He is delicacy itself, and loveable & loving.

> Both Londons fought vigorously for Nakata's safe passage back into the United States when he was detained in New Orleans on their return home from the Mexican Revolution.

When we got to Glen Ellen, that was a new life beginning for me. Mr. London and I used to be alone quite a bit. Frequently when I went to call him he was already awake, but when he was not, I used to wake him. No matter how heavily he was sleeping, I would just touch him and he would wake up with that wonderful smile on his face as he looked at me. Sometimes I would go in the morning to his bedroom and we would talk together for quite a long time while he is drinking coffee or eating eggs. . . . I used to get up about five o'clock to get his breakfast because I didn't want the cook to get up so early. . . .

After that I would massage Mr. London's hands. Even after he got that skin trouble, his hands were kind of numb. They were harsh and hard, and I used to massage them for him with vaseline. Scales would come off. I think six layers of skin must have come off. I would go back to get my own breakfast and then I would dress Mr. London. Then he would go to work and that would be about 9 o'clock.

While he was drinking coffee he would talk to me about all kinds of things. He loved Omar Khayyam and bought a copy of the *Rubaiyat* for me. Every morning, he took about one-half hour to teach me Omar Khayyam. He used to read it and explain it to me. He explained it in his way, saying, "A lot of people explain this a different way, but this is my way." It was very interesting. . . . After he dressed, Mr. London would start to work. He had a certain way of writing, and it was the same every day. He has a cigarette in his left hand and a blunt fountain pen with a wire tube at the end—a stylograph. He always used this instead of a fountain pen. The idea is that he doesn't have to watch the nib to see if it was turning to one side. He writes very large. When he is writing he is always humming something or singing. It is called "Redwing." He played that all the time on the phonograph on the *Snark*, and at home he still hums and sings it. Then he puffs a cigarette and writes some more and he does that for twenty minutes and then he gets up and takes a drink of Scotch whiskey. Then he eats a Japanese fish, the small white dried fish called crepe iriko that they use for bait. He eats that once in a while and then writes. Every twenty minutes he counts the pages. He writes so big, I suppose there are a thousand words to about twenty pages. After he writes about an hour, he begins to count and then writes about twenty minutes again. About four or five times he does this, and then he figures he is finished with his work.

I had one of his pens but I lost it someplace. He had worn out the metal part by writing so much, and then the writing came too big and heavy. His handwriting is too big anyway. The manuscript of one short story would be about three inches high. After London died, a man in England bought all his manuscript [*sic*], paying quite a large sum. Mrs. London was very, very glad. There was so much of it, she didn't know what to do.

This manuscript was not very clear writing, but it was nice clean copy— nothing added and nothing scratched out. But the writing was certainly terrible. Although he didn't work very hard at writing, he would go straight ahead and when he is done, he is through. Before starting in the morning, he reads over what he wrote yesterday that has been typed by Mrs. London or me and the words counted, then he puts it in his bag. He reads it over but seldom makes a correction. When he does, it's usually my misspelling.

Mr. London never read proof. Sometimes Mrs. London did, but other times they just left that job to Mr. Sterling. Very seldom were there any changes made in the proof.

When London was traveling, he had a special bag made of walrus skin, a writing bag. He had four or five pens and ink and a cardboard box, the kind that typewriter paper comes in, filled with the manuscript of the book he is writing. He always carried about thirty small tablets on which he made his notes. When he had made use of these notes, then he threw them away.

It has been said when London came back from Australia he worked nineteen hours a day. On the *Snark*, he usually wrote about three hours a day and when we came back to California he did about the same. He worked regularly but he didn't work so terribly hard writing. Then he spends more time writing letters. When he dictated to my dictaphone he knew I wasn't good in English so right in the middle of what he wanted written he would say, "Nakata you had better look up this word in the dictionary. It isn't spelled the way you think it is."

I asked Mr. London once, "Why do you have to drink when you write?" Mr. London told me, "You know Nakata, after I take a whiskey I write along and after a certain time, I suppose that whiskey has gone out of me. I see nothing but whiskey and the point of my pen says, 'Whiskey, whiskey, whiskey,' so I take whiskey and then I can write again."

*

Usually he went to bed about nine o'clock and then he reads in bed until about eleven or so. When he didn't want to be called, he wanted to be able to sleep later in the morning without having to tell me before I left him at night. I made a false clock so that the hands could be adjusted from a distance by using string, showing that time he wanted to get up. That was so he could fix the clock for me without getting out of bed. He wanted to have light fixed up so that when he fell asleep the lights would go out automatically. He didn't want to have to put out the light. He said, "The very idea wakes me up. I want to read and just fall asleep." I told him all right, I would fix it up. I had a springwork attached that he held a strong cord with his toe and when he fell asleep his toe relaxed and in no time the lights went out.

He was very impatient that man. He wouldn't take the trouble to open the buttons on his shirts. I usually changed buttons to a smaller size so that when he took hold of the top and pulled, the buttons would slide out of the holes instead of popping off. He would undo the top button and then zzzzzup all the rest of the way down. He should have lived when there were zippers.

But when I changed to small buttons, then when he put back his shoulders and pushed out his chest the way he used to do, shoving his belt down with his hands, all the buttons would slip out of the holes. In those days, perhaps they didn't have crepe wide enough to go around him. I remember we had them add a four-inch strip under the arms to the bottom [of] the shirt, so that when he threw his chest out the buttons wouldn't slip out.

He used to order shirts made of Japanese crepe. Now, we have a hard time to get shirts as good as those we used to get for him from Yamatoya, the Yokahama [sic] shirtmaker who is famous throughout the world. He used to order a dozen a year, he wore them out so quickly. He never liked a stiff collar but always ordered a soft collar attached to the shirt. He always had about a dozen black ties. He had one kind of shirt and one kind of necktie, and plenty of them. He wore a broad black tie, not the regular tailor made kind.

Mr. London ordered ten suits practically the same, made of very good material by a Honolulu tailor. He would often order two dozen underpants and undershirts—that is, two dozen of each—of English broadcloth, the very best. It's rather heavy.

A New York tailor named Lyon sent a man from New York to Glen Ellen to take Mr. London's measurements and they sent him four or five suits of different styles and colors. I think they were the most beautiful I ever saw. He wore them all, but he didn't seem to care very much that they were such good suits. He liked rough things. The same way with gardens. He never liked this made-garden with mowed lawn, even near his house. He liked it wild and natural.

We had quite a hard time with his socks. He wore knitted underwear even in summertime and then this BVD came in about 1910 and everybody was changing to the new short underwear and then the problem came how to keep up the socks. We tried with Paris Garters but he complained that they pinched. In those days, they wouldn't just let socks roll down, so we used to sew on elastic at the top of the sock, but even at that he complained that it pinched, and stopped the circulation.

Those Yamatoya shirts which London used to wear were so good, I have one that is twenty years old and still as good as new. But London was very hard on clothes, and he perspired a lot too.

One time I met Mr. London on the street in Oakland and he said, "Nakata, I have two handkerchiefs; but I think I have a cold. I need some more. I'll need half a dozen more by night." He was looking all over for me to ask me to buy handkerchiefs because he didn't know what to get or where to buy them. It seemed to me the man got perfectly helpless in the little things like that.

He always smoked Imperial cigarettes. They had a factory in San Francisco. These cigarettes came in an open package, ten in one package. He told me it was started with cigar stumps collected from bar rooms in Market Street which they sterilize and put in cigarettes. They were supposed to be pretty good. Of course later on when they got selling large quantities there were not enough stumps so they must have used fresh tobacco.

London smoked about fifty or sixty cigarettes every day. He smoked in bed too and his nice wool pajamas were full of holes. He would smoke the cigarettes and the hot ashes would drop and fall on his pajamas and singe the hair on his chest, so it looked very funny. They were nice pajamas, too. His coat lapels got all burned also. One time he sent them out to an expert to mend but the expert didn't do a very good job so we had to discard them. I thought

I might as well take a chance, so I took threads from the inside of the trousers to mend the coat. It took me about two days to repair a couple of holes, but I made a pretty good job, although if you looked carefully it showed. I suppose London had to wear the coats because it took me so long to mend and it might hurt my feelings if he didn't wear them.

And shoes! As far as I remember, he never bought shoes. I always had to buy them for him. Shoe stores in those days were not so nice as nowadays. Now, the store will exchange you even if you wear the shoes a little bit but in those days they wouldn't. He always wanted the shoes a bit oversize so that they would be comfortable. He had no corns but suffered quite a good deal from ingrowing toenail. I remember he used to borrow my nail clipper, which I bought one time in Baltimore.

"How much did you pay for that?" he asked me.

"I think I paid four dollars or five dollars."

"Gee! Four dollars for a nail clipper? I paid one dollar for mine."

But one time his toenail was so hard he couldn't clip with his one-dollar one so he had to borrow mine, which I still have. The whole family uses it. It is made in Germany by Hinkle and trademark is three men put together.

I think Mr. London was the only one in San Francisco who used to wear the kind of shoes he did. They always used to wear boots, but he wore Oxford ties. I never saw one pair of regular high shoes that Mr. London had. He usually wore tan. He liked tan.

He would keep on wearing clothes if I didn't change them for him all the time. He was so careless about those things. Underwear, and things like that, he didn't bother about. He would just put them on and off and if I forget to change them, then he puts them on again, so I must always take away the old ones and put new ones in place of them.

We had a Japanese cook who never had to buy any clothes. London's things fitted him perfectly. Shirts, socks, shoes, everything we gave him. I have a picture of him in one of London's shirts with a big black tie.

London never wore suspenders. He always wore the belt and pants very much under the waistline, so the pants were all wrinkles. His habit was to stick his hands in the belt and pull down, throwing back his shoulders. He was sloppy but he always had someone to look after him, so in that way he kept rather neat. He didn't like to wear anything made of good material because then he had to think about where he could sit. He liked khaki pants and old shoes. He used to say, "What is the use of worrying about clothes?"

But when it came to pajamas, that's different. He likes to have nice pajamas. "They feel good!"

Although he was so careless about his own clothes, he was very particular about Mrs. London's, and she is too. When you read Mr. London's books, you learn a lot about Mrs. London. All his ladies are like Mrs. London. In *Burning Daylight*, Dede Mason is like her. She wears very feminine clothes at home, prefers the country to the city, loves cattails, mariposa lilies, and the piano, which she plays very well. Dede Mason has quick, birdlike ways, almost flitting from mood to mood; and she was all contrition on the instant [*Burning Daylight*, 237].

### NOTE

1. Charmian London, "Nakata" [Biographical Notes], Jack London Collection, Huntington Library, JL 337.

# Natura [Ernest Darling]

## Letters to Jack and Charmian London (1911)

Ernest Wilfred Darling, also known as the "Nature Man" of Tahiti (1873?–1919), started out as a sickly runaway from California fleeing his physician father, who constantly dosed him with medicines, and lived off the land. He eventually made his way to Tahiti, where he foreswore the customs, food, and clothing of American cities for the open air and vegetarian diet available on his plot of land near Papeete, over which he raised a red flag for socialism. He himself wore a red loincloth. Eventually the French colonial authorities had enough of his free living and razed his farm. London saw him afterwards, and Darling declared he would rebuild. He visited the Londons on the ranch, and he wrote to them in his own peculiar, pared-down version of English. The best summary of his life and activities is offered by Charmian in *Pacific Monthly*, in a letter she wrote in April 1937:

Sirs:

Ernest Darling has found a way out of sickness and death, to keep his health with a Return-to-Nature life, kept strictly. . . . [H]e had gotten hold of a tiny holding, a mere bit of shelf on an almost inaccessible mountainside in Tahiti, where we climbed one day. He tilled the bit of land, and was an asset to the careless community, because he improved on whatever he laid his hands on. He lived mostly from what he raised—bananas and coconuts and other vegetable products. And of course he fished. The French are poor colonizers, and did not appreciate him, because he was "queer." So they made life so hard for him, finally even closing his way to his perch, that he had to leave Tahiti. (They ought to blush at the inconsistency of it.) I should have imagined he was around 38 or 40 at that time (1913).[1] And he lived like the man he was supposed to resemble. He was SIMPLE, his mind had been slightly touched, but he was RIGHT in everything, and lived as nearly a Christian life as it is possible to one to achieve. A few years after we knew him in Papeete (1908) he left, practically driven out, and returned to California. He came up to the Jack London Ranch several times. He had on a few necessary clothes which he mostly discarded in favor of a loincloth he brought with him; he also brought his chosen food, and sat out-

> side the house on some wild grass. He came perhaps three times. Then he faded out of the picture, and wandered again into the South Seas region. He finally wound up in the Fiji group, in Suva, I have heard, the capitol [*sic*]. And he was ill there, and he died there. We had word once more, from Berkeley. He seemed disappointed in renewing acquaintance in an inimical climate, after the idyllic scene of our Tahiti friendship. We felt sorrowful for him. Ernest Darling was utterly a practicing Christian. I never knew a man who so lived up to his idea of human behavior, as he. Inexorably he patterned himself upon Christ's teaching and practice. Quite simply. Helpfully, to everybody. He never seemed to fall down in his principles and activities. He was piteous about the treatment he eventually received in Tahiti; but he never censured his tormentors. . . . [A] remarkable figure . . . . Simple he was, but no fool.[2]

Dear Komrads Jack + Charmian,

Thanks for "Cruise of the Snark" Beautiful!

Am getting so interested in "S" that I am trying to sel out so I kan kompleet my book (O excuse me. I'll finish in long spelling as I promised in former letter). I may return to Cal. Next year. I'v so many letters to rite & rows to hoe. So kiss me quick & let me go.

—Natura.

P.S. Kindly return enclosed portal if this reaches you O.K.
(Page 210) C's pictures in "Cruise . . ." is simple "kute." Of most attractive cut in the whole volume.

*

My Deer Jack & Charmian,

Just reed ur gd letter ritten at Catalina.

Hope ere this uv reed dried ban [Natura means bananas]? O.K. They shood be avakt (?) in rich milk 1 hr before eating.

Thanks for permission to make . . . about Nature Man. Shal likely wait myself of the kinds in a few mos.

Thanks also for kind invitation to visit Glen Ellen. Shood be delighted 2 do so.

My place looks well. Pool r fresh & deep now. Pahus growing beautifully.
Golden melons + bananas in abundance.

I'v many inquiring letters 2 (write) & many rows 2 ho.

Foa ito ito

—Natura.

\*

My Dear Jack + Charmian,

Just read your good letter, foto & booklet. I shall read + re-send out to the
sleep world.

Out of consideration for Charmian busy & perhaps overworkt eyes I have
tacked on the conventional e's so this might be read more easily(?) But cranks
like me can't wait for systems to develop. We just "Captain Slocum it" &
paddle our own canoe in the face of the . . . red lights on either side of us.

Yet, I make a willowy bend when a Charmian friend request me to. I spell
the good old round however it may sound & so get there.

Jan Hawlasa & Elsie his wife visited last year. I enclose her letter & some
fotos they sent me. He is a Bohemian writer, poet, socialist & broad-viewed
young man (26 yrs). He inquired much of you. Wish you could meet. Elsie
& Charmian r much alike in many respects. He wrote me up in his Bohemian
book printed at Prague his home.

Please tell me if there was any mold or worms on bananas, so I'll know
better how to pack. What expressly did u have to have? 25 letters to write &
rows to hoe so kiss me quick & let me go.

Natura

P.S. Your greatest service to humanity is to be good to, merciful to + fully considerate for yourself. They will never thank you for working "terribly hard"
for them. You two people are the busiest I ever met. But does this strenuosity
pay in the long run?

Yours for socialism which means to me maximum opportunity for the development of each person on whatever plane.

Natura.

*

My dear Londons:

Thanks again yours of May. Find enclosed stamp addrest envelope for reply.

By this time next year I hope to have my book "Natura" ready for press. Had I best run it thru some mag. Or send it straight out from my own hand?

What house will do me the best all-round job leaving out of consideration the $ question? My first book is simply to pay . . . but mainly to establish a "rep" that will pave for a second "stunner"! With this in mind would I do better in England? Would I need to see the publishers? Could I get much better work if on the ground when they are striking off my job? How is Kerr & Co? Who give you best all round satisfaction? You are the best judge I know.

### NOTES

1. Charmian must be alluding to a visit by Ernest Darling to the ranch.
2. Charmian London, Letters, *Pacific Monthly* (April 1937): 1–3.

# Theodore Dreiser

## Letters to Jack London (1909–1910)

Theodore Dreiser (1871–1945) was, along with London, Crane, Norris, and Wharton, one of the greatest of the American naturalists, with such radical new perspectives as that of Carrie Meeber in *Sister Carrie* (1900). Like London, Dreiser was determined to tell what he saw as the realistic truth about life, no matter what the censors had to say. But as in *An American Tragedy* (1925), his characters come up against forces in society that they have no chance of besting and overcoming them in a deterministic universe of loss and regret. As they show characters at their morally weakest, both authors came under scrutiny regularly for impropriety, while each defended passionately the freedom of expression of the literary artist. When he dashed off a few notes to London, Dreiser was employed at *The Delineator*, a women's magazine.

My dear Mr. London:

I read "The Sea-Farmer" and I read it with a great deal of interest. It is a mighty fine story, and I should certainly like to have it, but I feel that I would hardly do for a women's magazine. For that reason only am I returning it. I wish you would let me see something else. Thanks very much for sending me this.

Very sincerely yours,
Theodore Dreiser
Editor.

*

My dear Mr. London:

I want to know if you can be induced to join a group of contributors already in mind in presenting your one most dramatic event under the caption of "The Most Dramatic Event In My Life." Herewith I am enclosing a proof of an article under this caption by Lieutenant Peary. I have in the office articles by John Mitchell, in which he describes his conference with the President; Orville Wright, who descants on his first flight; and Hiram Maxim, who tells of one of his discoveries. I do not know, of course, whether you would be willing to do this, and I trust that you will not consider me overofficious. The article need not be more than three thousand words in length, and the subject any interpretation which you care to put on it. For such an article we would be glad to pay you five cents a word, or $150.00. Will you kindly let me know whether you would care to undertake this, and obliged,

Very sincerely yours,
Theodore Dreiser
Editor.

# Ed Morrell

From "Statement of Ed Morrell Made to Jack London
in the Office of Schwartz & Powell at Oakland,
California, on the 19th Day of December, 1913" (1913)

Ed Morrell was the pen name of Edward H. Morrell (1868–1956). He was a member of a notorious gang in the San Joaquin Valley of California at the end of the last century that robbed the Southern Pacific Railroad. Captured and sentenced once to Folsom, then to San Quentin, for grand larceny for two years, he was released in 1893, but he robbed another train and was this time sentenced to fifteen years at San Quentin, including five years in solitary confinement. He endured other tortures. Upon his pardon in 1908, which London supported, Morrell became a sort of folk hero because the Southern Pacific Railroad was so hated by the locals, as portrayed in Frank Norris's *The Octopus* (1901). He was an outspoken opponent of solitary confinement, straitjackets, and other prison abuses. He published articles about his prison life and in defense of himself and other notorious inmates at San Quentin, and eventually a book about his ordeal titled *The Twenty-Fifth Man: The Strange Story of Ed. Morrell, the Hero of Jack London's "Star Rover"* (1924). London met him for lunch at Saddle Rock in Oakland, a favorite hangout, on December 23, just before he and Charmian departed by train for New York and Baltimore for the *Dirigo* voyage. Morrell even rode with the Londons on the train as far as Sacramento. Then Morrell had his story transcribed, as below, to an attorney. London used Morrell as the inspiration for his hero in what is sometimes called his "reincarnation novel," *The Star Rover*. Darrell Standing, straitjacketed and in solitary confinement, establishes rapport with other men silenced in solitary and learns to achieve "self-hypnosis" or "astral projection," taking him back to many different lives or reincarnations. (London himself averred that he personally did not believe in reincarnation.) London had a lot of unpublished stories or novel ideas, and he wanted to use them.[1]

Now, Jack, I am going to give you the first preliminaries of you might say the foundation of what has worked out in later years.

I was in solitary confinement at San Quentin. Oppenheimer[2] and I were scheming to get away, to make a getaway, so I was slowly working upon a project to cut the floor of the cell, which was steel, by the use of uric acid, in other words, urine. I went to work and made putty out of the bread and made a trough, just a little trough and day by day, for twenty-four hours, I would clean off the groove and take off the rust that had corroded; in the course of about eight or nine months the results started to be shown on the floor but they had a system of changing us from one cell to another so I kept two going all the time. Finally it was discovered, in other words betrayed. I hit upon a scheme, the thought came to me, one substance that is harder than another will overcome that substance and I thought here is steel, if I could get something harder than that steel I could cut that steel. The next question was what could I get to cut that steel and the only thing that appealed to me was anything within reach. I was lying in the bed one evening thinking and like a flash from a clear sky came the idea of a needle and back in my mind I remembered a story that had been told to me by a Siberian convict and the solution of the whole problem was there. But how to get the needle? I telegraphed to Oppenheimer,[3] of course the code, I telegraphed to Oppenheimer and I said "Jake, do you think you could get hold of a needle?" He says "I don't, why?" I says "If I can get a needle I can cut this door." That passed away, that was settled. That was the first inspiration that Oppenheimer ever got in regard to cutting the door with a needle. I forgot it. During one of those long periods of torture I was lying in the jacket one night, I was in bad, what we call a semi-conscious condition; this may seem far fetched but I heard as clear as if you spoke to me right now; "Poor weak little boy, poor, weak little boy, how long will you buck against the pricks? Don't you know that you are yourself your own worst enemy and all these conditions that you are chafing against, all this torture and everything else is purely with yourself, self-created? The people that you regard as your enemies are not your enemies; they are brought here by you and they are only instruments to chastise you. Control the instruments and everything else will be easy. The solution of your problem is not in the guards, not in the bolts or bars or doors that are holding you, but simply within yourself. Control your conditions and you can walk out of this cell."

For the first time in my present experience had I ever shown any inclination to meet the watch-dog halfway and when the guard came in the morning to put the sup of water between my teeth, he was surprised that I met him with a smile; I smiled even in my agony. I smiled and he reported that and I guess it shortened my time in the jacket.

After the jacket was taken off and I was able to stand on my feet, which was two or three days, I had to lie there like a helpless, bruised mass; all the time my brain was actively working. This message would come to me and I would think "I am going bug house; that was all purely of my own creation, purely imagination; I was just wondering, delirious, and I am taking this seriously." Yet back it would come to me, "why buck against the pricks, why?" All the time that eternal question, why? got me thinking. For weeks and weeks I tried to unravel the solution of this enigma to me, but it would not come; I said "How can I solve my problem when everything is utterly hopeless? I am in here in prison for life incarcerated in solitary for life, without a friend in the world to help me and no outside influence that can come to my support?" I says "It is absurd, I dismiss it." But as quick as I would dismiss it up would this picture again.

Finally the way started to come; I began to see, I began to live as if I were in another life, in another world. "I will put this to the test and if even the first preliminary steps justify me then I know I am right and I will go right along and work out the solution." That was the starting of the new condition. . . . After leaving the prison I remember walking up Market Street, it was after the fire and the ruins were spread out in all directions and for the first time in sixteen years a feeling came over me that I would like to cry. I felt my eyes soften. I went into a saloon, the poor man's club, the outcast's haven of rest; there were no place else to go; I was a stranger, alone. I sat down at a table and all the time I was feeling that everybody was looking at me. I should have stepped up to the bar and ordered a drink but I sat there at the table and finally the bartender kept noticing me so long that I raised my hand as an indication that I wanted him to come over and ask me what I would drink; I was undecided whether it was a glass of beer or whiskey or what, so I said "Give me some whiskey" and I took a few sips of the whiskey and the first sensation was dizziness, the next was to throw it up. Sitting there at the table there was one thing in my mind and that was my suit case; I had a suit case, I had my papers all in that, and I was fearing to leave that suit case any place; I had arrived at that stage where I suspected everybody. Finally I went up to the man and asked him if I could leave my suit case in his charge, he says "why, sure." He didn't seem to think it anything at all; I thought it was a wonderful thing and I felt rather squeamish about parting with that suit case. After he took the suit case I went back to the table and sat down and the first thing I knew my head was lying on the table and I started to cry. I thought it was one of the strangest sensations that I ever had; a feeling of relief came over me. I said "That is funny, why haven't I cried in the past?" I remember when I stepped outside of the door I turned and looked at the building to locate it and be sure I couldn't be wrong. I took down the number in a note book so that I would not lose track of that suit case. Then I walked and kept on walking and walked until it was dark.

### NOTES

1. This is particularly the case with Standing's immersion in the story of Christ as a Roman legionnaire of Danish origin. London and his friend Mary Austin both wrote what they called "Christ novels," perhaps inspired by the great success of Lew Wallace's *Ben-Hur* (1880). Austin published hers serially in the *North American Review* in 1915 as *The Man Jesus, Being a Brief Account of the Life and Teaching of the Man of Nazareth* (see Jack London, *Letters*, 1513-1514). When Austin wrote London to complain that no one appreciated her Christ novel, he was not sympathetic: "The majority of the people who inhabit the planet Earth are boneheads. I have read and enjoyed every bit of your 'Jesus Christ' book. . . . What if it does not get across? I have again and again written books that failed to get across." See Campbell, " 'Have *You* Read *My* "Christ" Story?' "

2. Jacob Oppenheimer (1872-1913) was a serial murderer and robber who not only attacked civilians in Oakland and San Francisco—including his live-in girlfriend—but murdered inmates, attacked guards, painstakingly sawed through his cell bars, and nearly escaped while at both Folsom and San Quentin. It was because of Oppenheimer that a law was passed requiring the death penalty for assault on other inmates or guards. Despite considerable intelligence, public support, and an excuse for every deed he had done, Oppenheimer was executed on July 11, 1913.

3. The prisoners in solitary confinement at San Quentin worked out a code system of rapping with their knuckles.

# Ed Morrell

## Letter to Jack London (1914)

Encouraged by Morrell, London continued to pursue and heighten his long-time criticisms of the California state prison system and campaigned for reform on such issues as straitjackets and the automatic death penalty for inmates who assault another inmate or a guard.[1] In letters London described Morrell and the effects of prison upon him: "More than once I have seen the hundreds of scars on his body, caused by the straight jacket" (*Letters*, 1520). London answered Morrell's plaintive December 22, 1914, letter below on December 24, but without much encouragement for Morrell's own attempt to write his story. London wrote: "I am returning herewith the opening chapter of your autobiography. I have just finished reading it. I hate to tell you this, but I tell it to you in all kindness. Anybody can throw 'the bull-con.' I refuse to throw the 'bull-con.' I state what I believe from my knowledge of the writing and publishing game. You have the stuff in your head and in your experiences, but, believe me, you are not bringing it out in so far as I may judge." This sounds rather harsh as a response to someone who offered one a great idea for a novel, but the two writers and former cons Morrell and London kept up their correspondence at least through January 1915.

Dear Jack:

Just before I left the Ferry to day I tried to Phone you but could not get any reply, I wanted badly to have a few words with you before I left. I am in route East to New York, Where I expect to get in to the harness once more. This has been one long siege for me, havent earned a cent since the II of August, With doctor bill and all other sort of imaginable debt staring me in the face.

I sent you the first instalement of the life Storey and as I told you the last time we met I wanted you to read it over and see if you could do something for me with the matter, naturally I have been expecting to hear from you from day to day, because I have been expecting to leave for the East for some time. Now jack I would certianly appreciate the favor very much if you could spare the time to write to me and let me hear what you can do for me.

Another thing, if its possible for you to do it I want you to help me in any way you can in New York, I am going to Vaudiville, and you know that what ever publicity one can get it inhances your earning value that much more, I thought of the New York Journal Rover, and the fact of me being in the big burg Etc. Etc. Therefore, how about you dropping a line to the Eastern end to that effect, acquainting them of my presence there, Again: if you have any good scouts in the shape of friends or other acquaintance send me letters of introduction to them, every little helps in my ventures in the East and rest assured I shall appreciate all you can do for me in the way of helping me to get on my feet once more.

In starting out at the beginning of the coming New Year I feel it in every bone of my body that this will be the Banner year of my life, I ecpect to get before some of the largest Audances in my public career, and this time it will be for my own precous self, I am getting up in years now, and in taken account of stock that I havent even a roof over my head, So this campaign will be 75 for Morrell, and 25 for the work that I have given all to for the last six years. I suppose you seen the account where Lowrie was appointed as the Wardens Sectary at SinSing Prison, Well: I only hope he makes good, but if he dont fight shy of John Barley Corn I am afraid his tenure of office will be short lived, he has been going to the Devil hard and fast here on the Coast, and all that know his true state of afairs here welcome this Godsend of a change in his life.

In closing this letter let me express my heartfelt wish that in the coming new year all sorts of good luck will be in store for you and Charmain.

> With Love for you bouth I remain as always your sincere friend.
>
> Ed.

**NOTE**

1. See Williams, "On *The Star Rover*," which Williams aptly calls "a small symposium" of nine articles by writers such as Jacob Oppenheimer and Emma Goldman, plus his informative introduction and notes. He notes that "the relations amongst Morrell, London, and Oppenheimer are tied to the larger questions of prison reform, the death penalty, socialism and anarchism, the character of the criminal, and eugenics," and thus they remain a significant dimension of London's work (82). See also Golden, "A Day with London and Morrell."

# Sophie Treadwell

## "Is Jack London a Capitalist? No!
## But Is Certainly 'Magnifique, by Gosh!'" (1914)

Playwright and journalist Sophie Anita Treadwell (1885–1970) is distinctive as one of the first and only modernist female playwrights, especially famous for her expressionist drama *Machinal* (1928). Of Mexican descent on her father's side, she was one of the first well-known Latinas to use her family's history in fiction, as in her novel *Lusita* (1931). Treadwell graduated from the University of California in 1906 with a degree in French. Like London, she came from a "broken" home and struggled with odd jobs to put herself through school, including vaudeville singing and writing stories for San Francisco newspapers, such as this sketch of Jack London. The San Francisco *Bulletin* hired her in 1908. In later years she married and moved to New York, where she enjoyed success on Broadway with her plays and was active in the suffragette movement. In 1921 she interviewed Pancho Villa for the *New York Herald Tribune*, the same publication that had published London's Johnson-Burns and Johnson-Jeffries heavyweight fight coverage in 1908 and 1910, as well as his story "Lost Face" and his novel *Burning Daylight* (1910) in serial form.

"Magnifique, by gosh!"

One of the ranch men was driving me from the Glen Ellen station to Jack London's place in the hills. He was a French Swiss, who had lived in South America before coming to California; and he was giving polyglot expression to his love for the fields, the flowers, the trees, and Jack London. We had come to a crest in the road from whence we could see the startling ruins of the great brown stone pile London built for a home that was burned some months ago, just when it was done.

"Three years we work to build him and someone burn, What a tristesse for me! But Jack London say, 'Cheer Pierre, we build again.' 'Not for a life of you,' I tell to heem. 'There is not in me so bigness of heart for a work and a expense.' But already we cut the trees. One year to—what you call—season? Por Dios! Get up you lassie—Magnifique, by gosh!"

[250]

The Londons live in the sprawly old house of an ancient winery that was on the place. It is set in the midst of the quiet hills. Mrs. London has arranged it cleverly, and there is an air of comfort and happiness and work about it as well as sunshine and country calm.

At the end of a long hall running through the center of the house is a door bearing the legend in heavy black letters on a white card: "Hands Off!" Behind this mute but screaming protector the California author is secure until noon. One hundred dollars' worth of story writing is done there every morning—1000 words at 10 cents a word. This takes between one and two hours. Then the mail is gone through, and about then a dull booming South Sea gong sounds. The midday meal is ready. The forbidding door opens, an attractive looking man with an adorable smile comes out—tramp, political economist, rancher, philosopher, author—and laugher.

Mr. London was late for lunch this day, but when he got there he made up for lost time—from the point of view of the interviewer—talking swiftly and to the point. I suppose he ate, too. That's what he was there for; so no doubt he did it. Action and directness seem to be two of his many middle names.

London answers every question one puts to him, quickly, directly and without hedging. Yet he is a very difficult man to interview. The very minute he came into the room, in spite of the blue eyes, in spite of the smile, in spite of a very charming expression, I knew that I was in for it. He has a steel-trap body and a steel-trap mind. He turns this battery on you, and lets it go at you, slam-bangs his own success and self-confidence. And he laughs.

"What have you come to ask me? Out with it! I know your paper didn't send you up here for nothing. Just to talk to Jack London? Here in California? I'm only interesting to interviewers away from home. All that the papers here can do for me is to misquote and belittle me! No? Say, I know what I'm talking about.

"So you know that when a university girl wandered into the hills in back of Berkeley and was attacked by a tramp the papers said it must have been Jack London? Don't know about that, eh? Well, do you know that when some Italians sought to play the badger game—do you know what the badger game is? All right! Well, these Italians tried to pull the badger game, and when the victim didn't come through with the money they cut him up in pieces and dumped him in the bay, or tried to, when they were interrupted. Do you know what the papers said then? That it must have been Jack London who did it. You don't believe that? Well, look it up in the files! How long have you been in the newspaper game? It was before your time. But it's the God's truth.

"Do you belong to the Woman's Press Club? No? Take a harp! Take two harps! Ever hear that story of Bierce's about the woman who had committed every sin in the book and went up to be questioned by Saint Peter? He told her to tell all and was just going to send her below, when she said she had been blackballed by the Woman's Press Club. 'Come in,' said Peter. 'Take a harp! Take two harps!' But they are no worse than the men's press club. Of all the flat-footed, bone-headed pinheads! Do you know that they knocked me consistently for twelve years; never as much as invited me to their club, and here the other day I got a letter asking me for $2000 for their clubhouse! Can you beat that?

"My new novel? I think I'll call it *The Jacket*: It's a punch against prison conditions in California. What I have to say in it is just what is said by every well-known criminologist in the world. Everybody who thinks knows it, and they have been hiring little halls and telling it to each other.

"What's the use of people who all more or less, think the same, getting little halls, and agreeing with one another?

"I'm trying to get some of these ideas over to fiction readers. Do you know that today it is possible to sentence a man to solitary confinement in California? That it is possible for us to hang a man for assault and battery? That, in fact, last year in 1913 we did hang a man for assault and battery? Jake Oppenheimer was hanged for assault and battery here in your own State, in California. The straitjacket still obtains in our prisons. Didn't you know that? Do I put any constructive ideas for prison reform into this novel? No, I do not. I just draw the picture of conditions as they are now. Have I any constructive ideas along those lines? Of course I have. I would turn prisons into hospitals. My basic belief is one of pure determinism. Each person moves along a line of least resistance. We do what is easier for us to do than not to do. We can't help doing what we do.

"If I'm short-sighted and bump into posts, I'm not to blame. It's because of my short sight. I ought to get glasses? Of course. That is just it! If I break our so-called laws, I can't help it. I do it because I am sick. There is something wrong with me, I'm a sick man. And I need doctors. I need all the skilled science of the twentieth century to investigate and see, and try if anything can be done for me to keep from doing what is hurtful to the whole body of my fellow-creatures. The whole school of scientific criminology is with me in this. It's only the fools who are not.

"Do I believe in capital punishment? No, I do not. It is too silly. I saw a man hanged because he killed another man. And he killed the other man over 25 cents. One said that the other owned the 25 cents. That one said he did not. They began to quarrel and finally, like two bulls in a pasture, they got to fighting; and in the fight one killed the other. So the state hanged him. Oh, the pomp and circumstances with which they stretched that man's body at the end of a rope! And when it was all over the warden said: 'Gentlemen, take your hats off!' It was then that I laughed.

"Am I still a Socialist? I'm in the same position that I've always been. Now they call it Syndicalism. I'm a Syndicalist. I believe in taking over, by whatever means necessary, the existing forms of government. The Boston Tea Party was an expression of that kind of feeling. Revolution? What about it? Our Pinker-tons [*sic*], our police, our soldiers — they are all organized for an allied purpose, the purpose of banging an offensive foreign substance into another man's body. But after all, Syndicalism is only a blind expression of personal feeling, of emotion.

"I have been interested in the Western Fuel case. And I'll tell you the point that got me, in that — the absolute horror and consternation of those men when one director was finally found guilty. Well, why not? They feel that they haven't done anything wrong. And they haven't. This is their society. The United States is their clubhouse. That same game is going on by gentlemen members all over the clubhouse. Why should these men go to jail?

"Yet, other men are going to jail — thousands of them — every day. And some of them are going, denied the right of trial by jury, denied the right to plead guilty or not guilty. You don't believe that? But it is true. I myself have been sent to jail, denied the right of trial by jury; denied the right to plead guilty or not guilty. And my name is legion. What was I doing? Nothing. Absolutely nothing. Walking along the streets of a city, when a cop hauled me in.

"What was I booked for? 'Vagrancy, yer Honor.' I tried to plead not guilty, to explain. The judge didn't even look at me. 'Thirty days.' And I was yanked aside while the judge went down the line. You must have seen men sentenced like that, dozens of times, haven't you? Then why do you look at me as though you doubted when I told you men were sentenced to jail without the right to plead? You have heard too much Fourth of July oratory. Be more brass tacks! Lose some of your illusions!

"It's your education that's to blame for your lack of brass tacks, not you. What a training we give to children! If I had a son I would not send him to school until he was ready for the last year of grammar school, and then only that he could get used to our form of democracy. No, I wouldn't give him a free choice of what he wanted to learn any more than I give a colt a free choice! I'd train him—freedom—but within limits. No, he would not go to a university; not unless he could run faster than I.

"The reason I quit the university was because I did not have money enough to get through and because I wasn't getting anything there that I wanted. Do you know what happened to me over there, in that State university at Berkeley, supported by the taxes of the people? I was called out before a whole regiment of students undergoing, as I was, enforced military drill, and I was publicly humiliated by an officer of the regular army because my uniform was shabby, because I lacked $40 to buy a new one. My uniform was a second-hand one. I bought it from a fellow for five dollars, and he had bought it from one before him. It was handed down from one poor student to another, and no doubt it did lack style. But was that any reason why the poor boob who had to wear it because he couldn't get a better one should be humiliated?

"Do you know who are the arbiters of American literature today? The failures of American literature! Men who could not get a half cent a word for a story of their own, dictate to men who get ten. When I was in New York this time a $6000 a year editor tried to tell me what to do. His magazine pays me $24,000 a year."

After luncheon Mr. London drove to the station. He drove a light team and handled it well; with all the firm ease one would expect of him. Conversation turned to farming. As the rig wheeled smartly down the country roads, Mr. London would wave the whip hand over the landscape.

"My land goes to the crest of those mountains there. We stretch the length of that valley. I have 500 acres in vines. These are my eucalypti. I put all these in. Got several hundred acres of them. This road isn't bad, is it, considering the rains we've had? This is my private road. Wait until you come to the county road—a fright. I always keep my own roads up—and my gates."

"Mr. London," I asked, widening my eyes to the breadth of valley and mountain that he calls "mine." "Is there such a thing as a Socialist capitalist?"

"I don't know," he answered easily. "When I was in New York I met a man who told me he was a bourgeois anarchist."

And I was just making a mental note about a clever hedge—when he burst out:

"You mean that for me. But I'm no capitalist. What is a capitalist?"

"One who has capital," I ventured weakly.

"No, a capitalist is one who lives off capital, who makes money earn money. I don't. I live off wage, the wages that I coin out of my Own brain. And you don't think this ranch earns me anything, do you? Why, if I'd die today you wouldn't believe it if I'd tell you how much in debt I'd be. But that's my way of getting ahead of the game. If I die owing $200,000 I'm just that much ahead of the game, am I not? If you die owing eight dollars, you'd be just eight dollars to the good, wouldn't you? Of course, one can take pride in always paying their bills and all that, but somehow that slide to eight bones as a possible debt capacity for me didn't thrill as it might."

"What are your ideas about marriage?" I asked. That's always a good way to change the subject.

"I believe in marriage. The march of civilization has proven out monogamy and shown it to be the best proposition along those lines for the human race. I insist that all the people that work for me be married. I'm not going to have any promiscuity around here."

"Nor celibacy?"

"I hope not."

I wanted to ask him if there is such a thing as a socialist dictator, but I knew he was laughing at me.

For there is something that I haven't been able to put into this interview, the undercurrent of laughter that is new in Jack London—that laughter that is born of vision and disillusion.

When I was on the train coming back the conductor came right away to punch.

"Was that Jack London?" he asked. "That man in the sombrero at the station?"

"That was Mr. Aristophanes," I told him.

"Guess Jack London isn't back yet. Pretty smart fellow, all right." I thought of the words of the French-Swiss ranch-hand:

"Magnifique, by gosh."

End of Interview.

# J. M. Lydgate

## "Local Writer's Opinion of Novelist Jack London" (1915)

In May of 1915, Jack London accompanied a U.S. congressional delegation on a visit to the island of Kauai hosted by local businessmen, to assess, among other things, the prospects of Nawilili Harbor in Lihue. London had never visited the island before, home to Kalalau Valley and one of his most famous heroes, Koolau the Leper. William A. Lydgate, son of the Reverend J. M. Lydgate (1854–1922), who received London as his guest, noted in his memoirs that "on May 13, 1915, a party of three distinguished gentlemen came to call. They were G. H. Gere, W. R. Farrington, later to be named governor of Hawai'i, and Jack London, then at the height of his fame as a novelist. London signed the guest book in a bold and masculine hand and opposite wrote 'Valley of the Moon, California, May 13/15.'" Reverend Lydgate published this account of his visit from London in the May 25, 1915, edition of *The Garden Island*, the local newspaper. The delegation were entertained by Olympic champion Duke Kahanamoku in a swimming race and feted at banquets and speeches. But reporters at the time noted London's staying out of the limelight, an indication of his worsening health from kidney disease. He did manage a long, winding drive to the beautiful town of Hanalei with Walter Sanborn, manager of the Princeville Plantation. As they drove along the coast, perhaps London reflected upon Kahanamoku, once his inspiration for surfing Waikiki Beach, and all that Hawai'i meant to him.[1]

I have been asked so many and such various questions about Jack London, that I have finally concluded to allay any remaining curiosity in this public manner. I may explain that I did not apply in advance for him or any other of my guests, but I am very grateful to the assigning powers for the allotment they made to me.

When Mr. C. A. Rice introduced me to Mr. London, he remarked to him jocularly, "He will fill you to the brim with Hawaiian folk-lore!" Somewhat alarmed at the strain to which I felt that my hospitality would be put, I hastily threw in the warning "Mr. London, if you never struck a dry spot before you've struck it now!" I may have been mistaken, but it seemed to me that his countenance fell perceptibly whether it was the supply of the folk-lore, or the lack of drinks, I couldn't say. However, he bore the deprivation very well.

I should say that he is about 40 years of age, though looking much younger, boyish off hand, natural and unassuming. Not by any chance would you take him for the Prince of the world's storytellers — rather for a drummer or a life insurance man, or even a book agent, except that when you talk to him, you realized that he wouldn't make his salt in any one of these professions, he is too modest!

In his talk, he is easy, natural, direct and simple, with a little hesitation at times as though he knew there was a better word if he could lay hold of it. There is no touch of the oratorical or the grandiloquent, no slightest recognition of an audience anywhere. More remarkable, perhaps, considering what he has come through, is the absolute freedom from slang and profanity. This must be the outcome of years of patient and faithful restraint.

Literature is the last thing, apparently, that he wants to talk about. If left to his own resources, he unfailingly drifted round to the interests and problems of his great ranch in California, "Valley of the Moon," where the difficulties and problems that run through the wide range of our own sugar estate problems here: problems of labor, cultivation, fertilizers, rotations of crops, plant food, chemical constituents, etc., subjects that carried me into such deep water that I immediately created a diversion by calling attention to the fine cloud effects over Haupu. He saw my limitation and dropped down to a lower level and told me how his sister really handled this ranch and did it far better than he could. All he did really was to put up the money for it, but that was quite a problem, it took so much frankly, so far, it had been a losing proposition, he had put in a great deal more than he had ever got out or perhaps ever would, but they had one redeeming consolation, they were steadily improving the place and would leave the land in much better shape than they found it, for when they found it, it had been ruined by slovenly cultivation.

Next to the problems of ranching come the experiences of deep sea sailing. A yachting trip in the "Snark" through the perils of the South Seas is one long trail of glory in his memory. With a local native pilot at the mast head himself at the bow with the lead and his wife at the wheel to pick a perilous way through reefs and channels and currents, with danger on every hand, this had the thrill of a continuous adventure, the more so when they outdared and out-ventured the native pilot, and sailed through places where he said they couldn't.

One long dream was the trip 'round the "Horn" — 5 months of release from the burdens and restraints of civilization and conventional life.[2] This was the chance for recovery, to make up lost time and lost ground in reading and study. He made a liberal provision on the basis of 3 books a day. Not that he would necessarily finish that many, but it was best to be on the safe side; there was always chance of accident or delay that might extend the voyage beyond the original expectations. He never allows himself to be separated from his books. He keeps one on hand all the time as a resource for any lull or delay in the program and this redeems many an hour that would otherwise be wasted.

Professionally, he works two hours a day, in the morning, rain or shine. Sundays or holidays, the only exception being when he is off on a trip like the congressional outing, and these little actions generally grow tiresome, he would be glad to get back to his work again. This two hours, of course, does not by any means, cover the whole of his activity. The business end of literature in these modern days, scattered as it is throughout the whole world, involves a lot of work in correspondence, etc. While he escapes as much of this as possible, he still finds that he has a great deal to do that is far from straight literature.

With his well-known socialistic sympathies it is not to be wondered that he is somewhat of a radical, or even iconoclast in literature. He holds very lightly the accepted canons and rules of literary practice. He claims that literature was made for man and not man for literature.

## NOTES

1. See Cook, "In 1915, Kauai Enthralled Jack London."
2. This was the Londons' 1912 voyage aboard the *Dirigo* from Baltimore to San Francisco.

# Joseph Conrad

## Letter to Jack London (1915)

> Born in Russia of Polish parents, Józef Teodor Konrad Korzeniowski, Joseph
> Conrad (1857–1924), became one of the greatest writers in the English lan-
> guage, one of many he spoke, having learned greatly from his days in school
> and in the French, British, and Belgian merchant marine. In the early 1890s
> he piloted a steamer up the Congo River and served on ships that frequented
> exotic locales such as Borneo, Singapore, and India. Many of his works, such
> as his most famous, *Lord Jim* (1900) and *Heart of Darkness* (1905), are nauti-
> cal tales. Though considered a psychological writer who probed the conscious-
> ness of the human mind like his modernist contemporaries Henry James
> and Virginia Woolf, and not grouped among naturalist writers like London,
> Conrad's unwavering ability to look at the worst in humanity and be able to
> verbalize the narrative of that humanity certainly relates him to the naturalists.
> London read his works throughout his life, beginning at least by March 1903.
> He and London share many literary affinities in their sea-writing: postcolonial
> disaster in the southern seas of the world, a mythic grasp of nature, and anti-
> heroes who mock romantic ones.

My Dear Sir,

I am immensely touched by the kindness in your letter—that apart from
the intense satisfaction given me by the approval of an accomplished fellow-
craftsman and a true brother in letters—of whose personality and art I have
been intensely aware for many years.

A few days before it reached me Percival Gibbon (a short-story writer and
a most distinguished journalist and corresp.) and I were talking you over
endlessly, in the quiet hours of the night. Gibbons who had just returned
after 5 months on the Russian front had been taking you in the bulk, soaking
himself in your prose. And we admire in vehemence of your strength and the
delicacy of your perception with the greatest sympathy and respect.

I haven't seen your latest—just the reviews such as come my way are en-
thusiastic. The book is in my house but I wait to finish a thing (short) which

I am writing now before I sit down to read you. It'll be a reward for being a good industrious boy. For it is not easy to write here nowadays. At this very moment there is a heavy brush of gunfire in Dover. I can hear for quick firers and the big guns—and wonder what it is. The night before last a Zep passed over the house (not for the first time) bound west on that raid on London of which you would have read already in your papers. Moreover I've just now a quonty wrist. This explains my clumsy handwriting.

And so no more—this time. Keep me in your kind memory and accept a grateful and cordial handgrasp.

Yours sincerely,
Joseph Conrad

# Edgar Lee Masters

## Letter to Charmian Kittredge London (1922)

After London's death, Charmian developed a friendship, almost exclusively by post, with fellow writer Edgar Lee Masters (1868–1924), a midwestern admirer of Jack London's work, whose own work could be called naturalistic albeit on the more Romantic side, such as his *Spoon River Anthology* (1915–1916). Masters saw in London and his literary legacy, and especially in Charmian as a "liberated woman," hope for the future. Like London and many other American fiction writers of the period, Masters had his start in journalism, with the *St. Louis Mirror*. He was editing newspapers and magazines in Chicago at the time he wrote to Charmian to acknowledge London as an influence and to praise her then recently published two-volume biography of her husband.

January 18, 1922
[Princeton, N.J.]
*The Book of Jack London* is something you may well be proud of, and one which you need never submit to any one in humbleness of spirit. The literary style is admirable, swift and fluent and condensed. . . . But . . . this book has made me blue, for the reason that I so well understand the flame and the power that strove with the American environment for life and expression.

I wish this book could fall into the hands of every boy in America contemplating a literary career. That would be its great use and its incalculable benefit to America, and to American letters. Strength that overlays itself, virility that regards itself as exhaustless, aspiration that must dodge waylaying, hope that must rebuild from disaster, tragedy, and so peculiarly American tragedy. Then this book so well portrays that Malice in life which entangles the soul. I see this in almost every one's life. One takes a wound in youth, or faces an obstacle. . . . [A]ll the rest is the work of the weird sisters who see and weave. You hint in places at advice which you proffered and which could not be taken. It is too bad that Jack London did not heed you as much as he loved you. He had done splendid and memorable books. His was a growing, an enlarging genius, a sense of ingeniousness and passionate for American expression; and it makes me hurt that the love and the intensity about which I first wrote you . . . drained the flame of all its oil. He had love in his life too.

# Milo Shepard

*From The Jack London Story and the Beauty Ranch (2001)*

Perhaps his dear friend, Earle Labor, captured Irving Milo Shepard (1925–2010), Jack London's great-nephew, best in the introduction to *The Jack London Story and the Beauty Ranch*, an oral history collection mainly of interviews of Shepard by Caroline Crawford of the Bancroft Library: like his family, "generous and heroic . . . in preserving 'for years to come' the lands restored by Jack London" in California's Sonoma Valley. And not only the lands that today form the Jack London Ranch, with its vineyards, and the Jack London State Historic Park, but London's literary legacy. As Labor notes, Shepard was the last literary executor of London's estate, and as such, in addition "to assuming the heavy responsibilities of managing the London Ranch along with the London/Shepard literary estate, Milo has become a leading force in bringing long-overdue recognition to Jack London as a major figure in American literature," especially through encouraging scholars from all over the world to visit him at the ranch and to use the research materials in Sonoma and at the Huntington Library and Utah State University Library. Shepard was a coeditor of the monumental *Letters of Jack London* published by Stanford University Press in 1988. Shepard, for a time a dairyman and a California state park ranger, returned to the London ranch where he was raised by his parents, Irving and Mildred Shepard, as a viticulturalist and executor. The interviews Crawford collected are important for understanding London's life: "Here is a man speaking honestly and directly from his first-hand experience. For example, herein we may accurately view, perhaps for the first time, Charmian London as she was seen by a man who knew her personally: a courageous woman who 'would challenge anything' but who 'never boasted' and 'never gossiped'—a woman who was gritty but 'feminine, very feminine'—one who was attractive enough in her eighties to turn men's heads," Labor notes. For those fortunate enough to know him, Milo was an extraordinary man, with a "genius for friendship," as Anna Strunsky said of Jack London. Crawford captures him beautifully as they walk through the fall vineyards while Shepard "talked about sustainable agricultural practices, bloom to harvest, and how his methods differ from those London used." As she relates, "Milo said, 'If you see a vine and it's wilted, it will die on you. If the color is changing, then it is crying for something. The vine tells you what it needs.' 'What did Jack London love about this country?' I asked. 'Its beauty,' he replied."

## Memories of Life on the London Ranch

CRAWFORD: Let's talk about your parents. What was their approach to the London association when you were growing up?

SHEPARD: When I was younger, Charmian was in the cottage, where Jack had his workroom, and where he died. When they opened the guest ranch in 1934, why, Eliza came up, and she had built the House of Happy Walls for Charmian. . . . [Then] my father sort of took over because Eliza was going downhill pretty fast. She died [in] 1939. So it was just sort of a progression.

\*

## Charmian, Jack, and Wake Robin

SHEPARD: . . . Where to start with Charmian? Charmian was always immaculate. Charmian always considered her body; was always very concerned about her body. And Jack London was, too. That's why they took all these drugs and stuff. If you look at the number of lists they took and drugs that they had—

CRAWFORD: What drugs?

SHEPARD: Well, you name it. Some were patented. Of course, in those days they would carry opium for broken legs. They had to do their own medications.

CRAWFORD: Opium as a painkiller perhaps?

SHEPARD: Yes, it was used commonly in those days. You didn't have to have a prescription to get it. That's what a lot of people don't understand, the use of those materials as basic medications.

The museum had to turn all the vials over because the kids would see what they were and say, "Oh, he was a hop head." [*laughter*] But Charmian was always dressed immaculate. She was very clean, . . . a large mouth and perfect teeth, [of] which she was very proud. She was proud of her hair too. You see the pictures shortly before she died. She's standing straight as can be. She was very concerned, caring enough not to carry any extra weight. She was always just about the right weight for her build.

CRAWFORD: She was tiny, wasn't she?

SHEPARD: Yes, she was small, but she was strong. She was very strong. She was very athletic. She was a natural athlete.

CRAWFORD: She must have been a wonderful rider.

SHEPARD: Oh, yes, she was a very good rider, and she was a rider who had no fear. I remember I was just a little kid down at the cow barn, the old cow barn, and I was with my father milking the cow and I heard her screaming. She had taken a horse down over the contours and she tried to jump this fence downhill, which is difficult. Anyway, the horse rolled over and she got injured.

CRAWFORD: How old was she then?

SHEPARD: Oh, I'd say she must have been in her early fifties or late forties.

CRAWFORD: How late in her life did she ride?

SHEPARD: She rode all the way up to—I think she stopped riding when I was in the service in 1944 or so. I think in 1945 she had another accident over at the House of Happy Walls, and they brought her back to the cottage, and I don't think she ever went back over to the House of Happy Walls. She was a strong woman, but she was a goer [Milo means she liked sex] as far as men were concerned. You have to realize she was an orphan. She stood on her own feet. She was raised by an aunt who believed in free sex and all that sort of thing.

CRAWFORD: That was Aunt Netta. Where was her resort?

SHEPARD: That was Wake Robin Lodge. Wake Robin is right at the corner—it would be the west, northwest corner of the Ranch. Part of Wake Robin was attached to the LaMotte place. . . .

You talk about the freedom of the sixties in San Francisco, Haight Street. Hell, San Francisco in those days—they were wilder than Haight Street. [*laughter*]

CRAWFORD: Yes. I just read Anna Strunsky's biography.

SHEPARD: . . . She led a very sad life. But for her to come out for the dedication in 1960 she was just like Charmian, small but her skin was beautiful. She was in her eighties but you wouldn't even know it. The twinkle in her eye—this is what Charmian had, this strength, inner strength, vivaciousness.

CRAWFORD: Returning for a moment to Joan; she said something surprising—she said she thought that Charmian had little influence on Jack London.

SHEPARD: Well, I'd say she had a terrific amount of influence on Jack London. Not only social influence, because Jack London could take her anywhere, and then she could hold herself up anywhere, from royalty on down, any social situation, but also London had a problem with writing descriptions, say, of the valley or, I don't know if I'm explaining correctly—I can't think of the word—but anyway, describing trees and using correct adjectives and tying things together. In *The Valley of the Moon*, Charmian did a lot of work on that. Some of the scholars have picked out places where Charmian assisted.

You look at the typescripts. Charmian typed from the holograph, and then she made corrections and then gave them to Jack. Jack would not allow an editor to work on his work. And then it was sent in to be published. You can see where she's changed things so they were a little smoother. Not really edited. I've seen what an editor can do to a manuscript!

The only thing I can say is, from what I've seen and understood from listening to her and Eliza and everything, they were what they called each other. They were mates. That's the best description for the two of them. And yes, they had their ups and downs, and people picked things out of context or they picked certain things—

CRAWFORD: He called her "Mate." Is that the reference? And she called him "Wolf"?

SHEPARD: Well, she called him "Mate Man," too.

### More about Jack and Charmian

. . . CRAWFORD: So there were infidelities.

SHEPARD: I don't think there were infidelities after Jack married Charmian. I don't think so. One time in New York, there was a woman, an actress in New York, and then Charmian received a telegram with no name on it that Jack London was running around with another gal.

You see, Jack London's time together with Charmian is so documented. That was about the only time that Jack London was away from Charmian. The woman happened to be a sixteen-year-old girl from the Baldwin family on Maui. And Jack London was just taking her to dinner, but whatever he did, he was newsworthy. You go to the Huntington Library and look at those large scrapbooks of all these articles about Jack London. It's just amazing.

He's been accused I don't know how many times of fathering children. It was impossible to know where Jack London was at that time. The last one was up in Seattle here, some woman said that Jack London was her father. No, he could have done that when he was single. He stepped out with Charmian when he was married to Bess. But after they were married, I doubt it. And Charmian didn't, either. She had affairs after London died.

CRAWFORD: She was young when he died. She was forty-five or so?

SHEPARD: Yes, and she was very sexually active her whole life, up to her death. So I'm sure — these trips and visiting people in Europe she probably had relationships. But she was very careful here.

CRAWFORD: Yes. She says here, in her book, "I sat at his feet and endeavored to come up to his standard of companionship, which he had missed even among men."

SHEPARD: Yes. I think what she's saying there is what Jack has written. It's sort of semi-autobiographical. In other words, his only companion and the closest person to him was Eliza, and when Eliza got married, she was sixteen, so Jack would be nine, and he took that very hard, very, very hard. From that point on — he writes in a way you think that there were long periods of time when he knew hardship; it was maybe three months. On the fish patrol was maybe six months or less. Working in a cannery was a couple of months. Shoveling coal was a very short period of time.

But he never was able to have any relationship with anyone. He loved his father, John London, and he considered him his father. But it wasn't till he became an author that he became close to — his closest friend would be George Sterling, who was a poet. But he craved a closeness he had never received, and I think this is what she is saying, I sit at his feet, and I'm not capable of giving — he was never capable of a close relationship. I think that's what I'm hearing.

CRAWFORD: And then something from one of his letters to her. He referred to, quote, "that old peace and rest you had for me, God — you had grit." . . .

SHEPARD: . . . Charmian was there. They were working together, day in and day out, traveling together. Not that Charmian was forcing herself on him; it was that he needed her. She took so much off his back, with the typing, getting material, all this.

Even when they went to Vera Cruz in 1914, they wouldn't let a woman on a U.S. Navy ship, so Jack arranged for her to go down in some steamer, and he went down on this U.S. Navy ship.

They were definitely a team. When you read Charmian's biography, that is what she tried to put in, that they were a team, but he was the leader. Charmian and Eliza were never in competition with him.

\*

## More about London's Agrarian Dreams

CRAWFORD: Let me back up a little bit, Milo, and read something from *Valley of the Moon*, just to get your ideas about it: "Across sheer ridges of mountains separated by deep green canyons and broadening down into rolling oak, orchards and vineyards, they caught their first sight of Sonoma Valley and the wild mountains that rimmed its eastern side." Does that sound like this topography to you?"

SHEPARD: Yes. The original Ranch was 1,400 acres. He bought seven ranches to make the one. However, as an agricultural entity, it was almost impossible to make money on it at that time.

CRAWFORD: Yes. He referred to the fact that the ranches were bankrupt, that he was buying these bankrupted properties, and his idea was to—

SHEPARD: They were worn out.

CRAWFORD: Who wore them out? Was it the Italians?

SHEPARD: No, no, no. This is long before the Italians. They were owned mainly by Scotch-Irish, who were originally homesteaders. . . . But there was no replenishing of the soil, and so that's what you call worn out.

The Ranch itself had very little agriculture land on it that you could work because, as he described it, you've got two running streams, two canyons. There's a fifty-foot waterfall. The canyons are 200 feet deep. The mountain was a volcano, a mud volcano that blew out on this side, and you can see it when you look at it.

So you have deep soils, and it flowed, it eroded, and you've got these steep canyons, steep, but you do have a flat plateau area that has about a couple hundred acres on it, and that was the main property.

CRAWFORD: This is a quote from Jack London. I want to know if you think it's exaggerated. He said, "I go into farming because my philosophy and research has taught me to recognize the fact that a return to the soil is the basis of economics. Do you realize that I devote two hours a day to writing and ten to farming?"

SHEPARD: I don't think that's exaggerating. However, when he says ten to farming, he did not farm himself. He may have spent ten hours thinking about what to do with his Ranch. Like he designed the pig pen, which is really extensive. He designed the stallion barns. He designed the planting, what he wanted, talking with other agricultural men. And then he turned it over to Eliza. Sometimes Eliza and the foreman in that department would look over what he was planning and put in ideas and go back to him. He did the planning, but he never did any physical work.

\*

CRAWFORD: . . . Well, I see various references in both books and letters to the fact that Jack London thought highly of Chinese farmers. He said in *The Valley of the Moon,* . . . "I'm getting results which the Chinese have demonstrated for forty centuries."
SHEPARD: Yes, contouring the land. He saw this in Korea. The farm pond, the contours; they used deep soils and didn't have them erode away.

Some of the first conservation work done out here was done by Jack London.

\*

## The Socialist Farmer-Writer and Dealings with Publishers, Ranch Guests, and Ranch Rules

CRAWFORD: It's from a letter to Fannie Hamilton that he wrote in 1906, very shortly after he bought the first property—he said, "I write seven days a week, I swim two hours a day, I sit in the sun naked and read, and ride one hour. Sometimes I box. I know great happiness. But still I'm the same revolutionary socialist, and more irritated by the smug and brutal bourgeoisie." Was that the pattern of his life?
SHEPARD: Well, I'd say it's the pattern of his life. Have you seen his "Rules of the Ranch"?
CRAWFORD: Yes. I want to ask you about those, too.
SHEPARD: Well, he dared do that. That was part of Charmian's job when people took Jack away from his work. She saw this. He had these wants, and the only way to get to them is for him to produce. You have a lot of the scholars criticized him for some of the work he did. Well, he admitted that he was writing for money. Classical authors never wrote for money in those days. That was terrible. You have to realize they were just changing from the pulp

magazines and the sensational stuff that was being written, into the short story magazines. London hit that market. He was great for it. That's why he wrote so many short stories, for *Harper's, Saturday Evening Post, Collier's.*

CRAWFORD: *Cosmopolitan.*

SHEPARD: *Cosmopolitan.* All those magazines were crying—and there were no authors.

CRAWFORD: And they paid good money.

SHEPARD: They paid good money.

CRAWFORD: They had to have paid well for him to have been able to do what he did.

SHEPARD: I'll show you this.

[*tape interruption*]

SHEPARD: All this is material on Jack London. These are copies of original "magazine sales, 1898 to May 1900," showing every one he sent . . . and what they paid. . . . He documented everything and added up all the words. He got so much a word. . . . For instance, here had 6,400 words, *The League of Old Men.* Paid $160. Went to the *Atlantic Monthly.* They paid him $160. "They corrected proofs and stipulated new publication," so he took less money to get it published.

In the one for *The Call of the Wild,* sold to Macmillan in 1902, he writes: "I asked $5,000. They offered $2,000, and they would publish it and advertise it." He sold it outright.

CRAWFORD: In order to get it out.

SHEPARD: Make him known as an author. This list here includes *McClure's, Cosmopolitan, Smart Set, Collier's, Youth's Companion, Country Life.*

# Works Cited

Anonymous. "London Honest and Straight as Boy—Johnny Heinold Mourns Author Friend." *San Francisco Chronicle*, November 23, 1916.

Atherton, Frank Irving. *Jack London in Boyhood Adventures*. Edited by James Williams. *Jack London Journal* 4 (1997): 14–172.

Bierce, Ambrose. Letter to George Sterling, February 18, 1905. Department of Special Collections, Stanford University Libraries. Reprinted in *The Critical Response to Jack London*, edited by Susan M. Nuernberg, 107–108. Westport, CT: Greenwood Press, 1995.

———. "Small Contributions." *Cosmopolitan*, July 1908, 220. Reprinted in *The Critical Response to Jack London*, edited by Susan M. Nuernberg, 135. Westport, CT: Greenwood Press, 1995.

Bishop, Del. Letter to Jack London, July 31, [unknown year]. Jack London Collection, Huntington Library, Pasadena, California.

Bond, Marshall Latham. "An Eulogy." http://www.london@sonoma.org. Accessed June 15, 2018.

———. *Gold Hunter: The Adventures of Marshall Bond*. Albuquerque: University of New Mexico Press, 1969.

Boylan, James. *Revolutionary Lives: Anna Strunsky and William English Walling*. Amherst: University of Massachusetts Press, 1998.

Brett, George. Letter to Jack London, December 27, 1901; January 10, 1902; June 10, September 25, October 22, 1906. Jack and Charmian London Collection, Merrill-Cazier Library, Utah State University.

Burbank, Luther. *The Harvest of Years*. Boston: Houghton Mifflin, 1927.

Campbell, Donna M., Panelist, Session 6-B, "American Literary Naturalism and Social Protest: A Roundtable Discussion." 29th Annual Conference of the American Literature Association, San Francisco, May 24–27, 2018.

———. *Bitter Tastes: Literary Naturalism and Early Cinema in American Women's Writing*. Athens: University of Georgia Press, 2016.

———. "'Have *You* Read *My* "Christ" Story?' Mary Austin's *The Man Jesus* and Jack London's *The Star Rover*." *The Call* 23, nos. 1–2 (2012): 9–13.

Conrad, Joseph. Letter to Jack London, September 10, 1915. Jack London Collection, Huntington Library, Pasadena, California.

Cook, Chris. "In 1915, Kauai Enthralled Jack London." *Kauai Times*, April 26, 1997, 1, 10.

Coolbrith, Ina. Letter to Jack London, January 2, 1907. Jack and Charmian London Collection, Merrill-Cazier Library, Utah State University.

Davis, Grace Monroe. "To Jack London." *Overland Monthly*, May 1932.

Dreiser, Theodore. Letter to Jack London, February 26, 1909; September 15, 1910. Jack and Charmian London Collection, Merrill-Cazier Library, Utah State University.

Fleming, Becky London. "Becky Remembers . . . Aunt Jennie (Daphna Virginia Prentiss.)." *Jack London Echoes* 4 (1982): 119–121.

———. "Memories of My Father, Jack London." *Pacific Historian* 18 (Fall 1974): 5–8.

Foner, Philip S., ed. *Jack London: An American Rebel*. New York: Citadel, 1947.

Ford, Alexander Hume. "Jack London in Hawaii: Rambling Reminiscences of the Editor." *Mid-Pacific Magazine* 13, no. 2 (February 1917).

Furst, Lillian, and Peter N. Skrine. *Naturalism*. London: Methuen, 1971.

Genthe, Arnold. *As I Remember*. New York: Reynal and Hitchcock, 1936.

George, Aleta. "Ina Coolbrith: A Mentor across the Centuries." *Jack London Foundation Quarterly Newsletter* 31, no. 1 ( January 2019): 5–9.

Golden, Harry. "A Day with London and Morrell." *Jack London Journal* 2 (1995): 115–117.

Griscom, Lloyd C. *Diplomatically Speaking*. New York: Literary Guild of America, 1940.

Heinold, Johnny. "Heinold Tells Early Life Was 'Barleycorn' Character." *Oakland Tribune*, November 23, 1916.

Hopper, James. "Jack London on the Campus." *California Alumni Fortnightly* 9, no. 18 (December 2, 1916): 278–279.

Jensen, Emil. "With Jack London at the Stewart River," November 13, 1926. Jack London Collection, Huntington Library, Pasadena, California.

Johns, Cloudesley. "Who the Hell *Is* Cloudesley Johns?" Edited and with introduction by James Williams. *Jack London Journal* 1 (1994): 65–109; 2 (1995): 39–63; 3 (1996): 169–188.

Johnson, Carter. "Eliza Will Do All Anyone Can Do." *American Legion Weekly*, September 22, 1916.

Johnson, Martin. Letter to Charmian London, October 27, 1917; March 14, 1932. Jack London Collection, Huntington Library, Pasadena, California.

———. Letter to Jack and Charmian London, November 25, 1909; October 20,

1911; December 7, 1912. Jack London Collection, Huntington Library, Pasadena, California.

———. *Through the South Seas with Jack London*. New York: Dodd, Mead, 1913.

Johnson, Osa. *I Married Adventure: The Lives and Adventures of Martin and Osa Johnson*. Philadelphia: J. B. Lippincott, 1940.

Kazin, Alfred. *On Native Grounds*. New York: Doubleday, 1942.

Kingman, Russ. *Jack London: A Definitive Chronology*. Middletown, CA: David Rejl, 1992.

———. *A Pictorial Life of Jack London*. New York: Crown, 1979.

Labor, Earle. "An Open Letter to Irving Stone," *Jack London Newsletter* 2, no. 3 (September–December 1969): 114–116.

———. *Jack London: An American Life*. New York: Farrar, Straus and Giroux, 2013.

Lasartemay, Eugene P., and Mary Rudge. *For Love of Jack London: His Life with Jennie Prentiss—A True Story*. New York: Vantage Press, 1991.

Lewis, Sinclair. Letter to Jack London, August 27, 1911. Jack London Collection, Huntington Library, Pasadena, California.

———. Letter to Jack London, October 10, 1911. Jack and Charmian London Collection, Merrill-Cazier Library, Utah State University.

Link, Eric Carl. *The Vast and Terrible Drama: American Literary Naturalism in the Late Nineteenth Century*. Tuscaloosa: University of Alabama Press, 2004.

London, Charmian Kittredge. *The Book of Jack London*. 2 vols. New York: Century, 1921.

———. "George Sterling: As I Knew Him." Special isssue, *Overland Monthly and Out West Magazine*, March 1927, 1–7.

———. Letter to Ernest Untermann, April 27, 1921. Jack and Charmian London Collection, Merrill-Cazier Library, Utah State University.

———. Letter to Joan London, May 1, 1917; April 29, May 5, 1919; March 26, May 10, 1925. Jack and Charmian London Collection, Merrill-Cazier Library, Utah State University.

———. Letter to Lorrin Thurston, May 18, 1925. Jack and Charmian London Collection, Merrill Cazier Library, Utah State University.

———. Letter to Upton Sinclair, October 10, 1931. Jack and Charmian London Collection, Merrill-Cazier Library, Utah State University.

———. *The Log of the* Snark. New York: Macmillan, 1916.

London, Elizabeth "Bess" Maddern. Letter to Jack London, August 2, 1905; March 24, 1908; October 9, 1916. Jack London Collection, Huntington Library, Pasadena, California.

London, Jack. *The Call of the Wild*. New York: Macmillan, 1903.

————. *The Complete Short Stories of Jack London*. Edited by Earle Labor, Robert C. Leitz III, and I. Milo Shepard. 3 vols. Stanford, CA: Stanford University Press, 1993.

————. *The Cruise of the* Snark. New York: Macmillan, 1912.

————. *Jack London Reports*. Edited by King Hendricks and Irving Shepard. New York: Doubleday, 1970.

————. *John Barleycorn*. New York: Macmillan, 1913.

————. *The Letters of Jack London*. Edited by Earle Labor, Robert C. Leitz III, and I. Milo Shepard. Stanford, CA: Stanford University Press, 1988.

————. *No Mentor But Myself: Jack London on Writers and Writing*. Edited by Dale L. Walker and Jeanne Campbell Reesman. 2nd ed. Stanford, CA: Stanford University Press, 1999.

————. "An Odyssey of the North." First printed in *Atlantic Monthly* 85 (January 1900); repr., *The Son of the Wolf* (Boston: Houghton Mifflin, 1900).

————. *The People of the Abyss*. New York: Macmillan, 1903.

————. *With a Heart Full of Love: Jack London's Presentation Copies to the Women in His Life*. Edited and with introduction by Sal Noto. Berkeley, CA: Twowindows Press, 1986.

London, Jack, with Anna Strunsky. *The Kempton-Wace Letters*. New York: Macmillan, 1903.

London, Joan. *Jack London and His Times: An Unconventional Biography*. New York: Doubleday, 1939. Repr., Seattle: University of Washington Press, 1975.

————. Letter to Jack London, October 22, 1911; January 21, 1912; September 13, 1913. From the private collection of Tarnel Abbott, *Jack London Journal* 3 (1996): 162–163, 163–164, 165–166.

————. Letter to Jack London, October 28, 1913. From the private collection of Tarnel Abbott.

London, Joan, with Bart Abbott. *Jack London and His Daughters*. Berkeley, CA: Hey Dey Books, 1990.

Lydgate, J. M. "Local Writer's Opinion of Novelist Jack London." *Garden Island* (Kauai), May 1915.

Masters, Edgar Lee. Letter to Charmian K. London, January 16, 1922. Jack and Charmian London Collection, Merrill-Cazier Library, Utah State University.

McClintock, James I., Jr. *White Logic: Jack London's Short Stories*. Cedar Springs, MI: Wolf House Books, 1976.

Morrell, Ed. Letter to Jack London, December 22, 1914. Jack and Charmian London Collection, Merrill-Cazier-Library, Utah State University.

————. "Statement of Ed Morrell Made to Jack London in the Office of

Schwartz & Powell at Oakland, California, on the 19th Day of December, 1913." *Jack London Journal* 2 (1995): 107–114.

Nakata, Yoshimatsu. "A Hero to His Valet." *Jack London Journal* 7 (2000): 26–103.

Natura. Letter to Jack and Charmian London, January 11, February 22, April 27, July 14, 1911. Jack and Charmian London Collection, Merrill-Cazier Library, Utah State University.

Pizer, Don. *Realism and Naturalism in Nineteenth-Century American Literature*. Carbondale: Southern Illinois University Press, 1967.

———. *Twentieth-Century American Literary Naturalism: An Interpretation*. Carbondale: Southern Illinois University Press, 1982.

Reesman, Jeanne Campbell. *Jack London's Racial Lives: A Critical Biography*. Athens: University of Georgia Press, 2009.

Shepard, Eliza London. Letter to Jack London, February 12, 1904. Jack London Collection, Huntington Library, Pasadena, California.

———. Letter to Jack London, March 4, 1904. Jack and Charmian London Collection, Merrill-Cazier Library, Utah State University.

Shepard, Milo. *The Jack London Story and the Beauty Ranch*. Interview by Caroline Crawford. Regional Oral History Project, Bancroft Library. Berkeley: University of California Press, 2001. http://content.cdlib.org/view?docId=kt8 p30068x&brand=calisphere&doc.view=entire_text2001.

Sinclair, Upton. "Upton Sinclair Pays Tribute to Jack London." *San Francisco Chronicle*, November 23, 1916.

Sisson, James E., comp. "A Chronological Bibliography of the Writings of Joan London," *Jack London Newsletter* 4, no. 1 (January–April 1971): 6–8.

Slocum, Joshua. *Sailing Alone around the World*. New York: Century, 1899.

Stasz, Clarice. *American Dreamers: Charmian and Jack London*. New York: St. Martin's, 1988.

———. *Jack London's Women*. Amherst: University of Massachusetts Press, 2003.

———. "Joan London: Publications." london@sonoma.edu. Accessed September 10, 2018.

Sterling, George. "In Tribute." *Bohemia*, no. 6 (1916): 171–172.

———. Letter to Jack London, April 18, 1906. Jack and Charmian London Collection, Merrill-Cazier Library, Utah State University.

Sterling, George, Jack London, Ambrose Bierce, and Gelett Burgess. "The Abalone Song." Music adapted by Sterling Sherwin. In *A San Francisco Songster: An Anthology of Songs and Ballads Sung in San Francisco from the Gold Rush Era to the Present, Illustrative of the City's Metamorphoses from Camp to Me-*

*tropolis, and Serving as Lyric Footnotes to Its Dramatic History*. Edited by Cornel Lengyel. San Francisco: Works Progress Administration of California, 1930.

Stone, Irving. *Sailor on Horseback: The Biography of Jack London*. Boston: Houghton Mifflin, 1939.

Treadwell, Sophie. "Is Jack London a Capitalist? No! But Is Certainly 'Magnifique, by Gosh!'" *Bulletin* (San Francisco), March 28, 1914. Reprinted in *Appeal to Reason* 21 (March 1914); *Jack London Journal* 3 (1996): 199–203.

Twain, Mark. *The Innocents Abroad*. 1869. Repr., edited by Shelley Fishkin Fisher. New York: Oxford University Press, 1996.

———. "Jim Smiley and His Jumping Frog." *New York Saturday Press*, November 18, 1865. Reprinted in *The Celebrated Jumping Frog of Calaveras County, and Other Sketches*. New York: C. H. Webb, 1867; New York: Oxford University Press, 1997.

von Tempski, Armine. *Born in Paradise*. New York: Duell, Sloan and Pearce, 1940.

Walker, Dale L., and Jeanne Campbell Reesman, eds. *No Mentor But Myself: Jack London on Writing and Writers*. Stanford: Stanford University Press, 1999.

Woodford, Charles Morris. *A Naturalist among the Head-hunters: Being an Account of Three Visits to the Solomon Islands in the Years 1886, 1887, and 1888*. London: G. Philip & Son, 1890.

Walling, Anna Strunsky. "Memoirs of Jack London." *The Masses* 9, no. 9 (1917): 13–14, 16–17.

Waters, Hal. "Anna Strunsky and Jack London (Based on Exclusive Interviews in 1963 and 1964)." *American Book Collector* 71, no. 3 (November 1966): 30.

Weston, Roger. "'Before I Die, I'll Have 1,000 Women.'" *Man's Magazine* 15, no. 2 (February 1967): 44, 60–64.

Williams, Jay. "On *The Star Rover*." *Jack London Journal* 2 (1995): 81–155.

Zola, Émile. Preface to *Thérèse Raquin*. 2nd ed., 1868. Reprinted with translation by Andrew Rothwell (New York: Oxford World's Classics, 2013).

# Index

Partington, Dick, 76–78, 164
Pasadena (California), 206
Peano, Felix, 164
Peary, Robert, 242
photography, 112–13, 114, 133, 194–96, 221, 222
Piedmont (California), 76–78, 87, 93, 130–33, 160
Piedmont Bungalow, 75, 131–32, 134
Pinkerton police, 253
Prentiss, Alonzo, 151
Prentiss, Mrs. Virginia Daphna ("Aunt Jennie"), 41, 130, 151–53
Princeville Plantation (Kauai, Hawai'i), 256
Provincetown (Massachusetts), 108

*Razzle Dazzle* (skiff), 58, 83
Rice, C. A., 256
Rich, Adrienne, 220
Roosevelt, Theodore, 112
Royal Hawaiian Hotel, 225
*Rubaiyat*, 323
Russo-Japanese War, 46, 93, 269

Sacramento (California), 244
Sacramento River, 79
Saddle Rock Restaurant, 244
Sag Harbor, 96
sailing, 61, 78–84, 88, 113, 135, 145, 154, 157–60, 167–68, 196–219, 257
*Sailor on Horseback: The Biography of Jack London*, 120
San Francisco (California), 41, 61, 86, 98, 112, 131, 148–49, 152, 164–70, 186, 197, 235–36, 265
San Francisco Bay (California), 62, 78–84, 131
San Francisco earthquake and fire

(April 18, 1906), 55, 96–97, 156, 164–70, 173
*San Francisco Examiner*, 46, 60, 84, 96
*San Francisco Post*, 75
San Joaquin Valley (California), 79, 82, 244
San Jose (California), 164
San Pablo Bay (California), 79
San Quentin Prison, 244–47
Sanborn, Walter, 256
Santa Clara Valley (California), 64, 66
Santa Rosa (California), 164
*Saturday Evening Post*, 75, 270
Sauk Center (Minnesota), 108
Seattle (Washington), 267
Sekine, Tokinosake, 231
Shepard, Eliza London, 41–47, 114, 130, 154, 159, 179, 180, 264, 266, 267–70
Shepard, Irving Washington, 42, 264
Shepard, James H., 41, 161–62
Shepard, Mildred, 263
Shepard, (Irving) Milo, 42, 263–70
Shepard & Company, 161
*Simba: King of the Beasts* (film), 220
sincerity, 51, 59, 90
Sinclair, Upton, 97, 101, 106–107
SinSing Prison, 249
*Sister Carrie*, 242
Slocum, Joshua, 172, 240
*Smart Set*, 270
*Snark* (cutter-rigged ketch), 50, 68, 74, 113, 139, 145, 168, 172, 196–219, 232, 233, 257
socialism, 64, 66, 87–94, 96, 105–107, 114, 116, 120, 126, 163–64, 240–41, 253, 254–55, 269–70
Sonoma Creek (California), 164
Sonoma Valley (California), 99, 263, 268

WRITERS IN THEIR OWN TIME